ADAMAWA
PAST AND PRESENT

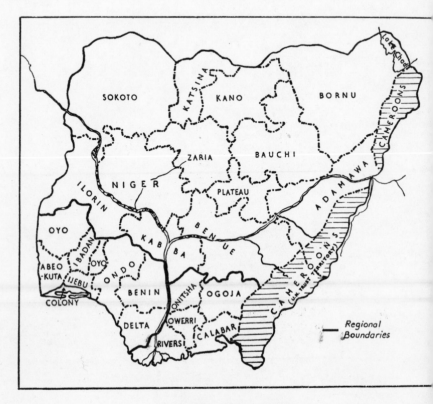

NIGERIA: PROVINCES

ADAMAWA

PAST AND PRESENT

AN
HISTORICAL APPROACH TO THE
DEVELOPMENT OF A
NORTHERN CAMEROONS PROVINCE

by

A. H. M. KIRK-GREENE

Reprinted for the
INTERNATIONAL AFRICAN INSTITUTE
by
DAWSONS OF PALL MALL
LONDON
1969

Originally published by the
Oxford University Press
for the
International African Institute

First published 1958

© *International African Institute* 1969

Reprinted 1969
Dawsons of Pall Mall
16 Pall Mall, London, S.W.1.

SBN: 7129 0398 4

66605

MADE AND PRINTED IN GREAT BRITAIN BY
THOMAS NELSON (PRINTERS) LTD., LONDON AND EDINBURGH

FOREWORD

MR. KIRK-GREENE's introduction to the history of Adamawa Province presents a straightforward and vivid picture of the Province as an officer in the Nigerian Administration has come to know it during several years of service and study devoted to its interests and problems. He describes its mountains and waterways, the character and occupations of its peoples, the political and economic conditions of the present day. He also sketches, in an equally lively manner, the history of the area over the past 150 years—a period in which it was the scene of the rise and warfare of the Fulani kingdoms, became of increasing interest to European trading firms, and was laid claim to by three different European powers within the short space of twenty-five years. For this part of his book the author draws on the works of French, German, and British travellers and explorers, on the reports and records of administrators and trading companies, and on Fulani texts and traditions, using verbatim quotations many of which are here translated for the first time.

While making no claim to exhaustive historical research or the presentation of new ethnographical material, this record of the varying fortunes of the territory, of the life of its peoples, the efforts and endurance of its explorers and the achievements of the early administrators, is of particular interest when the pattern of economic and political life in Nigeria is again being rapidly transformed.

London, 1957   DARYLL FORDE
Director, International African Institute

PREFACE

ADAMAWA PROVINCE was created in 1926, largely from the original Yola and Muri Provinces. A Gazetteer of Yola Province was published by the Nigerian Government over thirty years ago and one of Muri Province nearly forty years ago; a more recent account of the new province of Adamawa was clearly desirable.

This study has been compiled in the hope of giving the officer posted to Adamawa a background to the history of his Province and a guide to where he may be able to develop his interests and research. It also aims to provide a straightforward narrative, deliberately rejecting those ephemeral lists and statistics that so quickly grow out of date, and offering a chronicle of established facts and dates. On to this structure decennial supplements may be added; by virtue of the historical emphasis, revision and rewriting should not again be necessary, only extension.

A word on sources. Besides the valuable gazetteers quoted above and a useful typescript draft of the early 1930's, I have drawn extensively on two sources. One, the narratives and records of travellers to Adamawa during the past hundred years; the other, the local reports, files, district notebooks, and legends—even the accounts of eyewitnesses, for the history of modern Northern Nigeria has not yet reached the span of a man's days. The second source is available only to those who have had the privilege of serving in Adamawa. The first is open to all, and it is to encourage further acquaintance with such absorbingly interesting works that I have been so liberal in quotation and have listed these sources in a miniature bibliography of Adamawa literature, much of which has not been previously translated or catalogued.

I am particularly grateful to C. K. Wreford, Esq., C.M.G., Senior Resident, Adamawa Province, and to J. H. D. Stapleton, Esq., Senior District Officer (now Resident), without whose enthusiastic help and encouragement this book would have remained a might-have-been; to my *confrère*, R. W. H. du Boulay, Esq., District Officer, for allowing me to draw on his immense knowledge of

Adamawa; to those anonymous members of the library staffs in Kaduna, Cambridge, London, and Paris, who were so patient with me; and to the several editors for their kind permission to reproduce as appendixes, either *in toto* or in part, certain Adamawa articles of mine which have previously appeared in their journals and which seemed to be a suitable complement to this historical review. Finally, my thanks are due to the Government of Northern Nigeria for allowing me to publish this book, and to Professor Daryll Forde and Mrs. B. E. Wyatt of the International African Institute for the benefit of their wisdom and their unfailing support.

A. H. M. KIRK-GREENE

Yola, 1954–
Tunbridge Wells, 1956

PREFACE TO THE SECOND EDITION

This book was first published twelve years ago; it was written, taking advantage of library services to hand, during a sabbatical year back at Cambridge University in 1955–56; and it was based on materials collected during two tours of duty in Adamawa Province as a junior administrative officer during 1950–54. Thus not only is its formulation almost twenty years old, taking us back into a very different age of African historical studies, but its whole conceptualization relates to a period and to a purpose no longer extant. The publication of the first edition was manifestly within the tradition of those classics of their kind in the Northern Nigerian colonial context, the *Provincial Gazetteers*. As such it acknowledged debt to its predecessor volumes of the 1920's and to a valuable revised draft located in the Provincial archives at Yola. Yet it aimed at little more than providing, in perhaps a somewhat more sophisticated form, the kind of vademecum that I, along with many colleagues, so often wished we had in our pocket during those early years of extensive trekking in the hills and plains of Adamawa Province. That it claimed no greater pretension Professor Daryll Forde emphasized in his Foreword to the first edition, and two or three reviewers were quick to identify its proper place in the literature of colonial history as just an elegant super-gazetteer—one of them additionally lamenting the limited objective, expressed in the preface, of 'giving the officer posted to Adamawa a background to the history of his Province and a guide to where he may be able to develop his interests and research' and generously wishing that I had ignored 'those hypothetical future generations of District Officers and written instead a full-length history of Adamawa for the present generation of students'.

If, then, because of this book's dated and clearly circumscribed original objective, the decision to reprint it has come as a surprise, the same lapse of time since the fieldwork for the original publication has impressed on me the importance of qualifying this reprint with a contemporary preface. This is more than because of the firm views I hold on the straightforward republishing of out-of-print Africana without the intellectual insurance of an introduction placing the reprint in its proper setting and designed to reduce the danger of new mariners attempting to navigate the perilous seas of yesterday's history with the aid of today's charts and binoculars. It is, in this Adamawa context, because of the extensive changes that have taken place in the status of the former Northern Cameroons since this history of a predominantly Cameroons Province first appeared. These changes are physical as well as political: I can think of no country other than Nigeria which, on achieving self-government during that dizzy decade of African independence between 1957 and 1967, actually lost almost 5% of her territory and some one million of her population. For this reason, some sort of synoptic updating seemed to be imperative, and I am grateful to the publishers for their acceptance of this sole condition in agreeing to the reprinting of *Adamawa Past and Present*.

*   *   *   *   *

The events set out in these pages took the story up to 1955. While it is not the purpose of this preface to the second edition to narrate the details of Adamawa history over the succeeding fifteen years, it clearly lies within both the concern of the writer and the interests of the reader that a note should be included outlining the traumatic experience of Adamawa Province, as it existed in the 1950's, during the intervening period.

As Nigeria approached the agreed date for independence of October 1960, it became evident to the Nigerian Government as well as to the Colonial Office and the United Nations that the Trust (formerly Mandated) Territory status of the British Cameroons, administered as it was as an integral part of Nigeria (albeit with a specially created Ministry for Northern Cameroons Affairs in Kaduna since 1955 and a separate Commissioner for the Cameroons for longer still), presented a problem *sui generis* in the decolonizing process. Announcing this date to the United Nations in February 1958, Britain's representative made it plain that the United Kingdom did not wish to continue its trusteeship of the 'British' Cameroons after 1 October 1960. Hence a decision would be required on whether the areas of the separately [post-1954, when the Southern Cameroons gained the status of a quasi-federal region in the Federation of Nigeria] administered Northern and Southern Cameroons might elect to seek reunification with the 'French' Cameroun or remain part of the new Nigeria.

In October of the same year, France followed suit and notified the United Nations of her intention to bring to an end her trusteeship of the Cameroun. The triennial U.N. Visiting Mission was given the additional task of formulating proposals for 'the procedure for organising a consultation which would enable the people of the Cameroons under French administration to express . . . their wishes concerning the future . . .' Under Prime Minister Ahidjo's determined leadership, the Cameroun Legislative Council passed a resolution that affirmed support for reunification with the British Cameroons. It called for measures to be taken to consult *all* the peoples involved before the Cameroun achieved its independence on 1 January 1960.

At the special Session of the Trusteeship Council and at the ensuing 'Cameroons' meeting of the U.N. General Assembly held in New York at the beginning of 1959, which I had the privilege of attending in a supernumerary advisory capacity, the demands imposed by the timetable for Nigerian and Camerounian independence were resolved. Despite a split in the anti-colonialist ranks of the Fourth Committee over the role of *les Upécistes* and the need for a pre-independence general election in the French Cameroun, the final vote in the General Assembly on 12 March was 59:0: 12 endorsing the termination of France's trusteeship on 1 January 1960 without either a fresh election or special legislation for Dr. Moumié's party. On the less thorny issue of the British Cameroons, it was agreed that a plebiscite should be held in the Northern sector before Nigeria became independent in order to ascertain the wishes of the people. This decision was in accordance with the views of the 1958 U.N. Visiting Mission, which had recommended to the Trusteeship Council that, given the separately-paced and 'other-oriented' local government—the U.N. representative adopted the term 'Northern System'—of the two sections of the British Cameroons over the thirty-six years of mandate (there was not even a road connecting the two contiguous sectors), the wishes of their populations on their future should likewise be determined separately. Agreement on a similar plebiscite for the Southern Cameroons foundered on a difference of opinion between their two leaders, Messrs. Foncha and Endeley, on the nature of the questions to be put to the voters, with the result that the General Assembly could do no more than rule that there would be a plebiscite in both sectors of the British Cameroons before Nigeria became independent and urge the Southern Cameroons leaders to work out an accepted formula for their plebiscite. In the event, it was put off till early 1961. Beyond this summary, the Southern Cameroons story does not belong here.

Accordingly, in the British Northern Cameroons a plebiscite, supervised by a team of a dozen U.N. observers under a U.N. Plebiscite Commissioner, was held on 7 November 1959. The voters were required to answer 'Yes' to one of the two questions:

(a) Do you wish the Northern Cameroons to be part of the Northern Region of Nigeria when the Federation of Nigeria becomes independent on 1 October 1960?
(b) Are you in favour of deciding the future of the Northern Cameroons at a later date?

Out of the 87% of the Northern Cameroons electorate qualified to vote, the poll was 62% (70,546) against 38% (42,788) in favour of the second alternative. Within Adamawa Province, the voting was noticeably higher (69:31) showing the same preference. The Northern Nigerian Government was incensed at this unexpectedly substantial vote of no confidence in its administration. Its stunned dismay led its Premier to speak in anger and, exceptionally, to blame this open rebuff to his government on 'subversive activities on the part of the British officers who organised the plebiscite'. This was a direct reference to the U.N.'s decision that on the grounds of absolute impartiality all the returning officers would be expatriates and all the votes would be counted by expatriate missionaries, wives and non-officials, etc. Similar allegations were made by the Lamido of Adamawa and by the N.P.C. in petitions to the United Nations. Subsequently, and more accurately, a less intemperate evaluation of the protest vote saw it as a vigorous condemnation of the discriminatory administration by Yola and

Dikwa Native Administrations in their non-Fulani, non-Kanuri, 'pagan' districts. This was the explanation put forward at the U.N. by Sir Andrew Cohen. The official report by the Nigerian Government later phrased the rebuff in explicit political terms:

In view of the report of a United Nations Organisation Visiting Mission only twelve months before that public opinion within the Trust Territory almost universally favoured union with Nigeria, this may seem a surprising result. Its explanation lies in the fact that the inconclusive form of the second question made it possible for the political opponents of the Regional Government, and of Adamawa Native Authority, so to focus their campaign on local issues and meaningless promises of tax reduction that the future international status of the territory scarcely became a live issue at all. The local issues were mixed and differed from one area to another. In the Northern area it was objection to control from Yola and the campaign was partly organised and led by members of local Fulani families; in the Chamba area it became frankly a contest between the Chamba and the Fulani; and on the Mambila Plateau it was again objection to remote control from Yola, with underlying hostility of the farmer for the grazier who it seemed was protected by the Native Authority. Those favouring the second alternative made every effort to discredit the Native Authority in the eyes of the United Nations Observers without disclosing their own efforts to undermine its authority on which the maintenance of law and order very largely depended. Perusal of the Commissioner's report indicates that they very largely succeeded in their aim. The organisation of the Plebiscite, the ensuing political tension and the result have dominated the thoughts and actions of Adamawa Native Authority and of the Administration throughout the year. It was an ever darkening shadow that proved to be a cloudburst.

Such, indeed, was the ill-balanced phrasing of the question in the plebiscite that it is not implausible to read into the apparently anti-'Fulani', anti-N.P.C., vote the simple reaction of most humans to the momentous choice of 'do you want to commit yourselves for ever to X or would you rather have a little more time to think over such an irrevocable decision?' Understandably, men of sense jumped at the chance to postpone such a huge responsibility.

A high-powered Commission of Inquiry was at once set up, under the chairmanship of the Emir of Yauri. Regarded by the Nigerian Government as 'the logical sequence to the result of the plebiscite, which all are agreed was mainly a pronouncement on local issues', the terms of reference of this Tukur Commission were to probe into the local administration of the Northern Cameroons districts in the Yola and Dikwa emirates (the 1,386 square miles and 6,000 voters of the Tigon-Ndoro-Kentu area of the Wukari Division of Benue Province were too small to be of much importance), and far-reaching local government reforms were implemented with unaccustomed celerity and vigour.

No such plebiscite took place in the French Cameroun, but three months later a constitutional referendum was held. Seventy-five per cent of the eligible voters went to the polls, 60% (797,498) voting in favour of the new constitution and 40% (531,175) voting against it.

Meanwhile, Nigeria's own independence was just round the corner. There was not time enough to organize another plebiscite in the Northern Cameroons. So, on 1 July 1960, the 17,500 square miles of the Northern Cameroons were excised *en bloc* and re-constituted as a separate , thirteenth, Province within the Northern Region of Nigeria. Then, on 1 October, this Province was re-structured and restyled. A delightful anomaly in the history of accelerated decolonization now came about with the creation of a separate British-administered 'Trust Territory Province' within the body politic of an independent Nigeria, headed by a very senior British official (Sir Percy Wyn-Harris, formerly Governor of the Gambia) as United Kingdom Administrator—complete with Union Jack. Co-existent, as it were, was the standard administrative cadre of a Nigerian province, with its Resident and District Officers, responsible to the Northern Nigerian Government in Kaduna. This island of reluctant British responsibility within the sea of an independent Nigeria continued for the next eleven months, until the results of a second United Nations plebiscite, scheduled for February 1961, could be satisfactorily implemented, in accordance with Cameroonian wishes on how to utilize their independence. Once the October celebrations were out of the way, the Government of Northern Nigeria turned its attention to mounting an all-out campaign to win the Cameroons. Unequivocal warnings to the Northern Cameroonians were issued by the Nigerian Prime Minister on 'the dangers of going down the wrong road' and by the Sardauna against 'plunging yourselves and your people into misery and fear' if they did not cast their vote in the

Nigerian box. These and similar appeals were backed up by a lavish deployment of information media and adult education resources under senior members of the Government aimed at persuading the Northern Cameroonians of the advantages of trusting their future to the Government of Northern Nigeria, with its motto of 'One North, One People and One Destiny', rather than opting for reunification with their 'ethnically and religiously similar' and historically closer-linked kinsfolk over the 'French' border. Now the slogan *muna yi*, 'we are pulling together', was coined to replace that of *a yanke*, 'separation', heard at the previous plebiscite.

The second, and definitive, plebiscite in the British Cameroons, conducted in both sectors under elaborate United Nations observation, was held on 11 and 12 February 1961. The questions put to the voters this time were:

Do you wish to achieve independence by joining the independent Republic of Cameroun? *or*
Do you wish to achieve independence by joining the independent Federation of Nigeria?

In this final U.N. plebiscite, the Northern Cameroons voted, in an 83% poll and with women registered for the first time in Northern Nigeria's political history, by 60% (146,296) to 40% (97,659), to remain within the Federation of Nigeria, while the Southern Cameroons voted by 70% (233,571) to 30% (97,741) for their separation and eventual unification within the Cameroun Republic. Once again, the local distribution of the votes for and against are of considerable interest in our Adamawa context where, apart from obdurate Chamba's lone protest against years of Fulani over-rule, the Tukur local government reforms had worked their magic. In the comparative table on p. xvi I have brought together the figures for both the 1959 and the 1961 U.N. plebiscites in so far as they relate to the Northern Cameroons:

Kaduna was delighted, and in a statement to the legislature the Sardauna made no bones about the 'victory'. But if Lagos was shocked at its massive rejection by the Southern Cameroons, Yaoundé was harshly disappointed at this failure of the apparently 'anti-Nigerian' vote of 1959 to develop into full scale support for a Pan-Cameroon reunification. Their National Assembly passed

PLEBISCITE VOTING FIGURES
NORTHERN CAMEROONS 1959 and 1961

Plebiscite Area	1959 Plebiscite				1961 Plebiscite			
	Total Vote	Vote for Nigeria	Vote against Nigeria	Percentage Result for Nigeria	Total Vote	Vote for Nigeria	Vote for Cameroun	Percentage Result for Nigeria
Dikwa North .	14,671	7,575	7,197	52 : 48	33,327	22,765	10,562	68 : 32
Dikwa Central .	19,879	8,891	11,988	43 : 57	52,900	28,697	24,203	54 : 46
Gwoza .	10,129	3,356	6,773	33 : 67	20,669	18,115	2,554	88 : 12
Madagali/Cubunawa .	14,065	4,247	9,818	30 : 70	30,266	16,904	13,299	56 : 44
Mubi .	19,654	6,120	13,578	30 : 70	34,930	23,798	11,132	68 : 32
Chamba .	16,191	4,539	11,651	28 : 72	34,881	9,704	25,177	28 : 72
Toungo/Gashaka .	4,351	2,252	2,099	52 : 48	8,161	4,999	3,108	62 : 38
Mambila .	10,118	2,745	7,353	27 : 73	20,990	13,523	7,467	65 : 35
United Hills .	3,152	3,063	89	97 : 3	7,984	7,791	157	98 : 2
TOTAL Northern Cameroons	113,859	42,788	70,546	38 : 62	244,072	146,296	97,659	60 : 40

(*Source:* U.N. Documents A/4314 and T/1556)

an all-party motion protesting to the United Nations and doubting that such a result could possibly represent the true wishes of the Northern Cameroonians; a White Paper was issued, accusing the supervising officers of condoning irregularities in the registrations and conduct of the plebiscite; and Yaoundé charged Kaduna with malpractices, intimidations and strong-arm tactics during the pre-plebiscite campaign. At the United Nations, however, this special pleading made little headway, and on 21 April 1961 the General Assembly rejected the Cameroon's protest by a vote of 64:23:10. The U.N. ruled that the trusteeship of the Northern Cameroons should be terminated on 1 June 1961—a date to be observed for some years by the Cameroon Republic as a day of national mourning—and that the Southern Cameroons should end its trusteeship status and be merged with Cameroons on 1 October. Nevertheless, the Cameroon Republic was dissatisfied enough to take its case to the International Court of Justice. There, in December 1963, it was dismissed by ten votes to five on the grounds of the Court's lack of jurisdiction over an area where the General Assembly had already terminated trusteeship.

At a simple but dignified ceremony held in Mubi on 1 June in the presence of the Federal Prime Minister, Alhaji Sir Abubakar Tafawa Balewa, and the U.K. Administrator, Sir Percy Wyn-Harris, Britain's trusteeship of the Northern Cameroons was concluded, after 39 years, by the incorporation of the temporary Trusteeship Territory Province into the Federation of Nigeria. Renamed Sardauna Province in honour of the Premier of Northern Nigeria—the public competition to propose a suitable name had been quietly dropped—and promised the retention of its full, separate Provincial identity, it now comprised the six Native Authorities of Dikwa, Gwoza, Mubi, Chamba, Gashaka/Mambila and United Hills. In all, this political reorganization cost Adamawa emirate two-thirds of its territory. The truncation dramatically reduced the size of its N.A. staff and cut away the resources of its Native Treasury. Despite the Government's promise to the Lamido of Adamawa that such a monumental reduction of his authority would in no way jeopardize his historical status as a first-class emir, murmurs of discontent were understandably heard from the Yola Fulani, echoing the lament of Lamido Bobo Ahmadu who, fifty years earlier, had greeted the division of his territory into 'British' and 'German' spheres with the comment: 'they have left me merely the latrines of my kingdom'.

Although the Northern Nigerian Government had undertaken that never again would the erstwhile Trusteeship Territory be brought back under the hegemony of the Yola Fulani or the Dikwa Kanuri and Shuwa, and promised that none of the five Native Authorities established within the Trust Territory Province in 1960 would be 'subordinated in the future to any Native Authority outside the boundaries of the new Province', the Moslem population of Dikwa emirate soon generated sufficient protest and pressure to convince the Regional Government of the historical validity of their case for opting out of Sardauna Province and rejoining their kith and kin in Bornu Province. This transfer took place in 1963, leaving Sardauna Province as an association of five predominantly non-Moslem, ethnically conceived, and disparate Native Authorities.

In May 1967, the Supreme Commander of the Federal Military Government then in power in Lagos made a bold move to pre-empt the imminent secession on the part of the former Eastern Region. Abolishing the four Regions, Lieutenant-Colonel Gowon established twelve States in their stead. This reorganization was effected by the least cumbersome method at that stage, namely by linking certain provinces and restyling the joint administration a State, without in any instance interfering with existing Divisional boundaries. A delimitation commission, to take into account local wishes, was promised for a later date; but in the event the guarantee was overtaken by the outbreak of civil war and, at the time of writing, has still remained in understandable suspension. Under this new arrangement, the old Adamawa Province once again came into administrative contact with its offshoot Sardauna Province and, along with Bornu and Bauchi Provinces, they comprised the unwieldy North-Eastern State, containing 8 million people and 105,000 square miles—almost a third of the whole of Nigeria's land-mass and over a seventh of its total population. The new administrative organization came into active effect on 1 April 1968. Although this is currently [1969] the position, there is little to suggest that the more powerful elements of the present North-

Eastern State, which has re-assumed some of the frustrating features of stretched communications and awkward administration that unrelentingly taxed the authorities of colonial Adamawa Province alone, will suffer the continuance of an unwanted, unworkable and arbitrary amalgamation. Once the civil war is over and attention may properly be given to refining the local details of the rough-and-ready partition imposed by the States decree, it seems inevitable that this North-Eastern State will experience yet another alteration to its geo-political shape, its administrative responsibilities, and its local nomenclature. For Adamawa, these three features of administrative entity have been subjected to more frequent and more fundamental changes than in any other nineteenth-century Fulani emirate or twentieth-century administrative Province in the history of Northern Nigeria.

Such a résumé of Northern Cameroons history in the formative decade of 1958–68 is a necessary adjunct to any re-reading of the story of Adamawa Province as first presented. This Preface is no more than an historical gloss on the text that follows. Those who wish to examine in greater detail the mechanics and the impact of Britain's relinquishment of her responsibility for the trusteeship of the Northern Cameroons and the growth of the new Sardauna Province side by side with the *ichabod* fate of the rump of that old Adamawa Province which formed the original topic of this book, should consult the following fresh documentation (the first two entries also provide extensive bibliographical guidance to further reading):

Le Vine, Victor T. *The Cameroons: From Mandate to Independence*, University of California Press, 1964.

Gardinier, David. *Cameroon: United Nations Challenge to French Policy*, Oxford University Press, 1963.

Ardener, Edwin. 'The Political History of Cameroon', *The World Today*, August 1962.

Le Vine, Victor T. ' "P" Day in the Cameroons', *West Africa*, March 4 and 11, 1961.

United Nations. Report [of the 1958 Visiting Mission to the British Cameroons], Doc. T/1426, February 1959.

— Trusteeship Committee Report [on the future of the Cameroons], Docs. A/4094 and A/4095, Feb.–March 1959.

— Trusteeship Committee Report [on the plebiscite of 1959]. Doc. T/1491, November 1959.

— Trusteeship Committee Report [on the plebiscite of 1961]. Doc.
    T/1556, April 1961.
Provincial Annual Reports, 1955–   , Government Printer, Kaduna.
Njeuma, M. The Rise and Fall of Fulani Rule in Adamawa. (Un-
    published University of London Ph.D. thesis, 1969.)

A. H. M. KIRK-GREENE

St. Antony's College,
    Oxford, 1969.

CONTENTS

MAPS

I

GENERAL DESCRIPTION

BOUNDARIES

ADAMAWA PROVINCE, with an area of 31,786 square miles, is larger than Scotland. It ranks third in size among the Northern Provinces, following after Bornu (45,733 square miles) and Sokoto (36,477 square miles). Its pear-shaped land mass, with an extreme length of 350 miles and a maximum width of 165 miles, occupies the south-eastern corner of the Northern Region of Nigeria and lies between longitude 10° and 14° East. Its southern boundary lies at 6°30' North, the same latitude as Lagos; thence it marches north-eastwards, with the French Cameroons as its eastern boundary, until it reaches Bornu Province at 11°. Over a short sector between the two Adamawa areas of the Trusteeship Territory of the Northern Cameroons, comprising 10,970 square miles and administered as an integral part of the Province, the boundary is identical with the Anglo-German frontier delimited in 1909; elsewhere the international frontier of the Province is based on the Milner-Simon line of 1919. Within Nigeria, Adamawa marches on the north with the Provinces of Bornu and Bauchi and on the west with Plateau and Benue, while to the south lies the Bamenda Province of the Southern Cameroons.

POPULATION

The administrative capital of the Province is Yola, which with its port and *sabon gari* offshoot of Jimeta carries a population of just under 20,000. The 1952 census recorded a total population of 1,181,164, of whom 417,200 were in the Trust Territory. Density of population ranges from 210 to the square mile in Cubunawa District to only 3 in Gashaka.

A further breakdown of population statistics is given in Table I. It must be stressed that there is a considerable margin of uncertainty in both the classification and the counting.

TABLE I

Adamawa Division: 162 tribes have been listed at one time or another.
Muri Division: 26 tribes have been listed at one time or another.
Numan Division: 42 tribes have been listed at one time or another.

Recent returns show the leading tribes thus:

Tribe	Adamawa	Muri	Numan
Fulani	72,442	26,346	5,682
Hausa	19,054	13,300	2,304
Higi	63,745	—	—
Chamba	55,990	2,240	—
Marghi	45,004	—	—
Kilba	32,001	—	—
Gude	28,077	—	—
Fali	23,598	—	—
Bata	22,740	—	3,749
Mambila	18,027	—	—
Yungur	19,600	—	—
Njai	14,069	—	—
Verre	12,281	—	—
Higi-Fali	9,956	—	—
Kanuri	8,941	1,830	587
Sukur	5,052	—	—
Wula	2,871	—	—
Tur	2,522	—	—
Wagga	2,347	—	—
Ga'anda	7,641	—	—
Mumuye	8,364	92,866	2,028
Bura	4,502	—	710
Yendam	4,919	3,234	—
Dakka	4,995	2,940	—
Wurkum	—	24,880	—
Jukun	—	24,387	—
Jen	—	4,946	1,185
Nupe	—	826	259
Bachama	—	2,010	9,273
Ibo	3,030	994	373
Yoruba	—	508	23
Bolewa	—	1,257	—
Laka	—	200	261
Longuda	—	—	13,661
Mbula	—	—	7,861
Kanakuru	—	—	2,790
Lala	—	—	3,220
Piri	—	—	2,071

NATURAL DIVISIONS

Geographically, Adamawa Province may be divided into six principal areas:

(i) The low-lying valley of the Benue river, traversing it from east to west for over 200 miles at only 600 feet above sea level and constituting its major physical feature.

(ii) The northern highlands, rising to peaks of 4,000 feet and embracing the mountainous districts from Lala eastwards to Zummo and northwards to the Gwoza hills.

(iii) The Gongola valley, separating the northern highlands of Adamawa from the Bauchi plateau.

(iv) The southern highlands, including the 3,500-feet Alantika and Mumuye-Dakka ranges.

(v) The high-forest belt of Gashaka.

(vi) The Mambila plateau, boasting a mean altitude of 5,000 feet and summits up to 7,000 feet.

ADMINISTRATIVE DIVISIONS

The Province is divided into three administrative Divisions:

(1) *Adamawa:* area, 18,558 square miles; population, 799,150. It extends the full length of the Province along its eastern boundary from the Bornu border to that of Bamenda Province. The Provincial Headquarters at Yola and all the Trust Territory of the Province lie within Adamawa Emirate, which is coincident with the Division and is divided into 28 districts, ranging in size from Gashaka (4,134 square miles) to Yebbi (57 square miles) and in population from Mubi (77,988) to Belel (5,030). It contains some 50 miles of the Benue valley, the whole of the northern highlands except for the Lala District of Numan Division, the eastern half of the southern highlands, and the entire Gashaka area and Mambila plateau.

(2) *Muri:* area, 11,014 square miles; population, 260,288. It contains over 100 miles of the Benue valley and the western half of the southern highlands. About a third of the Division lies on the north bank of the Benue and consists of the south-eastern

escarpment of the Bauchi plateau, known as the Wurkum hills which rise almost directly from the Benue swamps. There are 11 districts, the largest in area being Bakundi (2,478 square miles) and in population Wurkum (42,000).

(3) *Numan:* area, 2,214 square miles; population, 121,438. It is encircled by the Adamawa Emirate and Muri Division, save for a brief sector to the north and north-west where it marches with the Biu and Gombe Divisions of Bornu and Bauchi Provinces respectively. The Benue splits the Division from east to west for about 60 miles, while 40 miles of the Gongola valley divide it from north to south. The Division has five districts, of which the largest in both area and population is Bachama, 945 square miles carrying 37,000 inhabitants.

At one time a considerable area of Adamawa Province was 'closed' under the provisions of the Unsettled Districts' Ordinance. For instance, in 1925 the Chamba, Mumuye, Piri, Longuda, Kanakuru, Yungur, Lala, Bura, Hona, Marghi and Kilba tribes were all defined as 'unsettled' with the exception of a very few areas, and the Mambiia, Alantika and northern touring districts were 'closed' *en bloc*. Numan Division was completely 'opened' in 1927. In Muri Division the Mumuye area west of the Jalingo-Lau road was "opened' in 1928, followed by part of Zinna District in 1931; the last part of Zinna District, the hills of Dong, was opened in 1954. In Adamawa Division, Ga'anda District was opened in 1927, Mambila District in 1936 and most of the northern districts in 1950. Today in the Province there remain only 150 square miles of unsettled districts in the Alantika area and some 400 square miles in certain villages of Madagali, Cubunawa and Mubi Districts lying to the east of the Uba-Bama road.

CLIMATE

In the northern districts of the Province, where the country rises to about 2,000 feet and the annual rainfall averages 42 inches, the climate is pleasantly free from the excessive heat and humidity caused by evaporation in the Benue valley. Along the Benue river evaporation produces a trying humid atmosphere throughout most of the year; shade temperatures of 110° are not unknown, and in Yola itself the heat is retained for long hours of the night by the abundant rock.

For most of the Province the seasonal cycle is that of the Northern Region generally: tornadoes and a few showers in the marginal months of April and October; the rains spreading from May to September, with perhaps a brief dry spell in August before the heavy rainfall of the succeeding month; lower temperatures during the harmattan months of November to January; and the hot and airless weeks from mid-February to the onset of the rains. This colourful description of the seasons is taken from a recent touring officer's report:

For five months of the year 50 inches of rain render travel by car virtually impossible; even by horse it is plodding and wearisome in the western spongelike swamps, wet and dangerous among the eastern hill torrents that are born in a night and live but for a season. May brings the first tornadoes, full of sound and fury, signifying little; June and July are a veritable spring, a time of rising sap and new birth and joy, when the country is swiftly and strangely changed to a green luxuriance. Then come three months of heavy storms and washouts, until one day quite suddenly there are no more dark clouds gathering over the Mandara hilltops: the corn turns brown and brittle, bush fires burn merrily along the hillsides at night like twinkling lights, and dead leaves litter the ground, for the dry season has come. November to February bring the invigorating climate of hot suns and chilly evenings, when the temperature can drop from 100 to 50 degrees within a space of hours. The harmattan veils the countryside with its mantle of Sahara-borne sand particles which infiltrate everywhere; shaving brushes stiffen while leather and paper curl at the edges, crumple and crackle. Thus into March and April, months when a cruel sun overwhelms all living things save the sturdy *Adenium Honghel* shrub; the burnt, parched earth bears no resemblance to the viridacious richness of earlier months; stifling nights bring little relief to a tense and nerve-taut community anxiously awaiting the onset of the first rains, which surely cannot be far behind.

There is another climatic zone in Adamawa, that of the Gashaka-Mambila region, where the prolonged rainy season approximates to the weather cycle of Southern Nigeria but with the plateau advantages of a low temperature.

Further climatic data are given in Tables II and III.

TABLE II[1]

Yola lies approximately 575 feet above sea-level, at 9°10′ N. and 12°29′ E.

Mean monthly rainfall, in inches, averaged over 35 years: line (a).
Mean daily maximum temperature, in degrees Fahrenheit: line (b)
Mean daily minimum temperature, in degrees Fahrenheit: line (c).
Mean relative humidity, per cent at 0600 hrs, G.M.T.: line (d).
Mean relative humidity, per cent at 1200 hrs, G.M.T.: line (e).

	Jan.	Feb.	Mar.	Apr.	May	June	July	Aug.	Sept.	Oct.	Nov.	Dec.	Year
(a)	0·0	0·0	0·3	1·9	4·9	6·2	6·8	7·7	7·8	3·2	0·2	0·0	39·0
(b)	95·1	98·4	102·0	103·0	96·9	90·5	87·4	87·2	86·2	91·1	96·9	96·0	94·2
(c)	65·2	69·4	75·5	78·8	76·1	73·4	72·4	73·4	71·5	71·9	67·5	65·1	71·6
(d)	35	33	34	55	76	87	90	92	93	91	71	47	67
(e)	16	15	17	26	39	61	66	68	69	60	29	19	40

[1] Taken from Appendix I to *Land and People of Nigeria*, 1955, which gives comparative figures for many large stations in the country.

TABLE III

Average rainfall: other stations in Adamawa Province

Month	Numan	Jalingo	Mubi	Gembu (1955)
January	—	—	—	—
February	0·22	0·29	—	9·04
March	0·52	0·64	0·05	—
April	1·35	2·68	0·30	4·35
May	4·66	6·14	3·60	7·82
June	5·36	7·79	5·47	14·98
July	5·60	7·99	7·30	8·21
August	5·65	7·24	10·24	5·46
September	6·71	10·57	10·56	6·83
October	2·87	4·98	3·40	8·68
November	0·07	0·19	1·31	1·13
December	—	—	—	—

VEGETATION

The general pattern is that of stretches of undulating country covered with thin, low-growing bush, intermittently broken by fertile valleys and abrupt massifs. These low ridges of well-drained laterite soil, which provide excellent grazing and arable land, may be regarded as an apron to the great granite hill systems of the Province.

The northern part of Adamawa is mainly Sudan savannah, with a patch of Guinea savannah in the Mubi-Biu area, while to the south lies Guinea savannah broken by islands of high forest in the Toungo-Gashaka region. This savannah, though profoundly affected in its physical appearance by farming and seasonal firing, is characterized by a continuous grass cover, in which stand abundant trees, generally of small size and of branched and twisted habit, and rarely providing an uninterrupted canopy. In the far south the grassland montane outriders of Bamenda merge into the Mbar plain and the Mambila plateaux.

Much of the Province is covered with secondary timber, a feature of the orchard bush of Northern Nigeria. The principal trees are acacia, shea-nut and locust-bean, with sporadic concentrations of deleb-palms and isolated baobabs. Remnants of true forest, in which mahogany and other hardwoods persist, are found in Gashaka and along the banks of streams.

On either side of the Benue stretch great marshlands, and the alluvial plain of the Gongola valley carries a rich layer of black cotton soil. Of the rice potentialities of Adamawa Dr. Dalziel wrote in 1910:

> The extensive marsh between the Benue and the long ridge on which Yola town is situated, some two miles in width and many miles in length, is alone capable of supplying the province with this grain, a fact which was pointed out to the late Emir by a party of Turkish exiles last year. From the deck of a river steamer one cannot fail to see extending from the edge of the natural channel almost endless areas of grassy swamps, little cumbered by trees, and limited only by the range of hills some 10 to 15 miles distant, areas which would appear to offer illimitable possibilities for the growth of this cereal.

Adamawa is blessed with valuable pastures, especially those of the Mambila plateau which support over 150,000 head of cattle. The fertile areas of the Gongola and Yedseram valleys have earned the name of Adamawa's granary; yam mounds are characteristic of the Mumuye country; and maize, tobacco and onions mark the riverain vegetation. There are, however, still large tracts of uncultivated bush, and in Gashaka and parts of Muri Division it is possible to do a day's trek without coming across more than a handful of huts.

RIVERS

The River Benue,[1] which with its tributaries waters nearly all the Province, rises in the 3,000-feet Ngaundere massif in the French Cameroons. Its name, Binuwe, means the 'Mother of Waters', though some scholars have sought to find its origin in a distortion of a Bachama word meaning 'The Big Death'. Its flow is rapid over the first 150 miles, with a fall of about 2,000 feet, but from its confluence with the Kebi the Benue proceeds more slowly. Shortly after passing the French town of Garua it enters Adamawa at a point some 30 miles above Yola and is joined from the south by the Faro which here marks the international boundary. This frontier follows the course of the Benue for a few miles

[1] See also Chapter VIII.

downstream, as far as the mouth of the Tiel, which constitutes the boundary northwards from the Benue for about 30 miles. Thence the Benue winds slowly westwards, amongst ever-changing sandbanks and with many a sweeping bend, until it meets the Niger opposite Lokoja and enters on the final stretch of its 800-mile journey to the sea. In the dry season, when the banks tower above as reminders of the earlier level, the river is shallow and can even be forded on foot by Yola; but in the rains, when a difference of over 20 feet has been measured, it swells to half a mile wide and is navigable by large river-steamers of 6- or 7-foot draught as far upstream as Garua.

In scenery the Benue presents a striking contrast to the Niger. Its waters untroubled by rapids or exposed rocks, its hills cut far back to reveal tongues of marshland running up the tributary valleys, its course undistinguished by the picturesque sequence of narrow gorge and expansive plain, the Benue bears signs of deep erosion and changing river beds. One traveller[1] has even hazarded that the break in the Bagale hills opposite Yola was once the bed of the Benue before the general physical upheaval.

The most important tributary of the Benue is the Gongola, which joins it at right angles opposite Numan and is navigable to light-draught steamers during the rains once they have overcome the considerable strength of the current at the confluence; in the dry season the Gongola contracts to a trickle.

Besides the rivers already mentioned, other important tributaries of the Benue include the Beti, Mayo Ine, Mayo Belwa, Kunini, Kilengi, Lamorde and Fan Manga. The Taraba and Donga rivers are navigable to river steamers at high-water, while the Pai used to serve as an evacuation route by launch for the galena mines at Zurak. It is noticeable that the southern tributaries are greater in number and size, since the river basin extends through broken and relatively well-timbered country as far as the verge of the Southern Provinces' rain-forest zone, whereas to the north it is brought up sharply against the stony central plateau of the Bauchi highlands. Incidentally, there is, just off the Mambila plateau and marking the boundary between Adamawa and Benue Provinces,

[1] Migeod.

a hidden and almost unknown waterfall, as spectacular as that of Assab on the Jos plateau, and estimated to be even larger in both fall and volume.

The north-east corner of the Province lies within the Chad basin and contains the headwaters of the Yedseram. This rises in the hills near Gella and within a few miles has broadened into a strong-flowing river, fed by numerous small tributaries from the Mandara range to the east of its fertile valley. Farther on, it meanders across the wide plain, here and there losing its identity in chains of pools and marshes, and eventually drains into Lake Chad. In general terms the boundary between the British and French Cameroons from the source of the Yedseram as far as the Bornu border is the watershed which separates the basin of this river from that of the Kebi river.

MOUNTAINS

The glory of Adamawa is in its mountain ranges.

Geologically, the prevalent formation is an exposure of the basal crystalline rocks common to Northern Nigeria, which in the northern and southern highlands emerge as granites and gneisses. In the elevated plains and the wider valleys that run between these ranges the basal rock is covered by a thick layer of laterite or by granite sandstone; shale and fossiliferous limestone of marine origin appear, associated with a more recent series of sandstone and ironstone, with here and there saline deposits. Much of Adamawa displays to perfection the geographical *Inselberglandschaft*, a series of isolated domes and kopjes set in a well-wooded plain.

Eastward from where the extensive Benue plain of Muri Division narrows near Lau there rise sudden and steep hills on both banks at a distance of 15 miles, developing on the right bank into the great barrier of the precipitous Muri range, whose peaks one explorer[1] has compared to the teeth of a gigantic saw. Farther upstream the eye is attracted by the curious and characteristic volcanic mounds of Gamadio and Giwana, and by the flat-topped, sugar-loaf sandstone outliers of Yendam Waka which, typical of the Niger country, are less common in the Benue valley.

[1] Lenfant.

The Kona and 4,000-feet Mumuye hills, which bound the plain to the south of the Benue, are largely granitic and present rounded contours, while the foothills of the tumbled Shebshi range are of quartzite and gneiss, creating more rugged outlines. These hills are the northernmost extension of the Mambila range, linked by the Toungo uplands which lead to the open grasslands of the Mumuye-Zinna system and gradually descend to the closely cultivated lower plateau round Zinna itself.

Approaching Yola, these central hills are breached by the plains of the Mayo Ine to the south and the Gongola plain to the north. They return on the right bank in the granite Longuda link with the Tangale system, in the long, tabular outlines of Libu, and in the terraced slopes and abrupt scarps of Bagale, while to the south rises the Verre massif, a solid mass fronting boldly outwards upon the surrounding plain with a continuous rocky face indented by a few deeply cut and narrow valleys. Behind it, and quite separate, tower the 3,600-feet Alantika mountains, whose mass can be seen 30 miles away from Yola, looming suddenly in sharp contrast to the broad Benue flood-plain.

North of Yola runs a high-level plain considerably above the elevation of the Benue, with generally hummocky country developing to a fine inselberg landscape. The curious local uplift at Song extends westward across the volcanic puys of 3,700-feet Mboi, with its line of small craters, to Yungur District, and eastward in rocky islets set in wooded plains to emerge as the Holma and Zummo-Malabu range.

Farther north the isolated, ten-mile, granite massif of the Kilba hills rears straight out of the plain, and many of the inselberge here afford excellent examples of exfoliation. For seventy miles along the eastern boundary runs the Mandara range, with peaks of 4,000 feet among its westward spurs of Maiha, Mubi, Cubunawa and Madagali Districts. This frontier escarpment is crowded with a fantastic series of pinnacles, culminating in the crystalline finger peak of Kamale, 700 feet high from its base and among the finest natural obelisks in the world.

The grassy highlands of the Mambila plateaux rise to over 7,000 feet and carry the best cattle ranges in Nigeria and some of its most majestic scenery. But this mountainous country, wild and hard of access, is so broken by the valleys of the Benue's southern tributaries that, to quote a recent traveller,[1] 'no one who has not actually performed the [Mambila plateau] journey can form any conception of its difficulty'. Nor can anybody who has trekked among these hills forget the superb panoramic view over the plains towards Serti or the storm-clouds rolling up over the undulating grasslands. The term 'plateau' is perhaps misleading, for once you have struggled up the escarpment the land is anything but flat; it is, rather, a saucer-shaped offshoot of the Cameroon highlands, where a trek from one village to the next may involve a whole day's laborious descent to the valley and the weary ascent of the opposite slope, though only a mile or so separates them as the crow flies.

The 6,700-feet trigonometrical point of Vogel Peak, so prominent on the map, is curiously elusive on the ground, according to reports from recent visitors. The Boundary Commission of 1907, however, reported 'two great blocks of mountains, those on the left culminating in Vogel Spitz'. An attempt was made by them to climb this mountain by way of a stream, but the waterfalls made this impossible.

FLORA AND FAUNA

For the botanical enthusiast there is plenty to discover and record in Adamawa Province. Especially beautiful is the *karya* or *adenium honghel* shrub, whose pink flowers are the pride of many a garden and give sudden delight to the traveller as they bloom in rocky wasteland even in the middle of the hot months. Grateful, too, to the eye is the yellow flower which springs up in the charred wake of a bush-fire, without leaves or visible stem. Other spectacular flora of the Province include the red and yellow *gloriosa superba*, the brilliant Flame of the Forest and the red silk-cotton tree, the frangipani and flamboyant so profuse in towns and gardens, and the water-lilies that float in nearly every village pool. Mambila has a flora of its own, among which figure an iris, several campions, a gladiolus and many orchises. At the end of the dry

[1] Migeod.

season the young leaves of the shea-nut and other shrubs burst forth in a startling kaleidoscope of colour.

The bird and fish life of the Province are particularly rich, but civilization has killed the description of Adamawa in the 'twenties: 'well-stocked with game, elephant, rhinoceros and giraffe being found in addition to the usual antelope and buffalo'. Adamawa, once famed for its ivory, used to be traversed by elephant paths, and there is at least one village in Mambila District which, up to a generation ago, used to support a community of Hausa ivory traders, but which disintegrated when the elephants in the area had all been killed and the hunters had moved on. There was a sizeable herd in Malabu in 1926. Rhinoceros at one time flourished in the Gongola and Goila areas; in 1939 they were still found near the Kilengi river, while giraffe were reported in the Benue-Pai bush of Muri Division only a few years earlier. Two hippopotami killed a man in Kiri in 1936. These animals can still be found in the Benue towards Garua, and a manager of the United Africa Company had an exciting encounter with them when he was touring in his travelling barge in 1952. Leopard are still common throughout the Province, and lion are plentiful wherever the population is sparse. In 1950 a lion strayed into Yola station and was shot by the Nigeria Police; in 1955 two errant bush-cows reconnoitred the Lamido's palace. An anthropologically-trained A.D.O. is said to have protested against his posting to the Southern Touring Area on the grounds that there were more wild animals than human beings there and his hobby was mankind.

Buffalo or bush-cow, roan, hartebeeste, water-buck, reed-buck, kob, oribi and the Senegambian gazelle are fairly commonly seen by the sportsman who works hard; the *barewa* or red-fronted gazelle still fearlessly frequents even Divisional headquarters. Wart-hog are found in the Benue valley and crocodiles are ever-present. Numan boasts of the manatee, and at Demsa, Kwa, and Yola, where many varieties of duck and geese can be counted, there is some first-class wild fowling. Bird shooting is good nearly everywhere, with abundant guinea-fowl and some francolin, sand-grouse, green and red-eye pigeon, and both the greater and lesser bustard.

There is excellent fishing in the Province. The principal game fish are the Nile perch—this *giwar ruwa* is a delicacy of the table—and the tiger-fish, which are found in the Benue and most of its tributaries. The silver catfish and several of its related 'electric' species afford good sport, and there is also a long, eel-like fish known as *dan sarki*. Perch may reach 300 lb., but the records with rod and line give Kilengi silver catfish 104 lb., electric catfish 90 lb., tiger-fish 32 lb., and perch 167 lb. This last-named was caught by G. W. Webster, Resident; it was weighed six hours after capture, was 68 inches long and had a girth of 54 inches.[1]

Although the best horses come from Bornu and Marua, the local Fulani are very keen on breeding horses, and there is excellent country round Yola and Jalingo for riding.

[1] See photograph in *West Africa*, 23 February 1918.

II

ETHNOLOGICAL NOTES

ADAMAWA—the name derives from Modibbo Adama, its first
Emir, who led the *jihad* in the south-east of what is now Northern
Nigeria at the turn of the last century—is historically neither the
amorphous mid-nineteenth-century Fulani kingdom of Fumbina
nor the reduced Province that we know today. The Fumbina
empire extended over much of the modern French Cameroons, as
far east as Lere and south as Ngaundere; its sway over many of
the acephalous pagan tribes in the Mubi and Numan areas was
but shadowy, with large tracts of disputed no-man's land between
it and the acquisitive kingdoms of Bornu, Muri or Bauchi.

The 1952 census emphasizes the religious pattern of the
Province: a Muslim minority ruling over a pagan majority which
is slowly turning to the socially advantageous creeds of Islam and
Christianity. It is reckoned that in Adamawa 30 per cent. of the
inhabitants profess Islam and 67 per cent. are pagan.

On the grounds of historical accuracy as well as geographical
entity, the history of Adamawa dates only from the *jihad*, and
Fulani genealogies rarely trace with conviction more than three or
four chiefs before 1800. Among the heterogeneous tribes of modern
Adamawa it is unlikely that any represents the aboriginal inhabitants, for all of them have traditions of migration from other lands.
There is still in Adamawa an unparalleled field of study for the
anthropologist. The ethnic history of the greater part of the
Province may be considered in terms of four more or less successive
waves of immigration, though many of the tribes probably preceded
these superimposed strata: Jukun, Chamba, Bata, Fulani.

JUKUN

The Jukun tribe, whose martial state of Kororofa was for some
centuries one of the great powers of the Nigerian hinterland and
carried its arms as far north as Kano and Bornu, had their first

capital at Bepi, on the western fringe of the Gassol District of Muri Division, about 15 miles north of Bantaji. Today no remains are visible apart from overgrown mounds and ditches representing the extensive walls of the old town. In the seventeenth century the capital was moved to Puje, near modern Wukari, and in the middle of the nineteenth century Wukari itself was built as the Jukun capital.

The war routes of the Jukun armies on their expeditions against the Hausa states and Kanem led through what is now Adamawa, and as late as 1908 trees that had grown up from the stakes which the warriors had thrust into the ground as tethering posts were still pointed out. This vigorous pagan empire—its military might was characterized in the legend that one of their kings was so powerful that since no horse could carry him he always rode a hartebeeste to war—suffered the vicissitudes of fortune common to all the Sudan states, and eventually crumbled away before the insidious advance of the Fulani, helped as ever by treachery from within. Buba Yaro of Gombe ravaged the Jukun country, and about 1860 Burba of Bakundi destroyed what was left of Kororofa. It is uncertain whether Wukari ever paid tribute to the Fulani, but it seems probable that, recognizing the paramount power, they were wont to send presents of slaves to the Emirs of Muri and Bauchi. The former Emir, Hamadu, established peace with Wukari by a marriage alliance, and in the reign of Nya the Muri forces combined with Wukari to invade the Tiv country.

The history of the Jukun empire is now of more concern to Benue than to Adamawa Province. There remains a Jukun bloc on the Kona hills of Muri Division, with settlements in western Gassol and round Lau; this town appears[1] at one time to have been a large Jukun centre. They are superficially assimilated to their Mumuye neighbours, with whom intermarriage occurs, though their political organization is more advanced.

CHAMBA

Linguistically there are two groups of Chamba. Some of the Adamawa Chamba, such as the Lekon tribe of Toungo, can be

[1] *Per* Mizon.

classified with the main Donga group, but those of Dakka, Sugu, and Nassarawo are in the second group, known as the Nyakanyare. It would appear that their main seat was originally at Lamurde Jongum (now in French territory), whence they were driven out by the Bata and crossed the Faro to the town known as Chamba, at the base of the Alantika hills. They were again expelled by the Bata, who had canoes while the Chamba had none. One section spread along the hills to Mapeo, another to the south of the Mumuye massif to coalesce with the Dakka, and a third remained on the eastern side of the plateau and fused with the Lekon.

Tradition has it that at one time in the early eighteenth century the Chamba, especially under their king Damashi, were the most important tribe on both banks of the Benue, and even after their expulsion by the Bata they remained paramount in the upper Mayo Belwa valley, where they still predominate.

BATA

The Bata invasion, before whose onset the Chamba retreated, appears to have consisted of two major waves. The first swept down through the Mandara hills and paused for a generation or two at Bazza in the upper Yedseram valley before continuing southwards to the Benue valley. The second wave also came from the north, but followed a line east of the Mandara hills down the Kebi valley and eventually settled at Demsa Poa (Old Demsa), a day's journey north of Garua, from which base they maintained their pressure on the Chamba. Under their chief, Kokomi, they became the most powerful tribe in Adamawa, but they were gradually driven westwards down the Benue by the Fulani campaigns. In the neighbourhood of Numan they built Demsa Mosu (New Demsa) and occupied the surrounding lowlands.

Tradition relates that at Demsa the tribe split as the result of a quarrel between the twin brothers of the royal family, whence originates the Bachama branch of the Bata tribe (see below, p. 168). The elder brother learned of a plot against his throne by the younger, whereupon the latter fled, taking with him the sacred pot which embodied the tribal rain-cult. Finding his brother already across the Benue, the elder called out to him: 'In future

you shall live on the north bank and I on the south. Yours shall
be the duty of guarding the Lares and Penates; mine shall be the
tasks of hunting and warring against the Fulani.' Even now the
religious rites are in the care of the Bachama chief at Lamurde.
The Bachama are sometimes referred to as the Bassama.

The Bata today occupy both banks of the Benue from Garua
to the Numan-Muri border, thus forming a 200-mile ribbon of
riverain settlements. People of partly Bata origin also inhabit the
Zummo-Malabu hills and constitute a strong element in Holma,
whither their forebears were sent as slaves to farm the rich volcanic
ground.

Before considering the final and most impressive stratum in
Adamawa's make-up, that of the Fulani, mention must be made
of some tribal movements which, though not appreciably in-
fluencing the core of the Province, are of significance on the
periphery.

MARGHI

When the Bata evacuated the Yedseram valley they were
replaced by the Marghi, who have a general legend of ancient
migration from the east. Those round Uba claim a Pabir origin;
the Wamdeo lineages are very mixed; in Huyum, Kofa, and Lassa
the predominant strain is Gazama, with its strong Muslim,
Kanuri influence; at Duhu and Gulak the Marghi stock has
coalesced with the immigrants from Gudur in the French
Cameroons; while at Bazza, which in pre-Fulani times was an
important Marghi centre, they have been largely replaced by the
Higi.

KILBA

One of the Marghi groups moved southwards to the hills and
plateau lying between the basins of the Hawal and Kilengi rivers
and became, under an alien Gude dynasty, the strong and effectively organized tribal kingdom of Kilba, whose reputation for
lawlessness was equalled by few other tribes in Nigeria. They
were never conquered by the Fulani, though there was an outpost
at Bila Kilba from which the Fulani used to carry out slave-raids

under the name of ruling. The Kilba did, however, suffer severely from the prolonged presence in their midst of Rabeh's son, Fad-el-Allah, at the very end of last century.

HIGI

Shortly after the establishment of the Marghi in northern Adamawa, another tribe, the Higi, invading from the east, occupied the central massifs of the Mandara range and drove the Marghi from its western slopes. The term *Higi*, meaning 'aboriginals', was conferred on them by the Marghi and was adopted by the Fulani in the form of *Hiji*; the people themselves, though using the word, prefer to be known as *Kakhumu* or 'people of the hills'. Their spiritual centre is now at Mukulu, on top of the spur above Bazza town.

There are several other prominent tribes in the hills of northern Adamawa. Foremost is Sukur, who claim to stem from mystic Gudur and whose *Llidi* or chief still wields immense spiritual authority as the supreme repository of the dynastic concept of priest-kingship. The Fali round Mubi were at one time a very important tribe, but, like the inhabitants of Tur and Wagga above Madagali and the Njai round Vokna and Maiha, they are now but an enclave whose main groups are to be found in the French Cameroons. Other tribes include a different branch of the Fali, round Kiriya and Mijilu; the Gude of Gella and Kwojja, also known as Cheke from the Fulani nickname for mat-makers; and the warlike, primitive Yungur of the Kilengi-Gongola watershed.

To the south of the Benue there are two other large tribal groups in Adamawa Division, the Verre and the Mambila. There is an immense difference between the various groups of the Verre, and again between the hill Verre and those of the Mayo Ine plains. The small groups of Vomni and Koma pagans in the Alantika mountains are still very primitive. Here alone in the Province the penis-sheath remains in evident use, suggesting an ancient connexion with the peoples of Plateau Province.

The large Mambila tribe occupy the major part of the plateau west of Banyo, stretching into Bamenda Province, whither they were probably driven under pressure from Banyo's slave-raiding. Prior to the formation of the Cameroons Trust Territory the Mambila had no relations with Yola, and those that became subject to the Fulani acknowledged only the governors of Banyo and Gashaka. Their wickerwork shields and curious swords are noteworthy, but they knew neither horse nor bow and arrow. Witchcraft plays a particularly potent rôle in their lives. The severity of their climate has taught the Mambila to evolve a technique of house-building superior to most in Northern Nigeria. There is a considerable difference between village and village, even their languages being mutually unintelligible, and the Mambila social organization is incohesive to an unusual degree.

MUMUYE

This is the principal tribe in the Muri Division and they account for more than 35 per cent. of the population. They occupy the eastern massif to the south of the Benue, whence they are expanding westwards and are settling in the Jalingo and Mutum Biu Districts. There is a theory that they may stem from the Cross River region, and they are probably one of the original tribes of Adamawa. Their supreme rain-maker lives at Yoro, and much emphasis is placed on the fetish *dodo*. Around Jalingo there has been considerable intermingling of Fulani and Mumuye blood, and the long-reigning Emir, Muhammadu Mafindi, enjoyed great personal influence with the Mumuye, amongst whom he lived during his banishment at the turn of the century. They have a turbulent and primitive record, and as late as 1933 the Resident could write:

The Mumuye appear to have made little if any progress towards administering themselves since 1914 when they told me quite frankly that they wanted no interference and that they preferred their contact with Government to be limited to the payment of tax. Only in one respect do they seem to have departed from the terms of an ultimatum some of them gave me at Zinna then. They do not now maintain that they are at liberty to sell their offspring and any children they can kidnap into slavery, but this change of mind is due to the fact that there are now no slave markets.

Next come the tribes known under the generic term of Wurkunawa, of whom the principal groups are the Kulu and the Piya. The latter are reputed to have migrated from the Tangale-Waja area in order to escape the slave-raids of Emir Yakubu of Bauchi. Their recognized chief is *Ardo* Kirim, but like the Kulu, with whom they have intermarried, they deny having had any dealings with the Muri Fulani before the British occupation. The Kulu, centred round Bambur, were probably subservient to the Jukun at one time.

The Jen occupy a small area on both banks of the Benue at the eastern end of Muri Division. Tall and slender in contrast to the hill-bred sturdiness of their Wurkum neighbours, they are skilled fishermen whose general mode of living is similar to that of the riverain Bata. According to their own traditions they stem from Bornu, but there is a marked Jukun influence in their social organization. The Dakka derive from Chamba stock, though features of Jukun culture are discernible; they are ruled in their hill-top villages by their tribal chief, the *Ganzamanu*.

NUMAN

In Numan Division there are three other main tribal groups besides the Bachama and Bata. The Mbula inhabit the north bank of the Benue eastwards from the River Gongola, and they intermarry with the Bata and Bachama, though their language and superb physique differentiate them. The Kanakuru inhabit the eastern slopes of the Gongola valley. They have their capital at Shellen and the *Amna* is their chief. The Longuda occupy the fertile plain on the west bank of the Gongola and the high hills of the Longuda escarpment. Other tribes are the Piri, a backward people inhabiting the hills that run down to the Benue swamps, and the Lala, a shy people living in the elevated tableland in the angle of the Hawal and Gongola rivers. All these tribes at one time enjoyed a fierce and warlike reputation.

FULANI

A detailed account of the Fulani penetration into Adamawa will be found in the chapters dealing with the history of Adamawa and

Muri Divisions, but here their immigration and their government are treated generally as the fourth, and by far the most important, stratum in the known history of the Province.

The remarkable Fulani race has given rise to much scholarly controversy as to their origin, on which no definitive theory has yet been proved. One claim is that they are of the same Polynesian stock that colonized Madagascar; another connects them with the Zingari or gipsies of Europe and traces both races back to a common Indian origin; while a third imaginatively relates them to the Hyksos or Shepherd Kings who were expelled from Egypt about the year 1630 B.C. There are still more fantastic hypotheses, ranging from a connexion between them and the lost Roman legionaries to the ascription to the Fulani of the original colonization of Canada! Certain it is that the lighter skin, thin lips, narrow nose, long straight hair, and generally refined facial features of the Fulani indicate a non-negroid descent.

Though the Fulani may have entered the Western Sudan from the Nile, within historic times their movement has unquestionably been from west to east. The first record of their presence in Eastern Nigeria dates from 1300, when a party of them came from Futa Toro, near Melle, to Bornu, and the Arab historian Makrizi noted their presence there in the first half of the fourteenth century. The early migrations of the Fulani were caused rather by their need for new pasturage than by any idea of conquest. They used to pay grazing dues to the pagans in whose country they herded their cattle, to whom they often acted as herdsmen, and were generally so subservient that they are said to have acceded to the *jus primae noctis*[1] claimed by these chiefs. The general conversion of the Fulani to Islam was slow, owing to the innate conservatism of a pastoral people, and only a minority had become Muslims by the time Adama launched his *jihad* at the beginning of the nineteenth century. Numerous clans, though supporting their kinsmen in the holy war, retained their totemic cults, and today the Mbororo'en and Kesu'en remain predominantly pagan while the Kiti'en, who settled among the Gongola valley tribes, are scarcely Islamized at all.

[1] For an interesting study of the ritual aspect of this ceremony, see *The Oedipus Complex*, E. Westermarck, 1934.

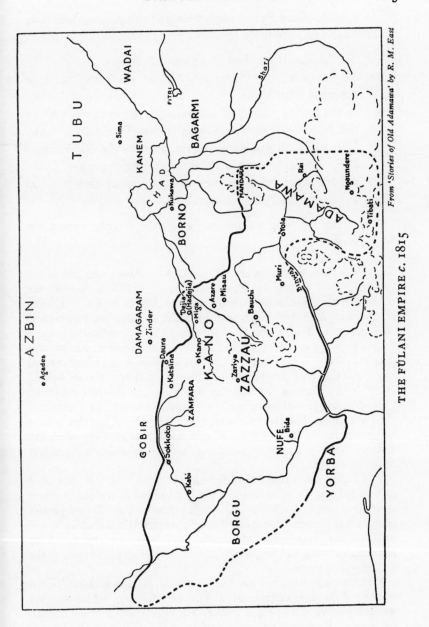

From 'Stories of Old Adamawa' by R. M. East

THE FÚLANI EMPIRE c. 1815

As a result of the Fulani migrations and campaigns, Adamawa in the 1850's fell into three clearly defined divisions:

(a) To the east, the Fulani kingdom of Fumbina.
(b) To the west, the Fulani kingdom of Muri and the area governed from Wase.
(c) In the centre, a block of unconquered pagan tribes, such as the Mumuye and the diverse tribes of modern Numan Division, with groups of pagans, such as the Kilba, Higi, Fali, and Koma, who maintained varying degrees of independence according to the inaccessibility of their hill-top villages to the Fulani cavalry.

The following observations on the Fulani dynasty were made by Lugard in 1902:

Early in the nineteenth century there arose a religious leader among the pastoral Fulani, named dan Fodio, the founder of Sokoto. To him the chiefs of the various Shepherd clans repaired, and he gave to each a flag of conquest. Armed with this sacred symbol, and inspired by fanatical zeal, each chief led his clan to victory, and the various Emirates more or less as they exist today were established. Dan Fodio is said to have prophesied that his green flag would be a passport to victory for 100 years, and that after that period the Fulani dynasty would cease to hold sway. It is a curious fact that this 100 years (by the Mohammedan Calendar) had just expired, and the Fulani are said to have expected their overthrow. The Habe dynasty, which they ousted, appears to have had a highly developed system of rule and administration which the Fulani adopted in its entirety, including the system of *alkalis* independent of the executive.

The Fulani never thoroughly conquered the country, and succeeded only in gaining the submission of the great towns in the plains where their horsemen were effective. The pagan tribes in the hills and broken country and even in large areas of the plains maintained their independence. They were constantly raided for slaves, and retaliated by attacking caravans and frequently carried the war up to the gates of the Fulani walled towns.

Wherever a Fulani army had been it left a depopulated desert. Greed was one of the chief characteristics of the new dynasty, and tax after tax was enforced upon the people. Bribery, corruption and extortion marked the so-called administration of justice, while the multiplication of harems and the growth of a large class of idle 'princes' led to nepotism.

It is improbable that the dynasty could have lasted long even had its collapse not been thus [campaign of 1897 by the Royal Niger Company] accelerated, for the passion of the Fulani for slave-raiding had denuded the country of its population. The truly awful desolation and destruction of life caused by this slave-raiding is apparent today: enormous tracts of land have gone out of cultivation, and one constantly sees the ruins of great towns now overgrown with jungle.

The system of Fulani rule was a feudal one, in which the right to all land was vested in the Emir, and fief holders paid a rent or tribute to the overlord. This in the case of Fulani holders appears to have been a tithe of the produce, but in the case of conquered pagans the amount was arbitrarily assessed and frequently doubled as a punishment for rebellion. . . .

In my view the tradition of British rule has ever been to arrest disintegration, to retain and build up again what is best in the social and political organisation of the conquered dynasties. I believe myself that the future of the virile races of this Protectorate lies largely in the regeneration of the Fulani. Their ceremonial, their coloured skins, their mode of life and habits of thought, appeal more to the native populations than the prosaic business-like habits of the Anglo-Saxon can ever do.

III

EXPLORATION

THE early European exploration of modern Northern Nigeria was primarily concerned with the elusive riddle of the Niger and its subsequent exploitation. Thus it was that the remote and dangerous regions of the Upper Benue were, apart from two or three explorers in the 1850's, quite unknown until the last two decades of the century when, during the scramble for Africa, Adamawa experienced an international interest that was decidedly embarrassing to more than one European government.

DENHAM[1]

The first European to come into touch with Adamawa was Major Denham (of the Oudney, Clapperton, and Denham expedition to Chad and Sokoto) who, during an enforced sojourn in Bornu in 1823, accompanied the combined Bornu and Mandara armies in their attack on the Fulani town of Musfeia (Masfel, now in French territory).

The Felatahs had carried a very strong fence of palisades, well-pointed, and fastened together with thongs of raw hide, six feet in height, from one hill to the other, and had placed their bowmen behind the palisades, and on the rising ground, with the wadey before them; their horse were all under cover of the hills and the town: this was a strong position. The Arabs, however, moved on with great gallantry, without any support or co-operation from the Bornou or Mandara troops, and notwithstanding the showers of arrows, some poisoned, which were fired on them from behind the palisades, Boo-Khaloum, with his handful of Arabs, carried them in about half an hour, and dashed on, driving the Felatahs up the sides of the hills. The women were everywhere seen supplying their protectors with fresh arrows during this struggle; and when they retreated to the hills, still shooting on their pursuers, the women assisted by rolling down huge masses of rock, previously undermined for the purpose.

[1] *Narrative of Travels and Discoveries in Northern and Central Africa, 1822, 1823, and 1824*, Denham and Clapperton, 1826.

Barca Gana, and about one hundred of the Bornou spearmen, now supported Boo-Khaloum, and pierced through and through some fifty unfortunates who were left wounded near the stakes. I rode by his side as he pushed on quite into the town, and a very desperate skirmish took place between Barca Gana's people and a small body of the Felatahs. These warriors throw the spear with great dexterity; and three times I saw the man transfixed to the earth who was dismounted for the purpose of firing the town, and as often were those who rushed forward for that purpose sacrificed for their temerity, by the Felatahs.

Had either the Mandara or the Sheikh's troops now moved up boldly, notwithstanding the defence these people made, they must have carried the town with the heights overlooking it, along which the Arabs were driving the Felatahs by the terror which their miserable guns excited; but, instead of this, they still kept on the other side of the wadey, out of reach of the arrows.

The Felatahs, seeing their backwardness, now made an attack in their turn: the arrows fell so thick that there was no standing against them, and the Arabs gave way. The Felatah horse now came on . . . We instantly became a flying mass.

Denham, wounded and separated from his companions, was seized by the Fulani when his horse fell under him. He was thrown to the ground and stripped naked: 'They were alone prevented from murdering me, in the first instance, I am persuaded, by the fear of injuring the value of my clothes, which appeared to them a rich booty.' He escaped while his captors were arguing over his clothes.

BARTH[1]

Barth, the remarkable German explorer, was the first European to travel extensively in Adamawa and to penetrate into its capital, Yola, in 1851. On 24 May he wrote from Kukawa his dispatch to the British Government, who had entrusted him with the mission of exploring Central Africa:

I have the honour to inform your Lordship that, on Tuesday next, I am to start for Adamawa, as it is called by the Fellatah (Fullan), or Fumbina, a very extensive country whose capital, Yola, is distant from here fifteen days south-south-west.

Passing through the border country of the Marghi, Barth caught his first glimpse of the Mandara hills:

[1] *Travels and Discoveries in North and Central Africa*, H. Barth, 1857.

The whole range of mountains, which forms the western barrier of the little country of Wandala, lay open before me at a distance of about twenty miles, while behind it, towards the south, mountains of more varied shape, and greater elevation, became more visible.

On 10 June he reached Uba, the northernmost Fulani settlement in Adamawa, whose governor impressed Barth less than did the tumbled rocks behind the town: 'Neither he nor his companions were dressed with any degree of elegance, or even cleanliness.' A week later Barth stood on the banks of the Benue, the first European to set eyes on the upper reaches of the Mother of Waters:

I looked long and silently upon the stream; it was one of the happiest moments in my life . . . it rarely happens that a traveller does not feel disappointed when he first actually beholds the principal features of a new country, of which his imagination has composed a picture from the description of the natives; but the appearance of the river far exceeded my most lively expectations.

Barth, 'in a state of mind not exempt from anxious feeling', entered Yola on 20 June:

. . . Yola is a large open place, consisting, with a few exceptions, of conical huts surrounded by spacious courtyards, and even by cornfields, the houses of the governor and those of his brothers being built alone of clay. Keeping along the principal street we continued our march for a mile and a quarter before we reached the house of the governor, which lies on the west side of a small open area, opposite the mosque, a flat oblong building, or rather hall, enclosed with clay walls, and covered with a flat thatched roof a little inclined to one side. Having reached this place, my companions fired a salute, which . . . was not very judicious.

The fact that Barth came from Bornu was the worst recommendation that he could have had, and the firing of guns on a Friday outside the mosque did nothing to improve matters. The Emir, Muhammad Lawal, refused to see Barth for two days; when he did receive him, the letters from Bornu caused such ill-feeling that Barth was obliged to return to his lodging without presenting his customary gifts. Later in the day he received a curt message from the Emir to say that as a vassal of Sokoto he could not entertain a stranger without express sanction. Despite his friendship with Mansur, a brother of the Emir, Barth was ordered to leave Yola without delay, and on 24 June he rode forth to retrace his steps to friendly Bornu, without the treaty that he had hoped to obtain.

Barth's travels in Northern Nigeria must rank among the great African explorations, and his account of this Adamawa journey remains a most fascinating and enthralling record.

VOGEL[1]

Vogel was sent out, with two N.C.O.s of the Royal Engineers, by the British Government in 1853 to relieve Barth and then to explore the Upper Benue as far as the Nile. Corporal Church quarrelled with Vogel and returned home with Barth in April 1855, while Corporal Macguire and his leader set out for Yakoba (Bauchi) and Adamawa. Macguire there deserted and was murdered by the pagans; the same fate overtook Vogel a little later. We know, however, that he succeeded in reaching Adamawa, for in a letter he claimed that on 30 April 1855 he crossed the Benue 'exactly on the spot from where the steamer *Pleiad* had returned, numerous empty pickle and brandy bottles giving sure evidence that Englishmen had been there'. Barth was of the opinion that Vogel had travelled extensively in the Hammaruwa, Yakoba, and Gombe triangle.

BAIKIE[2]

The news of Barth's discovery of the Benue, and his identification of it with the river hitherto known, from the Lokoja end, as the Chadda, determined the British Government to explore this new waterway, and to meet and assist Barth and Vogel. The Admiralty commissioned the veteran African adventurer, MacGregor Laird, to build and equip a vessel for this purpose. His instructions to his sailing-master advised him to 'make every exertion' to reach

---

[1] His papers were never recovered. There are, however, two rare books which have sought to re-enact Vogel's travels and discoveries from his correspondence: *Reisen in Central Afrika von Mungo Park bis auf Barth und Vogel,* edited by E. Schauenburg, 1859, and *Schilderung der Reisen und Entdeckungen des Dr. Edouard Vogel in Central Afrika,* edited by H. Wagner, 1860.

[2] *Narrative of an Exploring Voyage up the Rivers Kwora and Benue, commonly known as the Niger and Tsadda,* W. B. Baikie, 1856. Accounts were also written by T. J. Hutchinson and Bishop Crowther.

Yola. The vessel, christened the *Pleiad*, set sail for Fernando Po, where she was to pick up Mr. Beecroft who, as Consul, had been appointed to the command. He died before the *Pleiad* arrived and the command of the expedition devolved on Dr. William Balfour Baikie, R.N.

On 12 July 1854, the *Pleiad* entered the Nun mouth of the Niger, and on 7 August she began to make her way up the Benue, reaching the southern villages of Hammaruwa (Muri) on 16 September. Messages of welcome were received from the Emir, and after Baikie's party had returned from the town of Muri, he determined to visit the king himself. He describes the Fulani at length:

Their manners appeared to us, after meeting with so many rude tribes, cultivated and pleasing, and their persons were kept tolerably clean. Most of the men wear tobes, almost all have turbans, straw hats, or some kind of head-dress, and many sport loose trowsers . . . The women were certainly by far the best-looking whom we saw, and were dressed with some degree of taste . . . The ordinary language is the Pulo, but Hausa is also nearly universally understood.

The account of the audience with the Emir is interesting:

While approaching the palace we fired several blank shots, to the mingled terror and delight of the beholders . . . We were ushered into a large, substantial hut, the door of which was shaded by a curtain. We were seated on good Turkey rugs, and about were carelessly strewn cushions of bright-coloured European cloths and satins, red and yellow being the predominant shades. Across the capacious hut, immediately before us, hung a curtain of striped pink and white silk, which concealed his majesty from our view . . . I inquired of Sarikin Hausa whether the curtain was to be raised or not, but was told that, according to custom, the Sultan would remain unseen during our conference. The silk screen not being very thick, and as the king sat between me and an open door, I could see his figure and actions, though I could not distinguish his features.

The river was falling so fast that Baikie feared to take the *Pleiad* farther and, misinformed as to the distance to Yola from Gurowa, he tried to reach that city by gig. On 28 September he set out with Mr. May, the sailing-master, and his pet dog. They were hospitably received at Lau, but at Jen the natives showed unfriendliness and tried to detain them. The following day they rowed into the middle of the flooded village of Dulti where the natives, mistaking them perhaps for Fulani slave-raiders, threatened them with their weapons and prepared to rush them.

Suddenly my little dog, who had been lying quietly in the stern sheets, raised her head to see what was causing such a commotion. Her sudden appearance startled the Dulti warriors, who had never seen such an animal before, so they drew back to take counsel together, making signs to me to know if she could bite, to which I replied in the affirmative.

As it was clearly hopeless to attempt to reach Yola and the Faro, the adventurers turned downstream to rejoin the *Pleiad*. On arrival at her moorings no sign of the ship was to be seen, but they learned that the officers had decided, in view of the falling river, to withdraw to Zhibu, 120 miles downstream. They started out to row this distance, but came across the *Pleiad* hard aground on a bank opposite the mouth of the Taraba.

FLEGEL AND ASHCROFT[1]

In 1879 the German explorer Flegel, on board the Church Missionary Society's ship *Henry Venn* in command of their Niger lay agent, J. H. Ashcroft, made his first visit to Yola. Though the Emir refused point-blank to see any of the party, the diary of the voyage has much of interest about Adamawa. In Hammaruwa, where 'there seems to be a great lack of clothing, especially the female portion; and that speaks for itself against the men, who like to go about with about 15 yards round their head alone', Ashcroft had an audience with the Emir to explain the purpose of this missionary visit to the Upper Benue. He describes the royal executioner:

The headsman carried a club about 4½ feet long, two inches thick at one end, tapering to one and a quarter inches at the other, and he had a cord fastened to the club; it was about a quarter inch in diameter, just like our window-cord and just what is used for tying slaves when they are caught. I asked him how the men were killed, when he kneeled coolly down on the spot to show me. He went with a boy, and showed how they were first struck by him at the back of the head and stunned, and then

[1] For E. Flegel's first expedition (1879), see his lecture to the Royal Geographical Society in 1880. Ashcroft's diary is quoted in the Church Missionary Society's *Intelligencer* of 1880. For Flegel's subsequent travels in Adamawa, see his *Vom Niger-Benue: Briefe aus Afrika*, 1890.

how he took the sword that he had and cut off their heads. On our way back I found he alone had beheaded twenty-nine men, and three women who had murdered a favourite wife of their husband.

The royal messengers of Demsa, who brought him an ivory tusk as a salutation, were dressed in scarlet clothes, while the warlike Mbula sent out a flotilla of canoes to inspect the steamer. When the Emir of Yola refused to send a return present they continued up-river as far as Garua, arriving on 4 September, and from here steamed back down the Benue, ignoring Yola completely.

This episode brings to a close the first phase of European exploration of Adamawa, the purely geographical one. Between 1882 and 1883 Flegel,[1] who was a clerk in a German trading house at Lagos, travelled extensively in Adamawa as the first of the many explorers, English, French, and German, who sought to open up the commercial riches of the territory. He was twice admitted into the presence of the Emir of Yola and spent some months in the town before being peremptorily ordered to leave. Frail-bodied and tireless, his travels exhausted him and the final blow came when he found that the British had forestalled Germany in obtaining a commercial treaty with Sokoto, the liege of Adamawa.

ZINTGRAFF[2]

Another intrepid German explorer was Dr. Zintgraff, who left the Cameroons in December 1888 and, after a hazardous journey, reached Ibi in the following June. From there he travelled through Bakundi to Gashaka, whose ruler told him that only the Emir of Adamawa could give him permission to travel to Bali through Banyo. So Zintgraff set out from Gashaka for Yola, which he reached at the end of July.

I was greatly mistaken in thinking that I should have to spend a long time in Yola in seeking my requirements. Two days alone were enough in the English capital of German Adamawa to convince me that under no circumstances would permission be granted to me to travel to Banyo. True, of my actual reception I have no cause for complaint. The Sultan immediately on my arrival had a good compound prepared for me, and

[1] See also his *Lose Blätter aus dem Tagebuche meines Haussa-Freundes und Reisegefährten*, 1885.
[2] *Nord-Kamerun*, Eugen Zintgraff, 1895.

provided me with equally rich provisions such as sheep, chickens, butter, milk, beer, flour, and corn for my followers and horses. Like everywhere in Adamawa, I received on the very afternoon of my arrival many visitors, who enquired after my health and thence, though they had come themselves empty-handed, sought to obtain presents for themselves. . . .

The next afternoon brought certainty. The Sultan, after he had enquired the purpose of my visit, of which he was already well acquainted from Gashaka, declared that a journey to Banyo was not at that time feasible, as the Sultan of Banyo had shown himself rebellious. For two hours I exhausted myself in argument and counter-argument, and it required a great effort to remain quiet in face of the inevitable opposition of these people. Meanwhile I sat there, as with all the princelings of Adamawa, without a campstool, on a rug folded into a cushion, since it is not usual to offer stools or even chairs to distinguished visitors, who are obliged to squat on the ground. I did not remove my shoes, which is likewise a custom here where shoes are always left outside the audience chamber, since I would not have done so at home with my prince. On the other hand riding boots are retained, by the by, even by the Emir's own subjects.

The Emir, however, was obdurate, and Zintgraff deemed it wise not to tarry in Yola. He was back in Gashaka by 15 August, and reached the coast towards the end of the year.

MACDONALD[1]

In 1889 the British Government, as a result of many foreign and English complaints about the high-handed behaviour of the Chartered Company, sent out a special commissioner to visit all the treaty-chiefs and Royal Niger Company establishments on the Niger and Benue. Sailing up-river in the 400-ton stern-wheeler *Boussa*, they reached the wooding-station of Mairanawa on 10 August, where the Commissioner amused the Emir of Muri's executioner by asking for a demonstration of his art on his assistant. They stopped at Lau, Jen, and Numan,

. . . picturesquely situated and well-shaded by large trees, where the inhabitants fled from their village as we landed, leaving their chief and half-a-dozen followers to receive us alone.

A run of a few hours [from Geren] brought us to the anchorage at

[1] *Up the Niger*, Captain A. F. Mockler-Ferryman, 1892. He was private secretary to Major (later Sir) Claude Macdonald; the latter's own account was presented to the Royal Geographical Society in 1893.

Yola. We lay close under the left bank of the river, where a rugged range of low hills, covered with granite boulders and trees, obscures the view of the town. On the right bank the slopes of a magnificent group of mountains came almost down to the water. Yola itself lies three miles or more from the anchorage, though at this season of the year, the overflow from the river forms a huge lake, which extends to within a few hundred yards of the town, and which can be navigated by launches of light draught and canoes.

The Emir, sulking at the Niger Company whose trading hulk he had blockaded, refused to see the Commissioner, and while the party kicked their heels they went out after guinea-fowl on the bluff above the marshes.

The view was well worth the toil we had gone through and our first glimpse of Yola, visible two miles or more away, quite came up to our expectations. Isolated farms, surrounded by fields of corn, and dark green plantations of yam, lie dotted about in the foreground; behind these again acres of high yellow millet stretch away up to the scattered grass huts of Adamawa's capital. The town itself covers a large area of land, but owing to the numerous trees is almost hidden from view.

They steamed up to Garua and explored the Kebi. On their return to Yola on 25 August the Emir showed no sign of mellowing, and so they retraced their steps down the Benue, visiting Gassol and Bakundi on their way back to Lokoja.

The two large funnels [wrote Macdonald of the *Boussa*] sticking through the top of the awning inspired great respect in the Upper Benue, where so large a ship had never been seen before: the natives were under the impression that these imposing chimneys could be lowered from their vertical position at our own sweet will and fired off with destructive effect.

MORGEN[1]

The Germans were still striving to further their exploitation of the Adamawa hinterland, of whose potential value Nachtigal had first spoken in the early 1870's. In 1890 Morgen was commissioned to open the way for a big trading caravan which was being equipped by the German commercial houses of Hamburg, and he trekked from Yaunde, where Kund and Tappenbeck had erected the first inland station, through the Adamawa towns of Tibati and Banyo

[1] *Durch-Kamerun von Süd nach Nord*, C. Morgen, 1893.

across to Ibi on the Benue. His efforts to establish German control by asking the Fulani potentates to accept flags met with the firm reply that no such relationship could be entered into without the prior approval of the Emir of Yola.

STETTEN[1]

Another German expedition to Adamawa was led by Baron von Stetten who, accompanied by Lieutenant Häring, visited Yola in 1893 and concluded a treaty with the Emir.

UECHTRITZ[2]

In 1893 the German *Kolonialgesellschaft* sent out a private expedition under the command of Uechtritz in a final attempt to gain by treaty the legal claims for which their indifferent Government had been reluctant to make any sacrifices.

They anchored off Yola on 31 August, and were later allowed to disembark and encamp in Kassa village, on the plateau overlooking the Yola marshes.

A splendid view across the broad, green valley, the river and the mountains sparkling in the rays of the setting sun. We could not have wished for anything more beautiful.

There are rich descriptions of Yola, its crops and flora, its people, of interviews with the Emir and his diplomacy of presents and promises.

With several pieces of satin, lace strips and baft, and an Arabic book, Uechtritz presented himself before the minister. When, during the visit, Audu was about to hand over the book, the minister leaped up from his bed with a cry of *Allah*, threw himself to the ground, washed his face and hands with sand, and only then dared to receive, with pious awe, the holy book into the opened folds of his gown. The announcement that the book was not the Koran was unable to quieten his transports of ecstasy. 'The king,' he cried, 'will rejoice more at this present than at all the others you have given him, and he will surely send you a horse as a token of his pleasure!'

[1] See his articles in *Deutsches Kolonialblatt*, 1893 and 1895.

[2] *Adamawa*, Siegfried Passarge, 1895. He accompanied von Uechtritz as medical officer to the expedition. His monumental account is most rewarding to anyone who can work his way through 600 large pages of scholarly Teutonic prose.

Before they set out from Yola at the beginning of October to march with their 144 carriers to Garua, and thence northwards to Marua and southwards through Muri, an unexpected event threw Yola into panic.

Earlier in the day I had noticed brown clouds. As I was out walking on the following afternoon I suddenly found myself engulfed in a cloud of locusts. In their millions they hummed through the air, in their thousands they alighted on the ground, on bushes, trees and rocks, preferring the puddles and damp ground. At every step hundreds of them spiralled up and away, for they are timid, and even in flight will swerve away in front of people. In the fields women were running around like lunatics, shrieking and beating their calabashes with sticks and · waving enormous cloths in their attempts to frighten off the swarm . . . The damage that the locusts inflicted on the village was not very extensive, as nowhere had they settled long enough to devour much. The day enriched our cuisine with a new dish, namely roast grass-hoppers. Wings and legs were torn off, and the bodies turned for two minutes in the hot ashes with a stick. They tasted rather insipid and bitter, and in no way could be described as a delicacy. What is more, nowhere here were they eaten by the local people, and our own servants watched disbelievingly the preparation of this new dish.

MAISTRE[1]

At the same time as the Germans were pushing expedition after expedition into Adamawa, the French were equally active in their attempts to acquire this hinterland as a link in their dream-empire stretching from the Congo to the Mediterranean. Early in 1893 Maistre reached Yola after an epic march from the Congo through Garua; after a few days there he left on 3 February for the Chamba region, crossed to Koncha, and gradually worked his way back through Bakundi, arriving at Ibi on 6 March.

Maistre had expected to find the Niger Company at Garua, as with his 'one hundred and forty-nine half-exhausted men to drag along with us' the expedition was in a desperate state. The Com-pany's hulk, however, had been sent downstream, and Maistre had to march on to Yola to revictual and recuperate. The Emir was away on a campaign, so the town was quiet. Maistre left a silver coffee service as a present.

[1] *A travers l'Afrique Central du Congo au Niger, 1892–93*, C. Maistre.

In his standing orders for the expedition there is an interesting description of the line of march. Five riflemen marched ahead of the main column to act as scouts. Then came the advance guard of one section of sharp-shooters under the senior military officer, with Maistre himself. Behind them followed the scores of carriers, split into two groups, each with an escort of Senegalese riflemen, and under the command of the expedition's deputy-leader. Finally, another section of riflemen formed the rearguard. Commands to this serpent-like caravan, winding its way through the bush, were given by bugle calls; in case of attack a square was at once formed round the carriers, who would throw down their loads and lie beside them so as not to impede the field of fire.

MIZON[1]

There were other French expeditions to Adamawa—de Brazza tried to reach Yola by the southern overland route but was checked at Ngaundere in late 1892; Clozel and Poiret reached Yola in April 1893 from Oubangui—but none, either French or German, acquired quite such international notoriety as the two Mizon expeditions between 1890 and 1893.

Mizon, a lieutenant in the French navy, was appointed by the forward colonial party to secure for France the territories of Adamawa, Bornu, and Baghirmi, on the grounds that, since they were beyond the jurisdiction of Sokoto, the Niger Company's treaties were invalid and the region was therefore open to the first-comer. Attacked in the Delta by the savage Patani tribe, Mizon made a tedious journey with many delays up the Benue and eventually reached Yola in his cutter *René Caillé* on 20 August 1891. After an argumentative audience with the Emir he succeeded in obtaining permission to live in the Arab quarter of Yola town, where he was lodged in the same compound that Flegel had lived in. He settled there for over three months, making journeys to Numan and the Upper Benue, and eventually persuaded the Emir to sign a treaty with France. On 15 December he marched out of Yola, through Gurin to Ngaundere, and thence

[1] Material for Mizon's expeditions is hard to find. The best sources are *Nos Africains*, H. Alis, 1894, and the political polemics in the French and English press of the time. Mizon himself published only three pamphlets.

south towards the Congo, where he joined up with de Brazza on
7 April 1892.

Receiving influential backing in Paris, Mizon returned to the
West Coast in the autumn, despite the most vigorous representa-
tions of the Niger Company to whom his presence in Adamawa
was a thorn in the flesh. This time he brought two steamers, one
fitted out as a trading boat and the other carrying an unusually
heavy complement of French officers and arms. Proceeding up
the Benue on the flood, both vessels grounded near Zhiru in the
centre of Muri District at the end of September, where they
remained till the following rainy season.

Mizon wasted no time. He entered into relations with the Emir
of Muri, and established factories at Mairanawa and Kunini, and
on 23 November signed a treaty of protection with Muri. His
acidulous correspondence with the Niger Company was thenceforward written on paper headed 'The French Protectorate of
Muri', and he even held up the Royal Niger Company's mail
canoes on the grounds that they were passing through what he
asserted were French waters without carrying flags. Mizon
distributed arms to the Emir's officials, and on Christmas Day
1892 he landed his Senegalese sharp-shooters and two field-pieces
to aid the Emir in an attack on the pagan town of Kona, which the
Fulani had for six years vainly attempted to reduce.

When his vessels floated again in July, Mizon left 'a French
Resident' in Muri and went up to Yola. Mr. Wallace of the Niger
Company followed him upstream in two river steamers, armed
with troops and guns, seizing the French factories on the way.
August in Yola was a tense month, with Mizon wooing the Emir
and Wallace negotiating for the Niger Company: a spark could
have started an international war. Early in September Wallace
informed Mizon that he intended to seize his trading ship
Sergent Malamine. With the river beginning to fall, Mizon
proceeded down-river in the *Mosca*, leaving the other vessel as a
floating French station in Adamawa. Wallace at once confiscated
it, towed it down to Lokoja as a prize, and made sure that Mizon
and his party did not tarry in their journey to the Niger mouth.
All that remained of the French Protectorates of Muri and

Adamawa were a dozen Senegal soldiers under a Zouave officer in
Yola and two cannon, which were used against the British occupying force in 1901. The adventures of the piratic Mizon make
exciting reading in Adamawa history.

ROYAL NIGER COMPANY[1]

For the last few years of the century there were no more
expeditions to Adamawa, and the Royal Niger Company undertook little fresh exploration away from the Benue and its tributaries. Records are available, however, of two inland commercial
expeditions. In his speech at the 1892 General Meeting of the
Company, Lord Aberdare said:

The most recent British expedition to Lake Chad was that of the
Company the year before last. [It] started from Ribago . . . The distance
from that place to Lake Chad is only about 270 miles, but it was not
traversed by our expedition without risk, owing to the system pursued
by Bornu of encouraging the lawless pagan tribes of Marghis and others,
who occupy a broad belt of country between Ribago and Lake Chad.
This system not only serves to prevent the escape of Bornu slaves to the
southward, but also forms a barrier between that state and those provinces
of the Sokoto Empire which lie to the south and south-west of Bornu.

The expedition was a diplomatic failure.

Early in 1897 one of the Company's executive officers for the
Benue region travelled through Kentu in order to promote the
rubber industry and to persuade the people to come down from
the mountains whither they had been driven by Fulani raiders
from Banyo, Gashaka, and Bakundi.

The pioneering rôle of the Niger Company in opening up the
Adamawa country is fully treated in the next chapter, but quota-
tions from an account by their leading Adamawa agent, L. H.
Moseley,[2] may be a fitting conclusion to this period.

The country is flat and open, and splendidly fertile, little more than the
actual planting being required to bring forth the most luxuriant crop of
cereals. Guinea-corn, maize, rice, sweet potatoes, millet and groundnuts
are cultivated to a very great extent and form the chief articles of food.
Indigo is cultivated greatly, being used by the natives to dye their
cloths, which are made from the cotton plant, also freely grown.

[1] See Chapter IV.   [2] 'Regions of the Benue', L. H. Moseley, 1899.

In the town of Yola is a large native market, a stroll through which would show cloth, silk, salt, tinware, etc. of European manufacture, exposed for sale side by side with cloths and gowns from Kano and Nupe, beads, calabashes, looking-glasses, knives, etc., even to scents brought all the way from Tripoli. The Hausa trader predominates here, as this market forms a terminus of the great ivory caravan routes from the hunting-grounds and markets of Tibati and Ngaundere. An important item that should not be overlooked is that cattle thrive splendidly in this country. Large herds are to be met all over the plains.

The present difficulties to the development of this splendid country are: (1) The difficulties of transport to the coast . . . This is one of the many rich countries lying perdu for the want of a trans-African railway. (2) The Fulani race are not workers, and the pagan tribes who have no opportunities of making headway, owing to their persecution and oppression by the Fulani.

The climate is fairly healthy, though Europeans suffer from anaemia, caused by the heat during the months of December and January when the harmattan winds are blowing from the northern deserts. During this period I have known the thermometer to register at 5 a.m. 60° F. and 120° at one o'clock midday.

IV

THE ROYAL NIGER COMPANY

THE expansion of the Royal Niger Company from their Lower Benue district, centred on Ibi, towards the Upper Benue, followed by the international concentration on Yola during the scramble of the 1890's, makes the advent of the Company the principal influence in Adamawa between the Fulani *jihad* and the British occupation nearly a century later, and the activities of the Company dominate Adamawa history for the last decade or so of the nineteenth century.

CHARTER

After the signing of the Congress of Berlin in February 1885 and the declaration in June of the Protectorate of the Niger territories, the British Government had to decide between direct administration and administration by charter. The latter course appeared preferable, and in July 1886 a royal charter was granted to the National African Company, which had for some years been operating on the Niger and Benue rivers under the vigorous leadership of Sir George Taubman-Goldie, and which had been seeking this privilege since 1881. The company was thereupon renamed the Royal Niger Company,

. . . authorised and empowered, subject to the approval of our Secretary of State, to acquire and take by purchase, cession, or other lawful means, other rights, interests, authorities, or powers of any kind or nature whatever, in, over, or affecting the territories, lands, or property comprised in the several treaties aforesaid, or any rights, interests, authorities, or powers of any kind or nature whatever, in, over, or affecting other territories, lands or property in the region aforesaid, and to hold, use, enjoy, and exercise the same for the purposes of the Company.

STAFF

An executive staff was appointed under senior executive officers with wide administrative and judicial powers. The Company's headquarters were at Assaba, opposite Onitsha, with the Benue

district headquarters at Ibi, then in the Emirate of Muri. Mr.
William Wallace,[1] commonly known as 'Baba Wallisi', was in
charge of the Benue interests until 1887, when he was promoted
as deputy to Mr. J. Flint, the Agent-General, and was succeeded
at Ibi by Mr. Charles McIntosh.

'King Charlie' acquired great personal influence; he lived, so
the story goes, in considerable pomp, and wore—we are asked to
believe—a suit of chain-mail. Later chief agents on the Benue
between 1894 and 1899 included Messrs. A. J. Hill, F. J. Spink,
L. H. Moseley, and W. P. Hewby, the last-named joining Government on the revocation of the Charter to become the first Resident
of Muri Province.

POLICY

The administrative policy of the Company, with a small staff of
energetic young men largely engrossed in commercial development, was modest and simple. The aims were to maintain friendly
relations with the important Muslim chiefs, often by means of an
annual subsidy which ranged from £60 to Muri down to 30s. to
Numan; to keep trade routes open by any means feasible; and to
prevent, or at any rate check, the frightful slave-raiding among
the Benue pagans. Of this policy a company officer has written:

Every effort was made to put a stop to slave-raiding whenever possible
inside the Company's sphere of influence. It will be easily realized,
however, that this was a most delicate and difficult task when the custom
and religion of the powerful Fulani rulers up to that time is remembered.
Nevertheless, during the comparatively short life of the Charter great
success attended the Company's efforts in this direction, and it can be
confidently claimed that within reasonable control of the Company
raiding had been put down. It became an accepted ruling amongst the
former slave-raiding Emirs and chiefs that wherever the Company had
opened up or were interested in trade routes raiding would not be
allowed and would be punished.

To enforce their authority the executive officers had a small
force of constables officered by Europeans. Among the com-
mandants of this famous Royal Niger Constabulary were Major
Alder Burdon, who rose to high office under Government, Major

[1] He was later knighted when he acted as High Commissioner for Lugard.

Festing, who commanded the W.A.F.F. and became Resident of Kano, and Captain Moloney, who, crippled for life in the Brass raid on Akassa in 1895, became Resident of Nassarawa Province and was murdered at Keffi in 1902. Many other officers, such as Brackenbury, Arnold, and Parker, to name but a few, are well remembered in Nigerian history. A strong detachment of the force was stationed at Ibi.

EXPANSION ON THE BENUE

Prior to 1883 there had been a trading station at Loko, but it was in that year that the National African Company began to exploit the commercial possibilities of the river. Wallace, who was in charge of the venture, towed up to Ibi the wooden hulk *Emily Waters* as a base of operations. In the same year he went on to Yola, where he was warmly received by the Emir, Sanda, and, in exchange for many valuable presents, he obtained permission to trade in the town and the lease of a piece of ground on which to build a trading factory. In the following year Wallace's reception was cold, and when Dangerfield was sent up shortly afterwards with the building materials for the factory, he was astonished to learn that the Emir refused him authority to land them and would permit the Company to trade only from a steamer. It later transpired that the cause of the Emir's displeasure was that the Company's native agent, who had been left in Yola between 1883 and 1884, had been caught intriguing with the ladies of the royal household.

In 1885 the *Emily Waters* was towed up to Yola with a large stock of goods. On arrival she was ordered away, but, as the falling river made it impossible to retire, the Emir grudgingly gave his permission for trade to be opened. One Davenport and a native agent were left in charge, but almost at once the Emir formed a blockade of canoes round the hulk and crippled their operations. The Company persuaded the Sultan of Sokoto to address a letter of remonstrance to his vassal, and when the chief agent next visited Yola, in 1886, the Emir gave his consent to the reopening of trade on the hulk, promising that if all went well the Company should be allowed to build on shore.

The day after the chief agent left Yola in his steamer the Emir
suspended trade. It was then considered useless to open the
question again and the hulk was removed from Yola to Bubanjidda,
at the head of the Benue beyond Garua. Following upon another
stern letter from Sokoto, the Emir in 1887 allowed the Company
to bring the hulk down from Bubanjidda—the venture had been
a failure, owing to the misconduct of the agents in charge—to the
Ribago Province, where trade prospered. On the demarcation of
the Anglo-German spheres of influence in 1893 the Company
withdrew their stations above Yola, and Zubeiru, the new Emir,
perhaps jealous of Garua's affluence, allowed the hulk to anchor
off his capital. Not till 1896 did the Emir relent in his argument
that to allow the Company to build on his territory would be to
betray his patrimony: 'the river belongs to Allah, but the land
belongs to me'. The hulk left Yola at the end of the 1896 rains, and
after the treaty of 25 August 1897 the Company attempted to
establish itself on shore. To quote from Hewby's report:

I have made a treaty with the Emir, form No. 12, which he signed
without demur. I have paid him his subsidy for this year and I believe
that any Frenchman arriving at Yola [the reference is to the Mizon
affair], unless provided with a present of rifles and cartridges for the
Emir, would have a bad reception. It must be admitted, however, that
the Emir would probably have been less pleased had he known for
certain that the hulk was not going back there. If the Emir does not turn
unpleasant when he finds the water falling and no hulk, we should
purchase a good deal more rice and potash . . . for which purpose I have
landed 25 tons of salt there. A clerk and six soldiers remain to keep the
flag flying.

While the Yola venture experienced these vicissitudes, other
stations had been gradually opened up. By 1889 there were factories
at Kunini, Lau, Mairanawa, and Bakundi as well as those already
mentioned at Bubanjidda and Garua. Numan had been an important
wooding station since the treaty of 19 July 1885, and in response
to their wish for a factory, the *Nigretia*, one of the two new steel
hulks which had been specially built for taking the ground in the
dry season, was allocated to the Bassama venture in 1889 while
the other was sent up to Garua. In 1891 relations with Muri

became so strained that the Emir sacked the trading stations in his territory; not till 1895 was a *rapprochement* effected.

Major Arnold explored the Gongola river in 1895 and reached Shellen in a barge; the first steamer went up the river in September 1897. The Company made fresh treaties with Bachama and Demsa in 1896, granting them annual subsidies of £15 and £10 respectively, and in the same year Hewby engaged the village-head of Mbula to be purveyor of wood to the Company. The Bachama and Demsa subsidies were bought out in 1897 at a total cost of 18 cwt. of salt, then the most highly prized of all commodities.

MURI

In the oldest of the Company's territories on the upper Benue —the Muri treaty was signed on 30 January 1885—the situation with the Emir, Muhammadu Nya, had become difficult by 1890. The Emir viewed with suspicion the growing influence of the Company, their stronghold at Ibi in his territory, and their attitude towards his turbulent kinsmen in the Taraba districts. His precarious control over Jibu, which was continually in revolt, came to an end when the Company occupied the town, without the Emir's consent; *en revanche*, the Emir destroyed the factories at Lau and Kunini in 1891 and broke off friendly intercourse with the Company. Ibi was fortified to withstand an attack, but the Emir was preoccupied in 1892 with quelling the Kona pagans with the aid of Mizon's guns and with seeking the material benefits offered by the 'French Protectorate of Muri'.

In 1895 Hewby visited the Emir to restore diplomatic communications, but in the event little real good resulted, as Nya's sole interest was to obtain a supply of rifles for use against the pagans and his relatives on the south bank. The following extracts are from Hewby's report:

1st Meeting, 12/6/95. We had a most enthusiastic reception from every one, and the Emir did not conceal his satisfaction at meeting the Company's people at last.

2nd Meeting, 13/6/95. The Emir wore a concealed revolver on his left arm. He declared all relations with the French entirely at an end; he denied having made a treaty with them, and says that all papers received from them were burned by fire, which I believe is true. He says he never

intended to form definite relations with the Frenchmen, who told him
their real business was with Yola; they presented him with 42 rifles,
some revolvers, and 20 suits of mail . . . I asked the Emir to state fully
his desires as to a settlement with the Company, and his reply was:

(*a*) a re-establishment of trade.
(*b*) we must do what he says is good, and leave what he dislikes.
(*c*) in small wars or disputes with other peoples (pagans) he will be
    making no trouble with us, and he asks for no interference.
(*d*) finally he wants trade and no double-dealing, proper friendship,
    not as in McIntosh's time; no interference.

3rd Meeting, 14/6/95. After an interview of four hours a new treaty
was signed. The Emir would not sign with his own hand, but made the
Alkali (who signed for him the original agreement in 1885) sign it in the
usual way. I might perhaps have got his own signature by more pressure,
and the payment of a special sum, as was done at Yola; but I did not
want to enter on any pecuniary haggling, which had been avoided all
this time, and his Alkali's signature is perfectly valid from their own
point of view . . . Considerable trouble was caused by the young prince
Tafida who so far got the ear of the Emir as to insist on the signature of
the documents being delayed while a letter was sent to the Company
requesting rifles and ammunition: so greatly has Mizon's wholesale
importation of these weapons influenced these people that the idea
started by this young man for some time took hold of the Emir and his
people, who had either not thought of such a demand, or had not had
sufficient nerve to bring it forward, and for some time I thought the
treaty would fall through . . .

I have agreed to pay the Emir the subsidy for this year; and rather to
my surprise he expressed his desire to relinquish any claim to the subsidies of 1892, 1893 and 1894. Whether this is from any feeling of
penitence, or from an idea that he would not obtain payment, I am
unable to say. I gave him to understand that you wished to forget past
disputes, and were willing to overlook his reprisals on our stations . . .
The Emir told me more than one downright lie: one of which was that
he really did not quite understand how the Company's goods were
plundered at Lau, as he had kept the store locked up—he had removed
the powder merely because the rain was beating on it! . . . The Emir
promised to hoist the Company's flag which I sent him.

Finding little improvement in Muri's behaviour, the Company
proceeded to appoint a new chief of Ibi without any reference to
the Emir and refused to allow recognition of the latter's authority
west of the Donga river. Muhammadu Nya died and was suc-

ceeded in 1896 by Hassan, 'with the approval and moral support of the Company'. He, too, signed a treaty with the Company. In the following November letters were received from Sokoto urging the Emir to expel the Niger Company from their territory. To quote Hewby once more:

This Emir does not want us to leave, but he knows that his disobedience will be followed by instructions from Sokoto for Bakundi and the other independent divisions to unite and overthrow him. He therefore wants our support, and has not had the Sokoto letters read in public until he hears from the Company, whose reply I promised within a month. All the Benue states know well that the Company is the supreme power, and they really care little for Sokoto's orders, if not to their advantage. My view . . . that the best course to pursue now is to give Muri all moral support and retain our footing in the country; whereby we shall be able to retain our gum trade. It will take two months and a half from now for further instructions to arrive from Sokoto; and although we have only forty C.S.T. at Ibi, and can get no more, I expect to be able to keep things smoothly . . . The amount of 'bluff' that it will be advisable to employ with Muri I shall be better able to determine when I get back to Ibi and see how Yola is acting . . . Bakundi has sent in here to say that he has received orders from Sokoto to stop the roads to all ivory caravans coming from the south bound for Ibi.

The last few years of the life of the Royal Niger Company in Muri were occupied in enforcing law and order by means of a number of punitive patrols referred to later.

ADAMAWA

The peripetia of the Royal Niger Company at Yola have already been described, and they form a useful canvas on which to paint in these personal touches from the memoirs of two of the Company's agents[1] stationed there.

The Emir at the time was Mallam Zubeiru, a powerful autocratic Fulani . . . The Company's relations with the Emir were at times very difficult, and much diplomacy was needed to avoid trouble and secure the carrying out of the treaty. Those in charge of the Company's interests were handicapped by the distance from the nearest forces, at Ibi, and also by the fact that the Emir was of very uncertain and changeable mind. Being extremely extravagant, however, he usually

[1] Hewby and Moseley.

came to heel when hard up for his subsidy. This was sometimes held back until he did the right thing . . . He had to keep pace with his master at Sokoto, and this was a continual drain on his resources.

Zubeiru was too intelligent to really fight the Company, but at times he did use threats. Only once was an attack really threatened (I was there at the time) but, although the Emir came down to the river in force—it was in the dry season—he changed his mind when he realised we were prepared and, cute as ever, said he had come to salute us.

According to local tradition, however, what finally prompted the Emir to think better of his sortie was the sight of the rampart of salt bags which Moseley had erected for the defence of the hulk: they were the commodity which Zubeiru most coveted.

It was for the Company a continual struggle to keep a proud Fulani chieftain on the straight path, his tenets and upbringing continually forcing us into conflict . . . The Emir really assisted in keeping order among his vassals and did all he could to prevent pillage and plunder on the roads. Like all his race, however, he could only regard the pagans as potential wealth and refused to understand our views regarding slave-raiding—although he was much handicapped in this respect as many of the surrounding tribes were sufficiently powerful to look after themselves, and did so on several occasions to his discomfiture. As the Company's sphere of influence continually increased so raiding stopped.

In the dry season of 1893–4 a party of four Arabs arrived at Yola on a special mission from the Egyptian Government to Rabeh, the recent invader and conqueror of Bornu. After months of delay in Yola, where Zubeiru refused to adopt a straightforward policy and detained them on one pretext or another, the Company, acting as agents of Her Majesty's Niger Coast Protectorate, brought the party back to Ibi and arranged for their dispatch from Amar to Bauchi and thence eventually to Dikwa. In 1895 an attempt was made by Rabeh to open up communication with the Company, and his messengers arrived at Lau; but when it was discovered that Rabeh's need was for little but gunpowder the overtures came to naught.

Zubeiru, however, mistrusted the Company's efforts to get into touch with Rabeh, fearing that these were the prelude to an alliance against the Fulani. The Company was equally exercised by Zubeiru's expedition to the north in 1897, at a time when it was rumoured that Hayatu, the rebel grandson of Bello of Sokoto, had joined Rabeh and that both had sent their sons on a mission to the chief of Marua. The anxiety ended with Hayatu's death in an attempt to wrest the power from Rabeh by treachery, and with Zubeiru's severe military defeat.

The Company had always assumed that their 1886 treaty with Sokoto included Adamawa, but after the uncomfortable activities of Mizon in Yola they concluded a separate treaty with Adamawa in May 1893. This treaty, while it provided for the recognition of the Company as the authorized government within the Emir's territories, neither emphasized the fact that it was the recognized agent of the British Government nor demanded the specific acceptance of the protection of the British flag. The subsequent treaty of 1897 rectified these omissions.

Towards the end of that year inflammatory letters were received by the Emir from the Sultan of Sokoto. The first read: 'You have seen what the Company has done to Bida and Ilorin—my territory. You are not to allow the Company to remain in any part of the country over which you have jurisdiction.' The second was even briefer: 'Behold! I have another vassal. Rabeh has joined me.'

Commenting on the situation Hewby wrote:

I have no further information as to Rabeh's attitude, but it is quite possible that the many months' interval since the Nupe campaign closed has been employed in arranging a compact with Rabeh ... It is hard to say how the Emir will take this. He may start our people off to Ibi at once. But it is quite likely that he may consider he will suffer more at the hands of the Company for obedience than at the hands of his suzerain for disobedience of the Sultan's orders. He has not been over-zealous in carrying out orders before. Anyhow, we can do nothing at present but go or stay as he says.

Hewby was correct in his surmise: Zubeiru decided in favour of the Company.

NUMAN

The Company appears to have maintained from the first fairly good relations with the Bachama tribe, though in 1891 Numan was burnt as a reprisal for an attack on the hulk anchored there. With the truculent Mbula, however, the story is a different one.

When one of the first launches of the National African Company was on its way to Yola a quantity of firewood was purchased from the Mbula, but after it had been paid for the people refused to allow it to be taken on board and drove the launch away. Two years later, in 1885, they attacked a surf-boat of the Company which was being paddled downstream from Yola under Davenport's charge. No lives were lost, though many arrows fell into the boat. In 1886 a fine of fifty sheep was imposed on the Mbula. The tribe refused point-blank to pay anything, and consequently one of their villages was shelled and fired by the Company's steamer *Kuka* and troops were disembarked to round up fifty sheep.

From then onwards the Mbula remained reasonably quiet. They concluded treaties with the Company and in 1896 Hewby achieved the nominal subordination of the tribe to the secular authority of a single chief by engaging the village-head of Mbula to be purveyor of fuel. He gave him a letter of appointment, from the possession of which the holder derived the title of *Mai-Takarda*. This account of the punitive expedition following an attack on the Company's vessels in 1899 was given by an Mbula greybeard in 1933:

And this is the story of our war with the White Men of the Company. The cause of it was this: some Nupe people had come with three canoes and landed at a town called Tassala. We went to look at them, and saw that there was salt in their canoes, whereon we mustered and attacked them, and wounded two of their people. They fled and we took all their salt. And they went back down-river and told the White Men what we had done to them. But we rejoiced that we had got salt for our soup, not knowing of the White Man's war that was coming upon us. This was about the year 1900; in the same year we learned that two steam-ships were coming, and rejoiced, thinking that we should get salt in abundance. Then we gathered five towns for war, Juren, Kolle, Gossala, Tassala and Tahau, the men of these five made ready our canoes to do battle with the steam-ships. Then the steam-ships stood in between Kolle and Gossala, whereon some of our people launched their canoes and making for the steam-ships cast spears at them. Alas! we did not know that there were 300 soldiers in the ships. When they saw that spears were being thrown they dropped anchor, landed and loaded their guns; when they had loaded they started along the road to Gossala. Soon they came upon our warriors, more than a thousand in number, our people began to cast spears, and the soldiers began to shoot. More than a hundred of our people were killed; some ran away, some took to the water. All our towns were scattered and the soldiers took more than a thousand sheep and goats. We returned home lamenting, some for the death of their kinsmen, others for the loss of their possessions. That is the end of the story of our war with the White Men.

MILITARY OPERATIONS

The Company's semi-military force has already been referred to, and this quotation from the Special Commissioner's tour of inspection in 1889 will serve as a useful background to the summary of the Company's punitive expeditions that follows.

At 8 a.m. the Royal Niger Constabulary paraded for inspection and went through a number of manœuvres, customary on such occasions, with great *éclat*. The force is officered by Englishmen and consists of about five hundred men—Fantis, Hausas and Yorubas—mostly recruited from the Gold Coast. They are well paid and fed, and are clothed in a khaki zouave dress. Their arms consist of Snider rifles and sword bayonets; and in addition to the infantry there is a very smart little battery of mountain guns, commanded by an ex-gunner of our navy. This miniature army has been called upon frequently to undergo some very rough bush-fighting, and has been found all that could be desired. The bachelors of the constabulary are quartered in comfortable corrugated iron barracks, and the married men live with their families close by in what is termed 'Soldier Town'—a quarter very similar to the 'lines' of an Indian native regiment.

Most of the towns against which military operations were carried out are no longer within the boundaries of the modern Muri Emirate. Jibu, a piratically disposed and insubordinate vassal of Muri at the mouth of the Donga river, was a continual menace to the trade routes. In the Company's first years on the Upper Benue, before a trained force had been established, Wallace boldly carried the town by assault. In 1888 it was again stormed by the Niger Constabulary, their first action on the Benue, and in 1891 it was finally broken, remaining banned and deserted until 1898 when the Company invited a local chief to repopulate the town.

There was heavy fighting in 1895–6 against Kachella, a stout-hearted renegade of the Takum ruling family, who repulsed the first column of Constabulary from Ibi but was killed himself during a later assault. The year 1897 brought patrols against Dankoro, a free-lance Sarkin Yaki among the Munshi clans, and in 1899 there were aggressive patrols against Wurio and Montol.

Three operations may be considered representative of the military activity that marked the last years of the Company in Adamawa. In 1898 a force was sent against Barua, in Gashaka, whose inhabitants had been charged with complicity in an attack on an ivory caravan which had resulted in the death of its leader. On the way, however, Captain Parker learned that it was the tribesmen of the Wunkae hills who had taken the principal part in the outrage and he decided to attack this tribe. He was met by their chiefs, who agreed to his terms, but a subsequent treacherous attack upon the column as it was marching to a suitable camp-site provoked a battle in which the Wunkae were severely defeated. This demonstration was considered sufficient.

The Wase incident of 1898 was more serious. Captain Parker was dispatched from Ibi with a force of forty men and one 7-pounder gun to defend Amar from a threatened attack by the king of Wase. When they arrived they found that the attack had already taken place, but Amar had been defended by two Constabulary men and two soldiers of the newly formed West African Frontier Force, who happened to have been passing through on their return from a recruiting tour in Bauchi. The Wase raiders, convinced that Amar was held in force, had retired, leaving several of their men and horses dead along the route. On receiving this information Hewby set out from Ibi with another fifty Constabulary and a maxim-gun, and the column then marched on Wase. The town was surrounded by a wall 10 feet high with five gates and had a ditch 3 to 4 feet deep most of the way round. Fire was opened on the town but the walls could not be breached. Early in the attack on the wall Parker received an arrow in the head. Soon after one of the gates was rushed and the town fell. On the following day the gates were completely destroyed by the expedition.

The Suntai patrol of 1899, besides being one of the Company's larger operations on the Benue, brought the death of that gallant Constabulary officer, Captain H. W. E. Parker, of the South Wales

Borderers. Sarkin Kudu, the weak and unsatisfactory chief of Bakundi, constantly complained of the disaffection of his villages and frequently requested the Company's permission to coerce them. When, at the beginning of 1899, his authority was again threatened, Captain Parker was sent with forty men, not to undertake any definite task but to demonstrate to the countryside that the Company supported Sarkin Kudu. In Parker's judgment it was advisable for him to accompany this chief in making a flag-march to Suntai (Bakundi's nominal vassal), where they were greeted by a shower of arrows. This insolence was too much for Parker, who advanced upon the town wall with his inadequate force. He immediately had two men killed and half a dozen wounded; Parker, who had been severely wounded at Takum, Wase, and in the Bachama country, and who had more than once encountered poisoned-arrow attacks with no medical assistance beyond that provided by his Ijaw servant who attended to the casualties with a razor and a bottle of carbolic acid, met his death from a spear wound while in the act of giving a leg-up to the top of the wall to his tallest constable. The patrol retired to Ibi with their dead officer in a hammock.

This disaster decided the Company that Suntai would have to be taken. A strong column of 3 officers and a medical officer, 100 rank and file, a 7-pounder, and a maxim-gun was dispatched against the town, which put up a most determined fight. The wall was found to be quite unclimbable, and where it was breached the defenders in the most daring manner attempted repairs under maxim-fire. In the final assault over this breach the force lost 3 men killed and 25 wounded, including an officer and the medical officer. After the capture of Suntai the column commander presented his sword to the chief in admiration of his plucky defence.

TRADE

Important as administration might be, the main object of a dividend-conscious Company was trade. Baikie's journey in 1854 had proved the wealth of the regions fed by the Benue, and Barth had cherished a dream of European influence and commerce penetrating to the very heart of Adamawa. The produce of the principal buying stations on the Benue consisted of ivory at Ibi, Bakundi, and Ribago (Garua); benniseed at Donga, Bakundi, and Kunini; gum-arabic and gutta-percha at Mairanawa, Kunini, Numan, and Ribago; and some tin at Kunini and Lau. The Company was particularly interested in exploiting the big ivory markets of Banyo and Ngaundere in southern Adamawa, which had hitherto been the preserve of the Hausa traders from Kano. These ivory caravans, which sometimes spent up to two years on the road, trading from place to place and often in slaves, sold their ivory to the Company at Yola in exchange for trade goods; at one time in the late 'nineties the Company was buying as much as forty tons in a year.

Moseley writes of the famous hulks that characterized the riverain trade:

Those days it was no bed of roses for the European officials of the Company, usually two. Stations were not built on shore as a hulk could always be removed, which was a very useful card to have in hand against the Emir's tactics: a threat to remove the hulk was a powerful lever, for it would have meant the loss of the big trade being done with the Hausas and others, which meant revenue to Yola. Also a hulk was safer and could be defended in case of attack. These hulks were specially built steel boats and armed for defence ... They used to be stocked every wet season and were so berthed that they floated all the year round.

V

THE BRITISH OCCUPATION

WHEN Lugard took over the administration of what is now
Northern Nigeria from the Royal Niger Company on 1 January
1900, one of his first acts was to divide the Protectorate into three
Civil Provinces, Kano, Middle Niger, and Benue, and two Military
Provinces, Bornu and Borgu. By August that portion of the
Protectorate over which effective occupation had been established
could be further divided into nine provinces. Under this re-
organization the Company's district of Benue was split into
Upper and Lower Benue; the former was under W. P. Hewby,
Muri's first Resident, and the Emirate was transferred from the
Military Province of Bornu. Yola figured among the four additional
provinces that Lugard planned to take in hand as early as possible
and for which he included staff, at the standard strength of one
Resident and two Assistant Residents (including leave relief), in
his advance proposals to Mr. Chamberlain, the Secretary of State.

The reasons adduced by Lugard for opening up the eastern
territories of Bauchi, Yola, and Muri were

mainly on the ground of their supposed salubrity and mineral wealth.
The necessity of checking the rapid depopulation by organised slave-
raiding, and of dealing with the problems offered by the advent of the
French on Lake Chad and the arrival of Fad-el-Allah (Rabeh's son) in
British territory are additional reasons. Though these provinces are far
distant from Lake Chad, they will afford a base from which we can, to
some extent, keep in touch with events in the north.

Political expediency demanded the formation of a local authority
to cover the vital lines of communication provided by the River
Benue and the caravan routes to Chad which were then swarming
with brigands.

There was, in addition, the semi-fanatical obduracy of the Emir
of Yola, Zubeiru, who refused to treat with the Niger Company

55

and whose slave-raiding propensities called forth from Lugard this indictment of the Adamawa Emirate:

There is, probably, no part of the 'Dark Continent' in which the worst forms of slave-raiding still exist to so horrible an extent, and the slave-raiders are not even provident of their hunting grounds, for those who are useless as slaves are killed in large numbers, the villages burnt, and the fugitives left to starve in the bush.

For the first eighteen months the Administration was fully absorbed in keeping the peace on the lower Benue, and Adamawa was left alone. Zubeiru flatly refused to recognize the authority of Government, and although he remained loyal to his agreement to refrain from slave-raiding within the area agreed as being under the control of the Company, now shorn of its title and dignities, in every other way he was as unco-operative as he could be. He was probably not sane[1] at the time, and was uncertain whether he would not do better to throw in his lot with the Germans or the French.

CAPTURE OF YOLA

Finally, towards the end of the rains of 1901, the High Commissioner was strong enough to strike.

Meantime, in the extreme east of the Protectorate, the Emir of Yola was becoming more and more impossible. This man was a fine type of the Fulani ruler, well educated, but possessed with a religious fanaticism, which rendered him extremely intolerant of European 'infidels'. In spite of his treaties with the Niger Company, he had compelled them to haul down their flag on their trading hulk (they were not allowed to have a station ashore). He and the neighbouring Emir of Bautshi carried on a traffic in slaves, which were imported from German territory in huge numbers and sent throughout the Hausa states, while the trade routes were closed, and the merchants appealed for forcible intervention. September is practically the only month during which the Benue is navigable as far as Yola, and, as matters had well-nigh reached a crisis, Mr. Wallace was instructed to organise an expedition to deal with the situation in my absence.

No man in the Protectorate knew more about Yola than Wallace. On 21 August he informed Colonel Morland, Commandant of the W.A.F.F. at Jebba, that the Secretary of State

[1] *Per* Moseley and Hewby.

had cabled his approval of the proposed military expedition. He
suggested that 300 men would be more than enough, and added:
'It is my intention to accompany this expedition.' The force sailed
from Lokoja on 26 August in the steamers *Liberty* and *Nkissi* and
consisted of 15 officers, including 2 medical officers who had
been transferred from Jebba to join the expedition, 7 British
N.C.O.s, 365 rank and file, four 75-mm. guns, and four maxims,
under the command of Colonel Morland in person. They anchored
off Yola on 2 September, and when the Emir refused to listen to
the conciliatory offers made by the High Commissioner the attack
was ordered.

One steamer tied up at the lone baobab on the north side of the
town, known as *Bokki Hamman Petel* and still (1956) standing,
whence the troops were ferried ashore in five smaller boats, while
the other ship patrolled the lake that lies to the east of the town.
The rains were exceptionally heavy in 1901. Soon the enemy
appeared in strength with cavalry and infantry and attacked the
British square, but they were received with such a galling fire that
they immediately withdrew into the town. The guns now opened
fire on the Emir's palace. A couple of badly aimed shots were fired
in reply from the two cannon that Mizon had given to Zubeiru
in 1892.

Colonel Morland considered it was useless to waste any more
shells and ordered his men to advance into the town. A cook to
one of the officers, who was a native of Yola, had climbed the
baobab and pointed out the way to the Emir's compound. Little
resistance was encountered, either at the *Kofar Magaji* or in the
twisting streets, until the palace was reached. This, a large
building surrounded by a high wall, was the scene of a short,
desperate fight. Zubeiru's bodyguard had been reinforced by
some sixty deserters from Rabeh's army, armed with modern
rifles, and the cannon, crammed with grape-shot, were effectively
discharged at about 30 yards' range. They were trained on the
main approach and fired on the assaulting party as they advanced
round the corner. One soldier's leg was carried away, but Major
McClintock charged and captured the guns before they could be
reloaded. In face of rifle-fire the sole entrance to the building was

stormed, and the Emir escaped through a hole in the rear wall. By evening the remaining defenders had surrendered.

The British casualties were Colonel Morland, Major McClintock, and 37 men wounded, and two killed. The enemy lost about 150 killed and wounded, and among the arms captured were Mizon's two 9-pounder guns, 105 fused shells, 60 French rifles with cartridges, and a ton of gunpowder. The mosque was accidentally struck by a shell and caught fire.

Zubeiru refused to parley. The High Commissioner succeeded in establishing contact with Bobo Ahmadu, Zubeiru's brother, who had fled before the troops, and persuaded him to return to Yola, where he installed him as Emir of British Adamawa on 8 September. On the next day he addressed a directive to Dr. Cargill of the Upper Benue Province, Yola, instructing him to act as Resident until the arrival of Captain Ruxton, Assistant Resident. Leaving 100 men of Captain Baker's F Company, 2nd Northern Nigeria Regiment, 'encamped on the hill to the north-west of Yola' where a fort was built, Wallace returned to Lokoja. By 10 September all the royal scions and head slaves had found their way back to Yola, and on that day at an open meeting called by the Resident in the town every man of note acknowledged the new Emir. At the end of September the following notice appeared in the *Northern Nigerian Gazette*:

I, William Wallace, Acting High Commissioner for the Protectorate of Northern Nigeria . . . do hereby appoint Captain F. A. Ruxton to be Acting Assistant Resident for the Yola portion of the Upper Benue and in such portion to exercise and discharge all the judicial powers and duties of a Resident. Provided always that the said Captain F. A. Ruxton shall have no jurisdiction to hear and determine any case which may involve a sentence of death, penal servitude, deportation, imprisonment for a term exceeding six months, corporal punishment exceeding twelve strokes, or a fine exceeding £50 without previous authority in writing or by telegram from me.

FLIGHT OF ZUBEIRU

Zubeiru, with most of his court, had ridden out of Yola as soon as he found the troops had penetrated to his palace, leaving by the *Kofar Bai* and heading for Gurin where he had a house. As they galloped past the present *'Id* maidan outside Yola the Galadima reined up his horse and suggested that they should return to fight, but Zubeiru spurred his party on to Rugin. The Beti was so swollen that they were unable to ford it and they turned back to Sebore, where Wallace's envoys caught up with them. Zubeiru refused to listen to them but advised his brother Bobo Ahmadu to accept the offer of the *sarauta* and to return to Yola before the rival claimants forestalled him. Bobo Ahmadu took with him most of Zubeiru's retinue, only Aji Samaki, Ardo Bakari his close friend, Maigari, who later became Lamido, and Bilingang, a slave, remaining with the fugitive king. From Sebore, Zubeiru turned to Tuki, thence to Limadi, Nyibango, Nassarawo, through Yeli and the Chamba country across to Garua, and northwards through the Fali country to Marua, never sleeping two consecutive nights in the same village.

Meanwhile Cargill, still endeavouring to communicate to Zubeiru the High Commissioner's offer to allow him to settle on his farm at Namtari, heard that he had started for Marua. A patrol was sent to Gurin to head him off and give the Resident's messenger time to reach him, but the Gurin people would tell nothing of Zubeiru's movements. From Sheboa, Zubeiru had written identical letters to the people of Yola, Girei, and Namtari —the last two villages were populated by his slaves. The Alkali of Girei refused to read the letter, but the Namtari one was publicly read in the mosque:

I am going to Marua, I shall return and we will drive out the heathen. If they prove too strong, leave Yola and follow me to a new country. The Koran forbids you to sit down with the heathen. What do the mallams think of the burning of our mosque? The heathen wish to obtain our kingdom. Have no dealings with them.

When the Emir at Yola showed his letter to the Resident he was advised to send all three back to Zubeiru without comment. In his report Cargill noted:

No one in Yola wishes to hear or see more of Zubeiru, and further epistles from him to the Yolans need not be taken too seriously. They should not be entirely disregarded. The Yola Fulanis only wish to live and let live, but heresy is a nasty thing to throw in anyone's face.

It is interesting to note that when the Germans reached Micika under Dominik early in 1902 they captured among Zubeiru's belongings a letter from the Sultan of Sokoto, counselling him to lie down under the rule of the Europeans, 'who bring no trouble, only trade'; this may, of course, have dated from the days of Zubeiru's quarrel with the Royal Niger Company.

It seems that Zubeiru had originally intended to throw in his lot with the French. After the defeat of Rabeh by Lamy's troops in 1900 he sent greetings and presents to Gentil. These blandishments were refused, so when the Germans first appeared in the neighbourhood of Garua, Zubeiru made friendly overtures to them. From Adoure he sent four bullocks with messengers, but when part of the German force reached this village Zubeiru had cold feet and fled, leaving the Germans to burn the village. In March 1902 Zubeiru instigated the Fulani districts to attack the German expedition which had occupied Garua. The Fulani were heavily defeated. It is said that when Zubeiru heard this news, he hurled sand into the face of the messenger who told him that he alone had escaped to bring this report to his master, and asked: 'Why did they spare you?'

The Germans followed up the routed Fulani to Marua where Zubeiru, with the faithful Ahmadu, Lamdo Marua, determined to make a final stand. The battle that followed is renowned in the annals of Fulani history. Four hundred and twenty-four of his picked corps of *Sikirri* (those vowed to die) made an heroic stand round the green flag and were shot down to a man by machine-gun fire. Zubeiru was rushed from the field by his immediate attendants and took refuge in the Mandara hills, still accompanied by Lamdo Marua.

From Mabas, on the present Northern Cameroons boundary, he turned towards Madagali, where Ardo Bakari refused to allow him to stay. Zubeiru and Lamdo Marua separated here, the former furtively making his way through Micika and Kilba to settle in Guduk in the Song country in about October 1902. Ardo Bakari was shot by the Germans when they entered Madagali for his suspected complicity in giving Zubeiru a free passage. It is said that while passing through Bazza the pagans robbed Zubeiru and

Maigari, taking them for ordinary travellers. A certain Kanuri, named Bukar, gave Maigari a spear as a defensive weapon on the road; when Maigari became Lamido over twenty years later he repaid this samaritan act.

ZUBEIRU'S DEATH

From Guduk, Zubeiru sent to Marua an assassin who, in an interview with the German Resident, Graf Fugger, on 5 January, wounded him in the leg with a poisoned arrow; Fugger died within twelve hours. During Ramadan, Zubeiru's emissaries dropped two letters in Yola mosque, which they had concealed in the hollow of a cornstalk, announcing that he was intending to go to Mecca.

Early in 1903 rumours of Zubeiru's return to British territory reached the ears of G. N. Barclay, who had taken over Yola Province as its first substantive Resident in the previous April. On 16 February he informed the O.C. Troops at Yola:

Zubeiru is raiding round Guduk for slaves and cattle and causing a great deal of political unrest, his presence being a serious menace to the peace and development of the Province. I should be glad therefore, should you consider it feasible, if you would arrange to have him captured or driven out of the country.

Dr. Meall, with Sgt. Lowe of 2nd Northern Nigeria Regiment and twenty-eight rank and file left Yola, ostensibly to relieve the Wamdeo detachment but in reality to rendezvous at Song with O.C. Troops and 25 Mounted Infantry who marched from Yola by night and reached the camp on 18 September. From there the combined force made a night march on Guduk, but as their guide under-estimated the distance it was 7.30 a.m. instead of daybreak when they came upon the village. A scout about 600 yards beyond the village opened fire on the troops, whereupon the defenders swarmed forth to occupy a small hill, from which they had to be driven before the soldiers could enter the village.

From this vantage point O.C. Troops saw Zubeiru and a handful of followers gallop away as the infantry entered the town. He at once gave chase with his escort of Mounted Infantry and caught sight of the party after three hours. He and his guide got close enough for him to empty his revolver at them, but the shots went wide. The horses of the Mounted Infantry, who had ridden the 45 miles from Yola to Song and thence across to Guduk in less than thirty-six hours, were by now exhausted, and Zubeiru gradually drew away from his pursuers. On the next day Sgt. Lowe took the troop out in search; they killed two of Zubeiru's followers, but Zubeiru again outrode his enemy.

Lieutenant Nisbet reported back to the Resident:

The Guduk people fought very bravely and the bayonet was used with effect before we cleared the hill. [The enemy lost 33.] Zubeiru had a tremendous influence over them but unfortunately for them our bullets did not turn to water . . . I am now waiting for more ammunition and the maxim as I hear Zubeiru has reached Gaanda: I am determined to chase till we kill, capture or drive him out of the country . . . Tiro [the Resident's messenger] asked that you will kindly send him a tin of biscuits.

Barclay told Nisbet not to pursue Zubeiru beyond Ga'anda, the only Fulani town likely to harbour him, as he was not prepared to sanction a hurried expedition into the wild pagan country. He advised that the troops should return to Yola. Nisbet, however, had other views, and had meanwhile ordered up another platoon and a maxim-gun from Yola. On receipt of the Resident's letter, his quarrel—one of several that marked the relationship between civil and military officers in the early years at Yola and elsewhere in the Protectorate—burst into the open.

I am unaware [wrote O. C. Troops on 2 March] that I should take instructions from a Political Officer as to the disposal of the troops under my command in Yola Province, nor am I aware that I am responsible to a Political Officer as to the extent the troops should be employed in any military operation.

Then came his trump card: 'The ex-Emir of Yola, Mallam Zubeiru, has been killed. All further information when I reach you.' The Resident replied that Nisbet's views appeared to be 'diametrically opposed' to his own, and since he understood that all responsibility in the Province was his, in his capacity as representative of the High Commissioner, he had referred the matter to Lugard. Meanwhile he added his congratulations and thanks on the successful and energetic operations.

What had happened was this. The reinforced column had set off from Song in the early hours of 27 February and camped outside Ga'anda on the following morning. The people promptly took to the hills, but were persuaded gradually to return and collect twelve sheep and some corn as a warranty of their good behaviour. Large numbers of armed pagans began to gather and a message was sent that they were unable to pay the fine, though thirty sheep were tethered within sight of the camp. Nisbet ordered the maxim-gun to open fire on the chief's house, 500 yards away; the warriors dispersed and the sheep were collected.

On hearing a rumour that Zubeiru had been killed by the Lala pagans, Nisbet marched his column to the village of Go, where he was friendlily received. The pagans told him that they had killed a Fulani who had camped in the bush near Sinteri and whom they took to be a Fulani slave-raider. They had surrounded his camp and opened fire; Zubeiru was struck by several poisoned arrows and fell in an attempt to reach his horse, and the rest of his few followers were either killed or wounded. The O.C. Troops identified the corpse by its 'enormous frame, greyish pointed beard and hair'. There are, however, still Fulani in Yola who are convinced that the decapitated body belonged to Bakari, Zubeiru's close friend, and that Zubeiru himself was mysteriously lifted to the skies in a thick protective mist sent by the guarding hand of Allah.

The High Commissioner, after congratulating Barclay, referred to the Resident's offered reward of cloth to the value of ten slaves for the capture of Zubeiru: 'I certainly cannot sanction a reward of £15 for a murder. I should like to know the circumstances of his death, whether he resisted capture and was killed in a scuffle or foully murdered.' In his Annual Report he wrote:

I should have wished, had it been possible, to have afforded a domicile to this brave though fanatical chief, but he was wholly irreconcilable and his death is beyond doubt a great blessing to the Yola Province, over which he had long tyrannised and where he was cordially hated.

In 1906 Bilingang, the last of Zubeiru's party, collected a band of outlaws and terrorized a large area from an almost inaccessible camp. The force was surprised by night, but all escaped; they were never heard of again.

In 1927 Zubeiru's gown and cloak were returned to the Lamido of Adamawa. They had been carefully preserved by a Mallam at Guduk, to whom Zubeiru had entrusted them with instructions to keep them till his return; but as the Mallam was now approaching death, he had asked the village-head to hand the relics over to the Lamido.

PATROLS AND PACIFICATION

After the fall of Yola the first concern of Government was to reopen the Yola-Lau trade route: above Numan the Mbula were active in highway robbery and below it the Yendam Waka and Bachama had closed the roads on both banks of the Benue. In October 1901 Dr. Cargill left Yola with a small escort and marched through the dangerous Zinna country to Jalingo, where the Emir promised to stop the passage of all slaves through his territory. He was accompanied by the outlawed Yerima of Muri, Muhammadu Mafindi, who volunteered to use the considerable personal influence he had acquired during his exile at Mayo Belwa to keep the south-bank road open. He had, perhaps, over-estimated his influence, for as soon as the patrol had opened the Lau route and returned to Yola raiding broke out again.

'With the exception of the capital (Yola) and of a few minor settlements', wrote Lugard in his 1902 report,

the greater part of this province is occupied by lawless pagan tribes whose pastime it is to fall upon travellers and traders and to kidnap them or each other for sale as slaves. Mr. Barclay, the Resident, has done much by travelling among them to gain their friendship and to induce them to forego these undesirable practices, but it is unfortunately true that the African savage in his primitive state can, as a rule, understand nothing but force, and regards arguments and verbal lessons as the weapons of the weak, to be listened to for the moment and set aside when convenient. If, however, he is once convinced by coercion that the white man has power to enforce his admonitions he will in future respect them—to some extent.

In the north of the Province matters were little better. The Marghi and Kilba had closed the trade route to Bornu, and it was in order to reopen it and to deal with the recalcitrant tribes along the banks of the Benue and Gongola that the Resident established a military post at Wamdeo and that the High Commissioner decided to divert the column operating in Bauchi and Bornu through Yola on its return journey in 1902. Strengthened by a detachment from Yola, the force, consisting of 7 officers and 130 rank and file with 2 guns and 2 maxims, was given the task of traversing the Bachama and Wurkum country. The patrol commander, Major Cubitt, was attacked by the Longuda pagans at Banjiram, which he shelled but did not reduce. 'When we left the place next morning,' observed the Resident, 'in spite of shell and maxim fire they hovered round and saw us safely off the premises, defiant to the end. . . . I am afraid we have hardly scratched them.' Opposition was also encountered farther down the Benue at Kwa, on the present Muri-Numan boundary, where the people had recently murdered seven traders. Thirty-two skulls were found here in one house. The column was again attacked in the Wurkum hills, but after several skirmishes the chiefs came in to beg for peace.

In 1903 a small force was permanently based on Numan. Its presence stabilized the Bachama unrest and put an end to organized opposition by the Bata, who for the first time visited Yola to offer their friendship to the Resident. In August Lieutenant Moran thoroughly explored the Gongola in a steam canoe without coming into contact with the hostile riverain villages.

By the end of 1903 the first phase of the British occupation was complete. With the conquest of the great Hausa states, the whole Protectorate was now under administrative control; law and order had been restored in all the sixteen Provinces, local trade was flourishing, and the tolls collected by the political staff in return for the protection of the roads were willingly paid by the traders, some of whom volunteered the statement that the amount was less than they would have been called upon to pay under the former régime.

A YEAR OF UNREST

The year 1904 was a particularly difficult one in Adamawa. First, there was the famine, which had prevailed among the pagan tribes since the locust infestation of 1899 and now spread to the Fulani areas. The distress was very great: pagans sold their children for a mere handful of corn,[1] while many people died from eating unripe crops, seed corn, and poisonous roots. The German Resident at Garua wrote imploring assistance as the people were dying of hunger. The Gongola area suffered in the extreme: here 50 per cent. of the tribes were estimated to have died and children were sold in large numbers or offered to travellers in exchange for food. The confluence with the Benue was choked with corpses, and Banjiram and Shellen, for example, were reduced from 12,000 to under a thousand inhabitants.

Secondly, there were serious hostilities in both the Yola and Muri Provinces. The three great trade routes of Muri, namely those from the salt mines at Awe and the kola plantations at Bafum and Kentu, and the cattle route from beyond Gashaka, converged at Wase. Various expeditions had been sent to protect these caravan routes, but the lawless Yergum and Montol tribes had virtually isolated Wase and had recently murdered a party of traders. To complete their mischief they killed and ate a government messenger (or someone in mistake for him) who had been sent to warn them to desist. A strong column was sent by Lugard to restore communications with Bauchi, accompanied by Mr. Vischer[2] as Political Officer, who saved the life of a soldier by sucking the poison from his arrow wound. Lugard commented:

I trust that the capture of their fastnesses, which they had supposed to be impregnable, the heavy fine inflicted (£460), the deposition of the chiefs responsible, the destruction of two brigand bands who terrorised the country and defied the authority of the chiefs, and, above all, the careful explanation of the reason of the expedition and the prompt rendition of all captives, will have a permanent effect.

Upon the temporary withdrawal of the military post at Wamdeo in the Marghi District—there had been some doubt whether the village was not really in German Uba—the Marghi and Kilba plundered a government caravan and blocked the Bornu road, which had never been safe for parties without an escort. This was

[1] In the great Mandara famine of 1921, the French authorities at Gider found that a Matakam girl had been sold by her uncle to a Fulani of Madagali for thirteen calabashes of corn.   [2] Later Sir Hanns Vischer.

followed by risings round Yola itself. The Yendam Waka pagans once more closed the Lau road, and the Verre tribes from Gurin, Guriga, and Bai Manga, emboldened by their new freedom from Fulani pressure, began to raid the plains, murdering seven persons and sending word to the Resident that they intended to destroy all Fulani villages in the vicinity of the hills. These outbreaks were subdued by military patrols, and posts were established to prevent their recurrence.

An expedition was sent up the Gongola, to exploit this channel of communication, which had in the previous year been found navigable to light-draught steamers as far as Nafada, and to open up the fertile valley to trade. Hostilities were avoided, but a patrol was necessary to coerce the Bachama of Lamurde.

Finally, the configuration of the international boundary caused endless trouble during these early years, and the final settlement of the 1904 Boundary Commission did little to ease matters. In Nyibango District, for instance, which the Commission had partitioned between Britain and Germany, the headman of the British portion allied himself with his son Maigari, at that time headman on the German side but later Emir of Yola, and together they raided the British area of Nyibango and the neighbouring Verre villages until called to account by the German Resident.

North of the Benue the boundary line was even more disastrous to the old Emirate of Adamawa. Not only was it deprived of its richest provinces, but the eastern line, following the Yedseram, Tiel, and Faro rivers, robbed many of the chiefs of the greater part of their territories. The Fulani had always tended to pitch their camps on the western bank of a river and thence expand eastwards. From their point of view, therefore, the amputation of the eastern districts could scarcely have been worse: 'They have left me merely the latrines of my kingdom', lamented the Emir. Uba, Holma, Bila Kilba, and Gurin suffered most: they were reduced from large districts to single villages, with the bulk of their farm-lands cut off from them. The Germans naturally installed their own chiefs, and the resulting intrigues of the rival branches were labyrinthine and nefarious. The southern boundary was not so politically mortal, but it left the richest grazing grounds on the wrong side of the frontier—as the Emir remarked to the Resident, 'They say they have left us the head, but they have cut off the body!'

CONSOLIDATION

Though there were occasional outbreaks of lawlessness—such as that of the Piri tribe, who in 1906 invited the Resident to visit them as they had eaten every kind of flesh and were now curious to see what the flesh of the White Man tasted like—by the beginning of 1905 the new Administration was firmly in the saddle and the extent and effectiveness of civil control were reflected in the considerably reduced military expenditure.

Though these formative years were inevitably bound up with military events, the work done by the exiguous political staff was monumental. When the Political Department was formed in 1900 there were only nine posts in the Estimates. From the outset the method of administration was indirect rule through the chiefs, and it was to accentuate this policy that the political officers were styled 'Residents' instead of the more usual 'Commissioners' of other colonies. Other departments were equally thin on the ground: the total budget of 1900 for the whole Protectorate of Northern Nigeria was under £86,000, and the total civil staff for all departments allowed for only eighty-five European officers. The average number of political officers in Yola Province was only 3·3 in 1906 and no more than 5·1 by 1912; even in 1920 the total number of European officials did not normally exceed twelve in Yola and seven in Muri Province.

What was this British administration? None is better qualified to present its essentials than its greatest exponent, Lord Lugard, who in one of his most famous Nigerian speeches thus defined its aims:

The old treaties are dead—you have killed them. Now these are the words which I, the High Commissioner, have to say for the future . . . Every Sultan and Emir, and the principal officers of State, will be appointed by the High Commissioner. The emirs and chiefs who are appointed will rule over the people as of old time and take such taxes as are approved; but they will obey the laws of the Governor, and will act in accordance with the advice of this Resident. Buying and selling slaves, and enslaving people, are forbidden. It is forbidden to import fire arms, except flintlocks. The alkalis and emirs will hold the law courts as of old; but bribes are forbidden, and mutilation and confinement of men in inhuman prisons are not lawful . . . The Government hold the right of taxation, and will tell the emirs and chiefs what taxes they may levy.

All men are free to worship God as they please . . . It is the earnest desire of the King of England that this country shall prosper and grow rich in peace and in contentment; that the population shall increase, and the ruined towns which abound everywhere shall be built up; and that war and trouble shall cease. Henceforth no emir or chief shall levy war or fight. I earnestly hope to give effect in these matters to the wishes of my King.

In conclusion, I hope that you will find our rule sympathetic, and that the country will prosper and be contented . . . You must not fear to tell the Resident everything, and he will help and advise you.

And what had this policy achieved in five years? To quote from the brilliant history by Lady Lugard:

Its duty has been to bring under control a congeries of states, of which the internal disorders necessitated, in the first instance, a resort to the plain argument of military conquest. The administration has not in the short period of its existence been able to do more than to affirm the conquest of the country, and to create a skeleton of the machinery of government which it will be for time to bring to its full perfection.

But a beginning has been made. The framework of administration has been established in all the provinces. A territory which we found in chaos has been brought to order. The slave trade has been abolished within its frontiers. Its subject races have been secured in the possession of their lives and property . . . There has been no great shock and no convulsion, only into the veins of a decadent civilization new blood has been introduced, which has brought with it the promise of a new era of life.

VI

WAR AND PEACE

A.—THE CAMPAIGN 1914–15

THE 1914–18 war impinged on Adamawa perhaps more than on any other Province of Nigeria, both during its actual course and in its subsequent charge of mandated territory. Militarily, the operations are now referred to as the Cameroons campaign. Since Yola was only 30 miles away from the Garua strongpoint and German territory ran along the whole eastern frontier of the Yola and Muri Provinces, the war was an intimate experience in Adamawa.

THE OUTBREAK OF WAR

The telegram was not received till 5 August. All leave was immediately cancelled and preparations were made to receive the troops forming the Yola column. S. H. P. Vereker was put in charge of intelligence, though it was another administrative officer, K. V. Elphinstone, who eventually accompanied the troops as Political Officer; both were later Residents. Besides deliberately inaccurate information spread by both sides, there was a great deal of false intelligence emanating from a love of boasting or of notoriety, or from fear and imagination. The Assistant Commissioner of Police and the Surveyor were detailed to organize supplies and transport; the second police officer was responsible for local markets, and every British subject—with a single exception—took the oath as a member of the Nigerian Land Contingent. The one German subject, Herr Schelske, who was trading in partnership with a retired Niger Company agent, was committed to open arrest on parole.

All road and river communication with the Kamerun colony was closed. The police patrolled the telegraph lines, and pony posts were organized to link Yola with Numan, Bauchi, and Bornu.

The clerical staff were removed to temporary grass huts and their quarters prepared for the new officers. The Niger Company redirected 50 tons of rice from Burutu destined for Kano, while 35 tons of grain and 1,200 carriers were assembled by the S. & T. Officers.

The Pirambi detachment of the 2nd Nigeria Regiment was recalled to Yola, and the Resident was asked to find out the strength of the German post at Garua. No military reconnaissance was undertaken, as Major A. H. Festing of the Niger Company was expected any day from Garua. He arrived on 15 August and reported that when he had hastily departed on 11th the Germans, whose garrison consisted of 10 Europeans, 70 soldiers, and 2 machine-guns, knew nothing of the declaration of war.

Two more companies of troops arrived on 14 and 18 August, and on 21st the Mounted Infantry rode in under Lord Henry Seymour. Reinforced by another company of infantry, the Yola column marched out on 22 August, leaving one section behind as garrison. The Nigeria Regiment had now taken up its positions along the German frontier in accordance with the pre-arranged defence scheme: in the north the Maiduguri and Nafada columns covered Mora, in the south there were concentrations of troops at Calabar and on the Cross River, while the central thrust would come from Yola, which with its force of 600 men, 5 machine-guns, and 2 mountain guns constituted the strongest column.

THE TEPE AMBUSH

The Mounted Infantry, who provided the advance guard, were told that there was a minor German post of about one section strength at Tepe. As the cavalry approached they came under a withering fire from close quarters. In the high corn the M.I. could do little when they dismounted, and Seymour saw that his only hope was to take two sections round the flank and charge across the more open ground. The Germans, whose strength was later estimated at three officers and fifty men, were driven out, but the casualty rate of the Mounted Infantry was appalling: out of the six officers, Captain Wickham and Lieutenant Sherlock were killed, Major Lord Henry Seymour and Captain Macdonald wounded. Only two troopers were casualties, and the Germans lost two officers and two soldiers.

REVERSE AT GARUA

After another skirmish, at Saratse, the column reached Garua, which Lieutenant-Colonel Maclear decided to attack by night on 28 August. It was an ill-prepared, unreconnoitred and confused affair. Maclear, who disregarded his officers' advice to press home the advance against the centre fort while there was still the cover of darkness, preferred to rest his men before a daylight assault. When dawn broke, his troops found themselves concentrated in a small area exposed to heavy fire across open ground from a hill only 400 yards away. In face of a vigorous counter-attack the men broke and retreated to their camp.

British losses were high. Five officers were killed, among them Lieutenant-Colonel Maclear and Major Puckle, who was shot by a German orderly as he was accepting the surrender of an officer; two officers were wounded; and Doctors Trumper and Lindsay were taken prisoner when they insisted on staying behind to look after the 600-odd British casualties. Captain Adams withdrew the demoralized force to Tepe on 1 September and embarked his guns and carriers on the Niger Company's sternwheeler *Kampe*, which Major Festing had brought up to Bilachi. The column marched into Yola on 3 September.

It is probable that had the one company of troops stationed at Yola at the outbreak proceeded to Garua by steamer without delay, they would have found a skeleton garrison in the town. But by the time orders were received from Headquarters at Lagos and the host of carriers had been assembled, it was too late. The Germans had recalled their troops from Marua, had obtained reinforcements from Banyo, and had put Garua into a more than adequate state of defence. The official history of the campaign blames the repulse on a series of tactical errors and omissions, and attributes the final panic of the troops at Garua to a loss of confidence in their leaders as much as to the strain of the heavy bombardment, for in this their first encounter with European-trained troops they had displayed courage and steadiness in the initial assault.

THE REGROUPING AT YOLA

The news of the set-backs to both the Yola and Maiduguri columns had an understandably adverse effect on local morale throughout Adamawa and beyond. Lugard, back from leave in early September, at once reorganized the W.A.F.F. command. Brigadier-General Cunliffe was appointed to command the Nigerian forces and he made a personal inspection of the troops at Yola before he regrouped the column. Major Webb-Bowen was posted to Yola on 10 September to take charge of all troops in the area, which besides the Yola column included the Maiduguri force and the company that had occupied the German frontier post of Mubi. His instructions were to ensure the safety of Yola in case of an attack and then to accelerate the fall of Mora as a prelude to an allied assault with the French on Garua.

To make Yola station defensible, redoubts and wire entanglements were undertaken and the extended line of communication was shortened. To quote from the Resident's report:

... impossible to defend the lengthy line of scattered buildings stretching from the Residency to Jimeta, a distance of over two miles. Consequently the Residency, old station and Jimeta were prepared for evacuation, with the object of all assembling within the fortified area at the new site should the situation so demand. All government and personal property, office books and records, stores, etc., that were not in daily use, were removed to the base depot at Jimeta. This naturally added considerably to the difficulties of carrying on political and office work.

Marua was being held by a small force of Mounted Infantry. In November Captain Fox, who was in charge of the troops investing Mora, requested urgent reinforcements from Webb-Bowen as the Germans were reported to have sent 200 men from Garua, whose defence they had completed, to recapture Marua. Webb-Bowen's column therefore set out on 12 November, comprising 45 British officers and N.C.O.s, 384 soldiers, 205 followers, 52 gun carriers and 1,300 porters, 113 donkeys, and 240 slaughter cattle.

ALARMS AND EXCURSIONS

Webb-Bowen left behind one company and one section to hold Yola, while another company was stationed at Numan to cover the enemy forces at Mayo Kalei which threatened the rear of Yola. At Malabu a German raiding party burned 500 bags of corn which had been stored for the Yola column. Early in 1915 the company of troops at Beli was attacked but drove off the enemy. There were a number of notable raids in which special mention must be made of the heroic part played by the Administration and police.

The Takum affair was the first British success in the northern campaign. The police post of Bakundi under Soper, an Assistant Commissioner of Police, and another party under Lieutenant-Commander Waters, I.O., accompanied the Resident of Muri Province, J. M. Fremantle, in a raid on Gaiama, just across the border. After four days' skirmishing they withdrew to Takum, where Major Churcher, D.O., had surrounded the town with a chain of small block-houses. The Resident returned to Ibi. On 17 September the police force of fifty-seven men was attacked by a strong German patrol of about seventy soldiers and a machine-gun, who were attempting to penetrate to Ibi. The attack was repelled without loss, the Germans losing one European officer and half a dozen men and retiring to Kentu. The police then withdrew to Chanchangi to cover the Ibi road. Preparations were made to evacuate Ibi but the news of the Takum victory reassured the Resident. Reinforcements were sent from Yola and Lokoja, and later the defence of the frontier was transferred from the Resident to the Ibi column, consisting of 500 troops and police with two guns under Major Mann.

The post established on the outbreak of war at Bakundi to protect the southern borders of Muri was soon withdrawn, and the Germans occupied about 500 square miles of the Province. In November an attempt to dislodge them from Gazabu failed, H. Q. Glenny, D.O., being mortally wounded as he led the attack. He is buried at Bakundi.

On 17 January 1915, a party of fifteen to twenty soldiers under a German N.C.O. raided Yola just before dawn. They entered the hospital, over which the Red Cross lights were burning, and attacked the sick in their beds. Many shots were fired into the hospital and a British sergeant narrowly escaped with his life. The troops in the barracks were too far away to give assistance, but the

Treasury guard opened fire and led by W. O. P. Rosedale, A.D.O., who was first on the scene, enfiladed the enemy before the troops arrived. The objective was apparently the Residency, but the Germans were misled by a man whom they had captured on the road. Local lore now has it that the Germans did, in fact, reach the Residency, where they shot the cook, missing the Resident who was sleeping some distance away in his mosquito-proof cage. For some weeks after the raid the Resident and the medical department retired inside the new fort, but towards the end of March the Residency was reoccupied and a double guard was posted.

The southern districts of Yola Province suffered constant harrying from the German post at Mayo Kalei, and C. J. Hebblethwaite, D.O., who was in charge of the border patrol of mixed W.A.F.F. and police, decided to attack the fort at dawn on 7 April. He had with him Chartris, Commissioner of Police, and thirty men. The fort was strongly defended and drove off the attackers, who lost Hebblethwaite killed and two wounded men. That day, however, the enemy abandoned the fort, the remains of which can still be seen on the Jada road, together with Hebblethwaite's grave.

A week later news was received of the German raid of 12 April on Mutum Biu, then headquarters of Muri Division. A large force of troops from Banyo, with two maxim-guns, advanced upon the town, which was evacuated just in time; the Divisional Officer and the Emir escaped with the treasury across the river. The government station was completely wrecked and about eight miles of telegraph line destroyed.

When the second expedition advanced to Garua in April 1915, a communication post was established at Gurin, consisting of 42 rank and file of the W.A.F.F. and police under Lieutenant Pawle and Sergeant Fraser, with J. P. F. Fitzpatrick, D.O., as Intelligence Officer. On 29 April a German force of 300 rifles and 5 machine-guns, commanded by the skilled defender of Garua, von Crailsheim, who was making a daring foray along the British line of communication, entered the town. The garrison withdrew into the fort and the enemy, knowing there was only a small police posse there, marched forward in close order. The action lasted for eight hours, when the Germans withdrew with thirty casualties. Lieutenant Pawle was killed at the outset and Sergeant Fraser severely wounded soon after, so the conduct of the defence devolved upon Fitzpatrick. A third of the British force were casualties. On hearing of the engagement, Major Booth, who was making for Yola with 600 carriers to bring supplies up to Garua, hurried with his small escort to Gurin, but the Germans had withdrawn. From Garua the Mounted Infantry covered the 27 miles during the night and a company of infantry reached Gurin by 2 p.m., only 21 hours after the news had reached military headquarters.

THE FALL OF GARUA

When Webb-Bowen's column marched out from Yola in November 1914, he found he was too late to save Marua. He patrolled the area round Demsa, Pella (where a military post had been established to deal with the recrudescence of lawlessness among the Kilba and Marghi), and Mubi, but was unable to join up with the French column until the middle of January. This very strong combined force then took up a position under the French Commander, Brisset, to cordon off Garua.

Lugard, aware of the disturbing lack of success in the Northern Cameroons, was anxious to secure the fall of Garua, and the campaign was discussed at an important conference at Duala in January 1915. As Garua was known to be very heavily defended and its fortified hills were beyond normal artillery range, a 12-pounder and crew from H.M.S. *Challenger* were sent all the way up the Benue, despite the low water, to Yola, where they arrived on 12 March. A French 95 mm. gun had an even more adventurous journey, coming all the way from Dakar. Cunliffe himself conducted the operations, spending a month planning the attack and reorganizing the intelligence section in Yola before he transferred his staff headquarters to Bogole, by Garua.

The German position, manned by some 600 men and 3 guns, was a very strong one. Each of the five Garua rocky peaks was a self-contained fort, with parapets revetted with sandbags, an armour-plated command post, a cement water-tank, and stores of ammunition and food. The main post was the citadel, with walls strengthened to 15 feet thick and enormous underground tunnels. A triple belt of deep pits, wire or thorn abattis, and a moat surrounded the stronghold. Against this fortress Cunliffe could muster an equally impressive force, of 11 British and French infantry companies, a company of the Mounted Infantry and a squadron of French cavalry, 5 guns, and 11 machine-guns.

Von Crailsheim made a brilliant sortie in April and, joined by a force from Ngaundere, terrorized Gurin and Chamba before returning to Garua on 8 May, having successfully eluded Cunliffe's patrols. From the end of May a heavy bombardment continued while the allied line was gradually pushed forward to a point so near the town that 2,000 carriers were employed daily to bring up water supplies from the Benue. Food was reported to be short and there was smallpox in the town. Attempts were made to break out on 9/10 June with all baggage and ammunition, but many were drowned in the flooded Benue.

On 10 June the white flag was hoisted. An offer to capitulate was turned down and two hours later the Germans, some of whose troops had mutinied after the allied bombardment, agreed to an unconditional surrender. Thirty-seven Germans and 212 soldiers were made prisoners of war, many troops having escaped.

THE END OF THE CAMPAIGN

Cunliffe returned to Yola on 15 June, leaving Brisset at Garua to support Lieutenant-Colonel Webb-Bowen's thrust towards the south. Koncha and Chamba fell, and on 28th the heights of Ngaundere were stormed during a terrific tornado. Tingere was captured on 24 July and on 16 August the British entered Gashaka. The Ibi column had meanwhile joined up with the Takum force, occupied Kentu and reorganized to help in the final advance. Bamenda fell on 22 October and Banyo hill was taken on 6 November after severe fighting lasting three days and nights, in which Captains Bower-Smith and Mackinnon, and Colour-Sergeant King were killed.

In January 1916 Cunliffe moved his headquarters to Fumban,

thus marking the end of hostilities as far as Muri was concerned; Yola had ceased to be a base on 21 November. By mid-February the Germans had crossed the border into Spanish Muni, where they were interned, and the gallant defender of Mora, von Raben, surrendered to the Maiduguri column after a costly and masterly defence.

AFTERPIECE

The contribution of the Native Authorities during the campaign was enormous. Besides voting substantial sums to the war chest, the Emirs constantly encouraged the supply and transport services which so largely depended on the Native Authorities for their success. The Emir of Yola, for instance, provided 140 horses, 800 heel ropes and 200 head ropes, as well as mats and potash for the Mounted Infantry when they were stationed in his capital, and rifle slings, cartridge belts and 800 pairs of sandals for the infantry companies. In 1915 subscriptions from all over Muri paid for a gift of kola nuts for the whole of the Ibi column, and after the fall of Garua the Emir presented the victorious troops with a present of cattle and kola nuts.

The Resident's report gives a picture of the scale of the commissarial activities undertaken by the Native Authorities:

In Yola some 750 tons of grain, 1000 head of cattle, 80 horses besides large quantities of material have been provided. In addition to some 500 carriers supplied to the column for permanent work, over 6000 loads have been transported to various depots.

Nor was the assistance confined to logistics:

The Emirate has also provided border patrols along the whole frontier, and dak runners to each column. One of these patrols had a sharp encounter with an enemy raiding party under Boboa, father of Maigari of Nassarawo and one of the principal native scouts and foragers employed by the Germans. Boboa was killed and his followers scattered.

Government was grateful, and generous in its acknowledgement. By 'an act of grace' the Governor-General authorized a grant of £250 to the people of Gurin, whose loyalty had been severely tested by their no-man's land vulnerability throughout the campaign and who had been pillaged in a vile fashion during the raid of 29 April 1915. The Emir of Yola was awarded the C.B.E. in recognition of his war services, and the Emir of Muri and the District Head of Nyibango received the King's Medal for African Chiefs.

B.—THE CUSTODY OF THE CAMEROONS

So much of modern Adamawa, nearly two-thirds of the area and over half the population of the Emirate, lies within the Cameroons that an aperçu of its unusual story—it has been administered by three European nations within less than twenty-five years—is germane to the general exposition of Adamawa's history. The form 'Kamerun' suggests that the Germans mistakenly accepted the word as an indigenous one, whereas Cameroons is in fact the anglicized form of *Camarones*, itself the Spanish variant of the Portuguese *Rio dos Camaroes* or river of prawns.

THE GERMAN OCCUPATION

By a masterly coup, Bismarck outplayed and outpaced the British, and in July 1884 the German flag was raised in Duala. The hinterland, much of which belonged to or bordered on the Adamawa empire, had been explored by Rohlfs in 1865-7 and by the celebrated Gustav Nachtigal in 1869-73. The early 1890's, as has been shown in the chapter on exploration, saw the rivalry of England, France, and Germany in the race for Chad, but by 1894 the Germans had given up hopes of penetrating Adamawa by the overland route of Zintgraff or by the Niger-Benue approach favoured by Staudinger, and were concentrating on possible routes from the south.

The map of the Cameroons was determined by the Anglo-German agreement of March 1894, modified locally by the joint Boundary Commission of 1903-4. Governor Puttkamer, a nephew of Bismarck, had at once set about bringing the interior under German control in fact as well as in name. Rejecting as utopian the policy of Woermann, the leading Hamburg trader in the Cameroons, who wished to open up Adamawa by the peaceful penetration of Christian missionaries, Puttkamer preferred a strong, military line. Two of his most brilliant lieutenants during these years of consolidation were Kamptz and Dominik, working in the region round Yaounde.

In 1899 Tibati finally surrendered to the Germans, and two years later Hauptmann Kramer von Klausbruck stormed Ngaundere. From there he turned north to Garua, where he defeated the fugitive Emir of Adamawa. Dominik took over the Upper Benue and in 1902, with Oberleutnant Radtke, routed Zubeiru at Marua, afterwards entering Mubi in January and raiding the Micika and Kilba districts. He was joined by Oberleutnant Pavel who, on the murder of Nolte at Banyo, marched north to occupy Dikwa. Graf Fugger relieved von Bülow as Commandant in Garua but he was assassinated in January 1903. Hauptmann Thierry, the new Resident at Garua, was killed by the pagans near Mubi and was succeeded by Langheld, who had been Lugard's opposite number in Uganda. Thierry shares with Dominik the distinction of being still remembered in the Adamawa section of the Northern Cameroons.

In German Adamawa the normal Cameroons administrative zone or *Bezirk* was replaced by *Residentur*, administrative districts under a commissioner charged with ruling through the sixty-odd Fulani princes whose loyalty to Yola had now been broken. Of these *Residentur* there were three. From Mora, the northern Fulani districts of Diamare, Marua, Mindif, and Kalfu, and the pagan areas of Wandala and Logone were governed; the central one, known as that of Adamawa, embraced the Benue districts and Ngaundere; and to the south-east that of Banyo controlled the Koncha, Gashaka, and Banyo districts. In 1911 the size of the German Cameroons was doubled by a Franco-German agreement: Bismarck's work had been crowned and schoolboys could jubilantly declaim:

> Ich bin ein Bub' von Kamerun
> Der deutschen Kolonie;
> Fürst Bismarck hatte viel zu tun
> Bis er erworben sie.

INTERREGNUM

When the allied forces moved south in the late rains of 1915 it became necessary to establish a government in the conquered

portion of German Adamawa, which was provisionally shared
between the Yola and Muri Provinces and France. In April 1916
Banyo was handed over to the French; Gashaka was incorporated
into Muri Division from November and an area round Kentu was
attached to Ibi Division; Adamawa Division assumed responsibility
for the Chamba districts and those immediately north of the
Benue; and the northern Mandara region was allotted to the
French. In August 1917 Gashaka was transferred to Koncha,
which was administered by the Yola Province, and the Kentu area
went to Bamenda Province. In the eyes of the Adamawa Fulani
such restorations were regarded as a partial righting of an ancient
wrong, the Anglo-German Boundary Conventions.

The temporary French administration of the districts lying
along the western slopes of the Mandara mountain system was
even sketchier than that of the Germans, who had confined themselves to a few tours of exploration and an occasional armed foray
in support of the Fulani chiefs. Little is known of their brief rule;
there was not much of it. A comparison between the German tax
of 1913 and the French rates imposed in the Mubi area in 1920 is
interesting. The former rate was 2s. male, 1s. female, 2s. horse,
1s. cow, 6d. donkey, 1d. sheep or goat; the latter: 5s. male, 3s.
female or 1s. if she had children, 2s. horse, 1s. cow, 6d. donkey,
3d. sheep or goat.

The boundary delimitation of the British and French spheres of
influence was completed in 1920. In July 1922 Britain received a
mandate from the League of Nations to administer the strip of
territory along Nigeria's eastern frontier, while the greater portion
of the former German colony went to France.

SOUTHERN MANDATED AREA

On the final settlement of the Anglo-French boundary nearly
the whole of Dodeo, the greater part of Laro and the town of
Koncha, were assigned to the French. The chiefs of Koncha and
Laro moved over the border into the respective portions of their
old districts remaining under British mandate, and these areas
became the districts of Toungu and Namberu; the latter was
embodied in Nassarawo District when its headman decamped to

Koncha to avoid the consequence of his peculations. At the same time the village groups of Gurumpawo and Yebbi, which had once been subject to Koncha and Nassarawo, consolidated the independence they had gained during the war by receiving recognition as separate districts. The pagans of the Alantika hills had been nominally under Nassarawo, but no attempt was made to administer them till 1926, when they were brought into Verre District on account of their ethnic affinity.

Thus in 1921 there was formed, for the new mandated areas, the Southern Cameroons Division of Yola Province, with the independent Gurumpawo and Yebbi Districts. In 1924 Gashaka was returned to Muri Province, to be handed over to the newly-formed Adamawa Province in 1926 when, with the Kentu District of Bamenda Province, it became a division in its own right and had its own Divisional Officer. In 1928 Gashaka reverted to the status of a district, and five years later it lost Kentu to the Wukari District of Benue Province.

At first all the mandated territory had been excluded from the jurisdiction of the Emir, but in 1923 it was decided to administer it as an integral part of the Province.

It is of interest to record that the Arnado Kabri still has in his possession a German rest-house book and a tax register, which he looks on as his badge of office; the rest-house book was issued on 24 December 1909.

THE CHAMBA PATROL

Though not ranking as an occupying patrol, as was that dispatched to the northern mandated districts in the following year, the 1920 Chamba patrol nevertheless included among its objectives the collection of tax arrears from the hostile pagans in the newly gained territory and an overall watching-brief on the Tibba villages on both sides of the border lest they should be influenced by the disturbing example of the Chamba of the Lamja hills. Three patrols had operated in the area since 1916, but for different reasons none was successful. In consequence, the prestige of the Lamja *tsafi*[1] stood high, boasting that neither Fulani messenger

[1] The local religious cult.

nor government officer had ever achieved his mission among them and that even raids on Fulani cattle and the murder of a herdsman had been carried out with encouraging impunity.

The patrol of 2 officers, 1 medical officer, 60 rank and file and W. D. K. Mair, D.O. Kwoncha, left Yola on 15 December. The Lamja hills operations lasted 26 days, 11 of which were spent in occupying recalcitrant villages. When clearing the final summit hamlets the pagans 'gesticulated wildly, flicked an arrow or two, whirled their slings and shrieked shrill defiance', but it was an accidental swarm of bees that finally stampeded the patrol. Mair continues: 'The men were defiant, fully armed and prowling in caves, around and below our outposts. The sentries were liable to get an iron-tipped poisoned arrow through them at short range at any moment.'

Two more months were spent in patrolling the Dinding, Binyeri, and Gurumpawo groups, with a major skirmish at Ngba. This hill had become an asylum for all warlike spirits and the patrol was met by a shower of boulders and abuse, challenging them to approach. It was afterwards learnt that these pagans had never heard of a rifle and, assuming the soldiers' weapons to be mere clubs, had planned to enslave such a defenceless party.

The patrol returned to Yola on 22 March, but the friction between the political and military officers of the patrol and the unfortunate phraseology of the report, which aroused gubernatorial anxiety, left an unpleasant stigma on the operations.

NORTHERN MANDATED AREA

When the British Administration took over from the French in 1920 on the basis of the Milner-Simon agreement of the previous year, the northern mandated area consisted of eleven districts: Madagali, Moda, Micika, Mayo Bani, Mubi, Vokna, Maiha, Kowagol, Sorau, Wafango, and Belel. Moda and Micika were ethnically one and were therefore amalgamated under the name of Cubunawa; Vokna was merged with Maiha on tribal grounds; and for similar reasons Mayo Bani was restored to Uba and Kowagol to Holma, their previous separation having been due solely to the arbitrary cleavage of the old Anglo-German boundary. Sorau was made a village area of Holma, under whose suzerainty it had once been. For a while Demsa was administered with Belel as a single district, but the final partition allotted it to the French. Jealousy among the different branches of the ruling house made it impossible to amalgamate Wafango with Zummo until the death of the latter's chief in 1931.

THE MADAGALI PATROL

While the southern districts of Yola Province's new region— known as the Northern Cameroons, Yola Section—were orderly enough, the northern districts of Madagali, Cubunawa and Mubi were in a sorry condition. 'The country taken over by this Province', noted the Resident in 1920,

are [sic] the most lawless, ill-governed places I have seen in Nigeria since the early years of the Northern Nigeria Protectorate. Slave dealing and slave raiding are rampant . . . chiefs of minor importance were given rifles with which they were encouraged to attack the wretched pagans [who are] hiding like frightened monkeys on inaccessible hilltops . . . of course, everyone goes about fully armed: spears, shields, bows and arrows, clubs, etc.

Captain Brackenbury, D.O., went north in December 1920 to take over the area from the French, and in the new year the Emir followed him to Mubi, with a reduced entourage of 300–400 attendants! T. F. Carlyle, the Political Officer who relieved Brackenbury, reported that he was convinced there would be determined opposition to tax-collection in several places where the terrain would be in the rebels' favour. The Resident's suggestion that the collection should be postponed was over-ruled as impolitic, and sanction for a military patrol of two platoons and a Lewis gun was accordingly granted.

The patrol left on 17 October. The Resident's instructions to S. H. P. Vereker, the Political Officer accompanying the patrol, were:

The troops are really only to make a better demonstration; the pagans that have never been subjugated, e.g. those living in the Mandara hills, are to be left untouched for the moment. The first thing to be done is to collect the Jangali and Haraji. The latter will have to be collected on the basis of the French collection, as there is no time to assess or even take a new census, H.H.'s instructions being that the tax must be collected at once . . . I leave it to you to decide on the best place for Headquarters for the troops: they will remain with you from 3 to 6 months.

Vereker chose Mubi, which he reached on 4 November, and from there he visited all the main villages on the route up to Madagali, assessing and collecting tax. Back at Mubi, he made treks to the Pakka area and down as far as Sorau and Belel.

Only at Bazza Tilijo was armed resistance encountered. Inspired by their *arnado*, the pagans had shown equal obduracy to both the German and French Administrations and now, after three months' overtures from Vereker, they remained so truculent that the only course was to arrest their chief. As the D.O. and his escort reached the top of the hill at daybreak on 4 February the pagans greeted them with arrows. The enemy began to gather for an onslaught, urged on by their *arnado*, whose commands, shouted among the boulders, were translated to Vereker by his interpreters. The patrol opened fire as the charge developed, killing the chief in the first volley, and then entered the village without further opposition.

The patrol was brought to a close on 22 February, and both Vereker and Captain Buchan received congratulations from Winston Churchill, Secretary of State for the Colonies, on their able handling of the operation.

TRUST TERRITORY

Under the League of Nations mandate of 1922 the mandated territories of Northern and Southern Adamawa were administered as an integral part of the Province. By virtue of the provisions of the Atlantic Charter and the United Nations Organization, a quarter of a century later, the emphasis if not the form has changed considerably, and from the inception of the Trusteeship Council[1] in March 1947, much prominence has been given to the Trust Territories. The Trusteeship Council, to quote from the report of its opening session, aims at

a practical, workable system of international supervision of the administration of Trust Territories . . . The United Nations and the Administrating Authorities now solemnly join hands in the great venture of

[1] U.N.O. Document T/1.

reassuring, by deeds, the inhabitants of the Trust Territories as to their future political, economic, social and educational advancement, and the ultimate realization of their aspirations towards self-government or independence.

From 1947[1] onwards the Nigerian Government, as the Administering Authority, has published an annual report on the Cameroons under United Kingdom administration. This is based on a formidable questionnaire[2] submitted by the Trusteeship Council and is of extreme value.

From 1949 a triennial Visiting Mission has travelled in the Cameroons as the supervisory emissaries of the Trusteeship Council. The reports of the 1949[3] and 1952[4] Visiting Missions make interesting reading and could be quoted at length to illustrate the immense progress made in Northern and Southern Adamawa during the past decade. The Lamido addressed a vigorous petition[5] to the 1949 Mission:

There is something which is actually operating in the minds of my people ... It is still a mystery to the inhabitants of Adamawa that their country is composed of two Territories, viz., a portion being British and another held in trust: before the advent of Europeans, so the part of Adamawa Emirate which was purely British and the part occupied by the Germans were one country ruled by the Lamido Adamawa ... A change of policy is requested, i.e., the total dissolution of Trusteeship, and annexation to Adamawa Emirate as all the portion now British and French Territory formerly belonging to Adamawa.

There was no Adamawa petition to the 1952 Visiting Mission.

In 1955 the Regional Government created the new Ministry for Northern Cameroons Affairs, and this was shortly followed by the establishment of the advisory Northern Cameroons Consultative Committee, on which five members from Adamawa Trust Territory are serving.

The report of the 1955 Visiting Mission has not yet been published, but it is worth while recording that the Lamido informed

[1] The first report, Cmd. 1647/1922, was issued in 1922. This was followed by annual reports of lesser interest, but since 1947 their scope has been considerably enlarged.   [2] Document T/1010.   [3] Document T/798.
[4] Document T/1109.   [5] Document T./Pet., 4/21.

the visitors that in his land the concept of Trust Territory was little more than Greek to him and that his people looked on Northern Nigeria as their country rather than that Cameroons so dear to Trusteeship Council parlance, a territory which to them signified only the Southern Cameroons.

VII

SOME LATER TRAVELLERS

THE earlier chapter on exploration treated of the records of travellers to Adamawa up to the time of the British occupation. During the present century, however, the country has continued to attract adventurous visitors, whose accounts shed a fresh and fascinating light on the Adamawa of later years. Nor is this enlightenment confined to the chronicles of those that pass in a night or play but tip-and-run with local history; many who have served long and loyally have narrated their experiences in memoirs and journals.

BAUER[1]

In 1902 the long-promised expedition of the *Kolonialgesellschaft*, the influential Berlin society that constantly prodded the German Government into action on matters colonial, was dispatched under the dual leadership of Bauer and Waldow, with instructions to establish a trading station at Garua and divert the Cameroons trade that at that time enriched Yola. They were able to erect warehouses on the Niger so that German goods might be stored without paying customs dues.

The expedition reached Yola on 4 September and continued up-river to Garua. From there they trekked south to Ngaundere, back to Garua and northwards to Lake Chad. This journey took them through much of what later became Northern Adamawa territory: Sorau, Pakka, Mubi, Uba, Wamdeo and so to Madagali, Bama and Dikwa, thence back to Garua through Marua. They returned down the Benue passing Yola on 1 July 1903 and Lau on the 6th. In his diary Bauer noted:

The greater population density here seems to be due to the greater fertility of the region, so that the path wound its way almost continuously through fields of corn. That we were in a more prosperous district was also shown by the mass of foodstuffs brought to us in Mubi: the Lamido

[1] *Die deutsche Niger-Benue-Tsadsee Expedition*, F. Bauer, 1904.

had collected in the compound allotted to us a pile of not less than 460 bundles of corn, besides which stood enormous calabashes of dried meat and beer, with several baskets containing dozens of fowls, a calabash of more than a hundred eggs, three enormous pots holding about fifty litres of the finest milk; on top of all this a medium-sized ox had been tethered to one of the trees. Such a welcome of course demanded that we should show our gratitude for this magnificent hospitality by producing our best tradegoods; but the Lamido seemed determined not to let us outdo him in generosity, for hardly had we delivered our presents than he sent again, this time a really spirited stallion together with several jars of honey.

Bauer, like Barth, comments on the jaded appearance of Uba, despite its size and importance.

LENFANT AND DELEVOYE[1]

One of the most remarkable geographical ventures of the period was the French expedition to Lake Chad undertaken by Lenfant, an enterprise much praised by Lugard. For over half a century geographers had maintained that there was a continuous waterway linking Lake Chad to the Benue. Barth was the first to raise the point: 'I am convinced that in 50 years European vessels will maintain an annual trade with Lake Chad from the Bay of Biafra. Nature herself has formed an almost unbroken connection.' The vital union was the Tuburi marshes, believed to drain northwards through the Musgu and the Kotoko flats into the Logone and Shari rivers, and westwards over the deep Lata cataract into the Mayo Kebi. It was Lenfant who succeeded, in the face of considerable difficulty and danger, in getting a light boat through these Tuburi marshes and thus proving the existence of an unbroken water route between Garua and Chad.

His expedition reached Yola on 22 August with the special steel boat, the *Benôit-Garnier*, in tow behind the *Liberty*. They went straight on to Garua, for the high water was imperative to the success of Lenfant's quest, but on their way back in February they spent ten days in Yola as the guests of the Niger Company's agent. Lenfant was given an audience by the Emir, who reminisced on the visits of earlier French explorers such as Mizon and

[1] *La Grande Route du Tchad*, E. Lenfant, 1905, and the chronicle of his second in command, Delevoye, *En Afrique Centrale*, 1906.

Maistre. Despite the vitality of Yola's market, which is described below, Lenfant noted that the true centre of commerce had moved to the river bank where the Niger Company had established their canteen.

Native cotton fabrics, woven fillets, cotton galore, raw cotton, rubber, honey, beeswax, brown sugar, sweetmeats, meat, dried fish, vegetables, onions, peppers, brass rods, beads of various sizes and colour—all these are in daily use. One of the oddest features is the assortment of medicinal plants hawked by old crones in small jars of worked ox-hide, most graceful and prettily ornamented: bark of mahogany, a kind of highly odoriferous garlic, Adamawa ginger, a potash that is boiled in soup and gives it a flavour, another plant which when burnt gives one's clothes a pleasant scent, a purgative root . . . Among the market trays you can find antimony, spatules of bone for painting eyelids and rods for scratching your back, long bone sticks for slaughtering the entomic inhabitants of your scalp, and needles for pricking your gums and tattooing them in black.

BOUNDARY COMMISSION 1903–4[1]

The combined mission left England in the new year and reached Lokoja on 10 February. On the Benue the engines of the steel canoes broke down, so that the journey to Ibi was completed in dugouts and on short rations. An escort met the survey party there, with horses and 300 carriers, and on 4 April Yola was reached. Here four months were devoted to astronomical work and triangulation of the area before the Commission set out for Lake Chad. Jackson considered the Fulani, who could hardly have been expected to welcome the dissectors of their empire, as the most untrustworthy people he had ever met: 'They are grasping but lazy, their intelligence is unproductive and seems to have found its vent only in ruling without governing.' The Commission left for England in April 1904.

BOUNDARY COMMISSION 1912–13[2]

This mission demarcated the boundary south from Yola to Obokium on the Cross River, which had been previously surveyed

[1] Articles by Colonel L. Jackson in the *Journal of the Royal Geographical Society*, vol. XXVI.

[2] Article by Captain W. V. Nugent in the *Journal of the Royal Geographical Society*, vol. XLIII, and by Leutnant Detzner in *Das Deutsche Kolonialblatt*, 1914.

by Colonel Whitlock between 1907 and 1909. An escort of one
officer and thirty rank and file, with a political officer and a medical
officer, and numerous carriers, guides, and horses had been
assembled at Yola. This party marched forth on 4 October to meet
the German mission at boundary post 17, the last on the Chad-
Yola frontier. On the 360 miles of the boundary they put in
116 pillars.

Slave raiding is still carried on in this country, advantage being taken of
the proximity of the boundary, which makes it so easy to evade justice.
Many of the carriers with our party were runaway slaves, and soon
after leaving Yola we had much trouble with female slaves who had
escaped from their masters and joined the headquarters of the expedition
where husbands and food were plentiful. Angry masters, mounted on
fiery horses, used to arrive in the camp at all hours of the day and night
demanding their lawful property. The ladies were for the most part
unwilling to return to the harem ... The Shebshi mountains are interesting for the fact that they would form the principal obstacle, a well-nigh
insuperable one, to the construction of a direct line of railway from
Calabar via Takum and Bakundi to Yola. Yola is one of the few important points in Nigeria which does not appear likely to be linked up with
the coast by a railway for many years to come. The German railway
from Duala to the north, if it ever does reach Garua, will pass to the
east of the Shebshis.

BOYD ALEXANDER[1]

The Alexander-Gosling expedition of 1905 aimed at crossing
Africa by boat and thereby demonstrating that the two coasts of
the continent were linked by a wonderful system of waterways.
Boyd Alexander skirted Adamawa on his first expedition, going
northwards and westwards from Ibi to Bauchi before striking
across to Bornu, but Gosling and Alexander's remarkable boy,
José, came up the Benue as far as Numan, whence they ascended
the River Gongola.

Lau is under the Sultan of the Muri Province. The last ruler made
away with the clerk in the Niger Company's store, and, appropriating
the key, sent in whenever he wanted supplies. He was never punished
and was still in possession when he died ... Next morning Gosling made
an early start and was well on his journey up the river when he was

[1] *From the Niger to the Nile*, Boyd Alexander, 1907; *Boyd Alexander's Last
Journey*, Herbert Alexander, 1912.

pursued by the Bashimas, bringing along the rods of his mosquito curtains which his boy had forgotten and left upon the bank.

This was the year of the great famine, and there was much trouble in finding polers to take the boats and canoes among the wild Gongola pagans: 'they feared that up the river it would be famine for themselves and food for the inhabitants'.

The expedition achieved its objects, but at a terrible price. Boyd's brother, Claud, and Gosling, dead; one native eaten by cannibals, and two more vanished, probably sharing the same fate; two drowned as the boats shot some rapids; and one death from sleeping-sickness.

Boyd Alexander's second journey took place in 1909. His objects were to climb the Cameroon peak for ornithological specimens and then, having visited his brother's grave at Maifoni,[1] to lead a caravan of camels through Wadai and Darfur to Khartoum. He arrived at Yola on 4 August, and after a week in the old station he went on to the Fulani town where the Assistant Resident lived and worked.

From the barracks it is rather a tedious journey; a leaky canoe takes one over a marsh about a mile in width, and then one has a journey of another mile of sloppy marshland, but of course this is only in the rainy season. I was met by the Eurema, the Emir's eldest son, with about a hundred horse, who escorted me up to Yola. The Eurema went first; then came the band, aligatas and drums; then myself, and on either flank troupes [sic] of horsemen, who at intervals would throw up and shake their closed fists in the air by way of salute, crying out at the same time with hoarse voices a welcome to Yola, while in front more troupes of horsemen would gallop forward and spread out like a fan, and then return at a breakneck speed to rein their horses up before the Eurema.

The trade of the Province consisted of gum, gutta, beeswax, and indigo, while the Niger Company was buying 6 tons of shea-nuts a week during the season of August and September. Kola-nuts from Ngaundere and Banyo fetched 5s. a hundred in Yola market, and cigarettes were of recent vogue, selling at 2s. a carton.

Boyd Alexander set out for Maifoni on 25 August. At Pella there was a small military post in charge of an N.C.O.

[1] The original military station of Maiduguri.

Had breakfast with Sergeant Hammond. How resourceful these non-commissioned officers are! The first dish he gave me was dry biscuits well soaked in milk and flavoured with a little nutmeg. To prevent the soaked biscuit from rising a small stick was spanned across the cup. It was really excellent, and I never realised, till he told me, that it was only made out of ship's biscuit.

Boyd Alexander was murdered by tribesmen at Nyeri, in Wadai, in April 1910. He and his brother now lie in the famed cemetery by the Residency in Maiduguri.

FREMANTLE[1]

Fremantle, who was Resident of Muri Province during the First World War, was transferred from Bussa to Yola in 1908. It took him eight weeks' poling to do the 820 miles! He writes of Yola's 'mysterious atmosphere' and its traditions of independence of Zungeru directives. The meeting with his opposite number from Garua is amusingly described:

15th Jan., 1908. Frantic messages, as the German Resident sent to say he was at Mubi and would see me there, which was not at all what I wanted; much relieved therefore when he wrote to say 'of course I will come to Uba', and turned up looking very fit and very friendly—with an escort of 15 rather fearful-looking Coast soldiers mounted, with lances and German flags to the fore. As they have been on trek two months, one must not be too critical, but their attempts at mounting guard were very comical and called forth sarcastic comment from von Krogh as we passed. V. K. is an excellent fellow and good company, and a thorough sahib.

They discussed various points.

'That be fine palaver we do today', was V. K.'s comment afterwards. I had a half-bottle of port left and we needed warming up, as it was fearfully cold (I was in my motor-coat all the morning). 'I vill write letter to Governor and say all palaver be cleaned at Uba, we finish the bounder trouble'. Then a match he was flicking à la bullet happened to hit me in the face, and I said after the manner of the Yola-Garua correspondence: 'I protest'. 'Zo—we must telegraph one time—letter say palaver be cleaned no be right—all be wrong—plenty palaver live at Uba'. He is keen on nothing but trekking and wants to go all round

[1] *Two African Journals and Other Papers*, J. M. Fremantle (privately printed, 1938).

Adamawa before the rains. He has talked like a father to all the chiefs and only expects possibility of trouble in one district, Marua, where he proposes to establish their headquarters.

KUMM[1]

Kumm came to Northern Nigeria in 1905 to secure definite information on the advance of Islam among the pagan tribes, and as a result of his report the Sudan United Mission was founded for fieldwork in the region, with stations at Wase (known as Rock Station), Wukari, and Ibi. The proposal to build a Freed Slaves Home at Jen, on the borders of Yola and Muri Provinces, fell through, and the first S.U.M. station in Yola was near Mbula.

As the sub-title of his first book refers to the 'Land of Darkness', it is not surprising to find that Kumm's main concern was with the vast mission field of Adamawa:

Its name sounds like music. But little or no music, little or no harmony lies behind the softly sounding name . . . Adamawa, there it lies bathed in tropical sunshine, or bright under its southern moon, stretching from the Kameruns inward to the centre of the Great Sudan . . . it forms the healthiest part of the whole Sudan. . . . The healthy mountain region of Adamawa, with its vigorous, intelligent heathen tribes, seems most inviting . . . a strong basis there for missionary work throughout the Central Sudan.

In March 1909, Kumm came up-river to Yola. 'The Resident of Yola Province expressed his sincerest hope that I might not be eaten by the cannibals, especially as I did not intend to take an armed escort with me.' After spending much time in dragging his boat over sandbanks and digging out channels for it, he gave up his attempt to pole to Garua; with the help of the Niger Company agent, fifty-five carriers were engaged and the party set off overland.

MECKLENBURG[2]

The German Central African expedition of 1910–11, under the leadership of the Duke of Mecklenburg, passed through Yola in

[1] *From Hausaland to Egypt*, Karl Kumm, 1910; less important is his *The Sudan*, 1907.
[2] *From the Congo to the Niger and the Nile*, A. Friedrich, Duke of Mecklenburg, 1913.

July 1910, complete with its collection of lions, leopards, monkeys, hyenas, and jackals.

The agent of the Niger Company received us and kindly placed at our disposal the little steamer *Yola*. We breakfasted with several English officers at the station and then, after paying a visit to the military commandant, we went on board . . . Every evening we encamped on the bank. Unfortunately Haberer's boy, Issonno, fell overboard without being noticed, and was drowned.

OLIVE MACLEOD[1]

Olive MacLeod, who might have married Boyd Alexander had he returned from his second expedition, bravely determined to visit his grave, taking out the headstone that had been carved in England. She got in touch with the French officers at Fort Lamy, who told her of Boyd Alexander's last days and handed over his diaries to her. She stopped at Yola on her way up to Garua, declining the Resident's chivalrous offer to turn out of his quarters for her. Olive MacLeod later married C. L. Temple, who became Lieutenant-Governor of the Northern Provinces, and continued her deep interest in the country by her writings on the northern tribes.

'LANGA-LANGA'[2]

'Langa-Langa', the pen-name of a Resident who later wrote the standard gazetteer of Ilorin Province, has left an account of his brief spell of duty in Numan in 1915.

Numan was a lonely little station on the right bank of the great silent Benue. In the rains it was almost an island, for the low-lying ground at the back became water-logged and almost impassable. There was little with which to occupy myself after office hours, and there was something about the sad, though glorious, sunsets of an evening which had an infinitely depressing effect on one's solitude. An occasional launch would be put in for fuel, and a chat with passing friends would liven things up.

Nor had other travellers taken kindly to Numan, as these quotations from the rest-house book show: 'As an *aviary* this rest-house leaves nothing to be desired', or 'stabling fair, but could not find rest-house'.

[1] *Chiefs and Cities of Central Africa*, Olive MacLeod, 1912.
[2] *Up Against it in Nigeria*, 'Langa-Langa', 1921.

OAKLEY[1]

Oakley, who was posted to Yola Province in 1921, gives an excellent account of the life of a Political Officer in the 'twenties, and many of his memoirs are concerned with the Benue and Northern Adamawa peoples. Of his time as A.D.O. Provincial Office he writes:

Office hours were nominally from 7 a.m. to 2 p.m., with an hour off for breakfast. It usually worked out that one had no more than twenty minutes for breakfast and stayed at the office until 3.30 p.m. or got back to one's house just in time for a cup of tea. Here one would find a *mallam*, a native scribe, garbed in turban and flowing robe, waiting to give one a lesson in Hausa. He sat on the ground and explained things with his fingers on the mud floor, or we read fables together, until one's head nodded, when he would tactfully make obeisance on all-fours. That would be the signal to rouse oneself and go out to the one tennis-court in the station. Here every one foregathered in the dry season, the Resident, the O.C. troops, one or two subalterns, the doctor and his wife, the Education Officer and his wife, the Commissioner of Police, and any D.O. or A.D.O. who might be in the station at the time. Often we could only muster a four, but we made as much use of the time from about 5 p.m. to 6.20 p.m. as we could to get exercise. When night fell the boys arranged the chairs for the 'Scotch Club', or we would repair to someone's bungalow to while away the time to dinner with 'small chop'. After dinner I usually found that I had work to do. There were times, of course, when I spent the evening with one or more in the station, and grand evenings they were, but more often than not I was burning the midnight oil trying to balance cash books or juggling with statistics in an endeavour to make them tally with someone's elusive figures.

During office hours, if I wanted to consult the Resident about anything, I had to walk across the station square to the Residency and could be seen approaching by him. Sometimes towards the end of the morning I could see him moving about his room, then on catching sight of me he would sit down hurriedly. My reception would be cold and haughty, for he was very dignified, with a smartly trimmed beard and the brusque manner of an admiral. After explaining my business he was usually rather testy, then, gradually relaxing, he helped me out of my difficulty, saying at the end: 'Well, it's lunch time now, what about a short sharp one?'

[1] *Treks and Palavers*, R. R. Oakley, 1938.

MIGEOD[1]

Migeod spent the first twenty-five years of the century in Africa, as both a Colonial civil servant and an explorer.

As to expense, I have now been on three expeditions and find that a man travelling alone, and not falling sick nor having any accidents, can do it at a rate of £2 a day for a minimum period of ten months, and yet be quite comfortable.

In 1923 he trekked through the whole of the Cameroons from Victoria, through Bamenda, Mambila, and Gashaka, up to Yola; in 1922 he had travelled from Yola to Bornu and Lake Chad. Migeod thus provides a fully documented source for contemporary Adamawa conditions besides recording much ethnological and linguistic information.

Of Numan he writes:

The old site of the native town was to the left of the Niger Company's factory. A road has been made round the low bluff to the few Government buildings, and protruding from the bank may be seen the bones of the former inhabitants buried there. From a natural history point of view Numan is interesting as being a place which the manatee frequents.

At Jimeta the caprices of the prostitutes are amusingly described:

There is such a mob of them at Jimeta. Occasionally the Emir is advised to decree that they should be expelled. The ladies submit and move down river to the next big town, and an equal number come thence in their place. They land from the steamer in gaily coloured clothes with a smile and a glad eye for all, and the drab toiling wives are filled with envy and jealousy . . . The hordes of prostitutes are really an administrative problem; as low as 3d. a visit is sometimes accepted.

Before fording the Benue, whose channel was knee-deep and only about 200 yards across, Migeod called on the Emir.

We had a talk in his reception hall, which was almost dark. All it contained were the Emir's mat, two chairs, and a big motor bicycle of great horsepower, which the Emir bought from the Niger Company but cannot ride. It would indeed be dangerous for a good rider on these roads . . .

[1] *Through Nigeria to Lake Chad*, 1924, and *Through British Cameroons*, 1925, F. W. H. Migeod. He was the brother of C. O. Migeod, Resident of Yola Province.

A hobby of the Emir's was to keep cats. He had some dozens, all said to be descendants of one given by a Niger Company's agent many years ago.

When in Northern Adamawa Migeod had to rebuke his Emir's representative for his over-zeal, telling him that

I did not want a chorus of furious shouting because an old, old man probably half blind, on a distant mountain top, had not fallen down and made obeisance; nor did I require persons with loads on their heads to put them down when I passed.

He has much of interest to say about Song, Pella, the Kilba, and Marghi, and the years have done little to change the appearance of Wamdeo as he described it:

A fence of a double row of a very tall straight cactus runs along in front, and inside it is a very tight fit. The paths between the mat walls of the compounds were not more than from 2 to 3 feet wide, and huts and boulders and clay pot-shaped granaries, always perched on a rock, were packed as tight as they could be. Even stacks of firewood were piled up between the huts . . . The whole idea seemed to me to be always ready to fight a house to house defensive engagement.

VIII

THE DEVELOPMENT OF GENERAL
ADMINISTRATION

PROVINCIAL ORGANIZATION

MURI PROVINCE dates from the inception of the Upper Benue
Province in 1900, and Yola Province was constituted on 1 August
1901. Up to 1914 the present Adamawa Emirate cannot be
considered separately from its neighbouring territories which now
form the Muri and Numan Divisions, since all policy and progress
were then based on the vital channel of communication, the
River Benue, and to a lesser extent on the caravan routes to Bornu,
with the opening of subsidiary routes and areas radiating from
these life-lines. The *de facto* concept of Adamawa Province as we
know it today can be traced to the conclusion of the Cameroons
campaign in the autumn of 1915 when, with the withdrawal of the
allied columns to the south, it became necessary to provide for the
administration of the conquered areas. A formal mandate was
not granted till 1922, though the southern areas had been under
British control since 1916 and the northern districts since 1920.

The modern Adamawa Province did not, however, emerge
de jure until the great reorganization of the Northern Provinces in
1926, which did away with the old Yola and Muri Provinces, and
aimed at providing, throughout the region, one administrative
officer for every 100,000 persons. Shani District, which had been
transferred from Bornu Province to Muri in 1921, was handed
back to Bornu; Muri Emirate with its mandated territory of
Gashaka and the independent district of Wase became part of
Yola Province; and the remainder of Muri Province went to
Munshi, later re-named Benue, Province. His Honour was of the
opinion that expressions such as 'Yola Province' and 'the Emir of
Yola' were considered pejorative by the Fulani, and he therefore
recommended that the new unit of the fused Yola and Muri

Provinces should adopt the name used by the local people, Adamawa. The Resident's wish to have only two Divisions under his jurisdiction, Yola-Gashaka and Muri-Numan, did not find favour, and 1926 saw the birth of Adamawa Province, made up of four Divisions: (i) Yola; (ii) Numan; (iii) Muri Emirate, with independent Wase and Mumuye; (iv) Gashaka. Though internal reorganizations have taken place since then, the Adamawa provincial boundaries have remained unaltered apart from the transfer of Kentu to Benue Province in 1933 and of Wase to Plateau Province in 1946.

Provincial headquarters have remained at Jimeta, the Government Reservation of Yola, despite an exciting chapter of vicissitudes and ventures.[1]

DISTRICT ORGANIZATION

The Emirates of Adamawa and Muri are divided into districts, each under a District Head holding office from the Emir, to whom he is responsible for the government of his area. Yungur and Chamba (1938) are subordinate Native Authorities. In Numan most of the independent pagan districts adopted a loose federation in 1936, and in 1955, after other forms of conciliar administration, the Numan Federation Native Authority was expanded and reconstituted.

A district, in turn, is subdivided into village areas, each under a Village Head, selected by the village council with the approval of the District Head and his council and confirmed in his appointment by the Emir. The village usually consists of a number of hamlets, under a hamlet head, scattered over a considerable area; in a few pagan districts the hamlet may consist of a single group of contiguous households. Towns like Yola, Jimeta, Mubi, Numan, and Jalingo require some special executive appointment in the nature of a *magajin gari*, whose office gradually demands the development of a town council.

THE EVOLUTION OF TAXATION

Before the advent of the British the existing forms of taxation were modelled on the Koran, while pagan communities paid their

[1] See Appendix A.

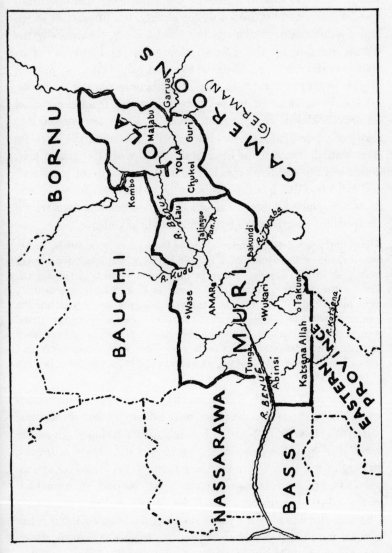

YOLA AND MURI PROVINCES c. 1910

tribute in slaves, given or captured. The principal taxes among the Fulani were: (1) *Zakka*, a tithe on corn, in theory due only from true believers and destined only for charity, but in practice levied and lavished indiscriminately; (2) *Kurdin Kasa*, theoretically the tribute payable by the conquered pagans; (3) Plantation Tax, levied on all crops other than the two that paid *zakka*; (4) *Jangali*, originally a 5 per cent. tithe due on cattle only and not on flocks; (5) *Kurdin sarauta*, an accession duty expected from every chief or office-holder on appointment, which by abuse deteriorated into a sale of offices; (6) *Gado* or death-duties, including the intestate estates which lapsed to the Emir in the absence of a recognized heir. There were in addition taxes imposed on every form of handicraft and extra fees due from specialists such as brewers, honey-sellers, prostitutes, and gamblers. Lugard in his two detailed memoranda on taxation[1] describes the traditional mode of collection:

The country was divided under a kind of feudal system into fiefs, and in most provinces the estates of a fief-holder were scattered at distances from each other. The fief-holder in most cases resided at the capital, and the taxes were collected by a *jikada* or *ajele*. The former usually went his rounds at the time the tax was due, the latter lived on the country. These tax-gatherers were the curse of the country, and practised oppression and extortion. In theory, they had no power; in practice, they terrorised the peasantry. They were also the agents, messengers and spies of the Emir or fief-holder, and reported deaths for the collection of *gado*.

But in the Yola and Muri Emirates, where the administration was mainly military and the towns were little more than war camps, this elaborate code of taxation had not fully developed. Even the *haraji* due from the conquered pagans was not always enforced, although periodic levies, in kind or service, were exacted for special purposes, and in Yola town certain craftsmen paid an annual fee in the nature of a licence. The Fulani chiefs of Rei, Ngaundere, Chamba, and Tibati sent a yearly quota of slaves to Yola, but many of these were often passed on as the Yola tribute to Sokoto, which was also paid by Muri. The new taxation policy of 1903 aimed at abolishing the intermediate *jikada*, allowing the district headman to collect tribute direct from each village head and to take it direct

[1] *Annual Reports of Northern Nigeria*, 1900–11, pp. 216–24, 790–814.

to the Emir, and at merging the former agricultural taxes into the general assessment of Moslem areas while independent pagans would pay more or less on a capitation basis.

In Yola Emirate the 1903–4 taxation took the form of a poll-tax on all adult males for the Fulani districts, and was not extended to the pagan districts till 1909, at the rate of a few pence per head. At the same time the Koranic *zakka* was collected on all village cattle and *jangali* of 5 per cent. on all nomad herds, including those pasturing in the independent areas, which were treated as belonging to the Emirate on the grounds that they were all owned by Fulani. The poll-tax was collected by the district and village headmen, aided by government staff and representatives of the Emir, on a census supervised by the Resident, while *zakka* and *jangali* were collected by those officials previously charged with the collection of Koranic dues.

For some years the whole of the cattle-taxes and a large proportion of the poll-tax were paid in kind. Half of the assessment was paid to Government, but in Muri, where the ultra-conservative Fulani were unable to understand the payment of regular dues by their own people, this was reduced in 1907 to a quarter, and it thereafter varied by districts until in 1913 the fifty-fifty basis was reintroduced for the poll-tax, and in 1919 for the cattle-tax. As late as the 1920's we find an officer writing of how he received the government share from the Northern Cameroons:

Two or three thousand pounds at a time would be brought in in two-shilling pieces, shillings, sixpences and threepenny bits, and sometimes in francs or marks and even Maria Theresa dollars. Sometimes the tax from the more primitive pagans was received in kind, such as corn, cowrie shells and brass rings. I remember once, after a busy day, just as I was about to close the office, on looking through the window I saw several hundreds of pagans sitting on the square outside, each with a goatskin stuffed full of corn . . . When the last skin was emptied and the tally told and all was found correct, they leapt into the air waving spears and bows and, chattering excitedly, . . . set out for home.

An attempt was made in 1905 to introduce some order into the distribution of the Native Authority share of the taxes by allotting to the various officials a fixed percentage of the amounts they collected; village heads 5 per cent., district heads 15 per cent. There was, however, no provision for other members of the Administration—except the *alkalai*, who retained all fees and fines—and they remained dependent on the Emir until the introduction of the Native Treasury system in 1911.

In 1907 it was decided to abandon the poll-tax in favour of a rough income-tax of 5 per cent. It was estimated that 5*s*. per compound would be equivalent to the desired rate; a count of compounds was made, the lump sum was announced to the elders, who were directed to divide it up among the householders in proportion to their wealth—and the experiment failed.

It was tried again in 1911, with some success. In the same year the payment of cattle-tax in kind was revoked, *zakka* being fixed at 1*s*. a head of cattle and *jangali* at 1*s*. 6*d*. This became 2*s*. a head on all cattle in 1913, was reduced to 1*s*. 6*d*. in 1931, and since then has gradually risen to the present rate of 5*s*. a beast other than the dwarf pagan cattle which, being unmilked, are now exempt from *jangali*. The incidence of general tax or *haraji* within the Province today ranges from 32*s*. in Numan Division to 26*s*. in Muri and Adamawa Divisions. Native Authorities are beginning to realize that there is room for a tighter assessment of the trader class in towns, where tax-assessment committees are now appearing.

Besides the poll- and cattle-taxes, various other taxes were enforced, and abandoned, during the early years of the Protectorate in order to raise desperately needed revenue for Government. From 1903 to 1907 a caravan tax of 10 per cent. on the value of goods was levied, which was paid at toll stations set up along the main caravan routes. On arrival at a station the caravan encamped in the open space prepared for it and declared its goods to the collector, who took his list to the Resident's office and made out a clearance paper. If a caravan passed through three Provinces and received clearance papers in each, it was exempt from further payment. In the same period canoe licences were authorized: the canoes were classified according to carrying capacity and an annual licence ranged from 5*s*. to £3, in exchange for which payment a disc was issued by the Resident to be affixed to the canoe. Hawkers' licences were issued to petty traders, other than purveyors of meat, in Muri Province up to 1913. From 1950 onwards, Native Treasuries have been turning their attention once more to the revenue potential of indirect taxation and licences.

NATIVE TREASURIES

The Native Treasury system was introduced in 1911 by the establishment of the Yola Emirate Treasury. Previously the share of taxes retained by the Native Authority had been devoted entirely to the remuneration of those engaged in the actual collection, but under the new system all revenue accruing to the N.A., whether from direct taxes or court fees, market dues, etc., was paid into a central treasury to provide funds for the N.A. services and fixed salaries for all N.A. employees from the Emir downwards. In 1912 a second treasury was established at Numan for the six independent pagan districts, and in the following year Muri opened its Native Treasury. In 1915 another treasury was approved, for Shellen, which was so greatly in advance of the other districts in Numan Division. The two Numan treasuries, however, were abolished in October 1921, for reasons of economy and the desirability of central control for public works, and a Provincial Treasury, with a staff trained at Kano, was set up, into which all Native Authority revenues were paid. This experiment, too, was abandoned in February 1922, as it was held that the pagan tribes who had maintained their independence against the Fulani would resent the merging of their revenues with those of Adamawa Emirate. A combined treasury for the pagan districts of Numan was re-established, and in 1934 Shellen again became a separate treasury until its decease in 1950. The Adamawa Native Treasury, which closed its sub-treasury at Gashaka in 1928, now has sub-treasuries at Mubi (1936), Gembu, and Jada. On the government side, there are a sub-treasury at Jimeta and local treasuries at Jalingo and Numan.

It is worth noting that in the first year of Adamawa Native Treasury the total revenue was £14,085, while forty years later it was £304,298; the complexities of Native Treasury finance, with its involved system of code grants and Financial Memoranda, have developed at an equally rapid rate from the days of the simple cashbook kept in Ajami script.

EDUCATION

One of the earliest reports from Yola lists 8 Fulani, 3 Arab, 2 Kanuri, and 2 Hausa schools in the town, all of them teaching the Koranic syllabus. At the end of October 1916, Captain F. W. Taylor came to Yola to open the Provincial School. This was in temporary quarters at Jalingo, the Lamido's summer residence, situated in the marshy area two miles west of the old government station. The school started with 6 mallams, but these had to be sent off to Bauchi when Taylor was seconded for war service. It was therefore not till January 1920 that the Provincial School really opened with 19 pupils, aged from 7 to 19, rising to 41 in the second term, though one had to be dismissed because he had a 'predilection for long vacations at short intervals'. This site was on the plateau where the Provincial Girls' School now stands.

This was followed in 1924 by the first rural school, at Mayo Belwa, and in 1926 a second was opened at Mubi; both had 13 pupils. Yet by 1940 there were only 1,286 pupils in all the Adamawa schools; three years later the school attendance figure was one per 1,000 of the population and included precisely six girls. Now there are over 9,000 children attending school, and in the last decade the number of schools has risen from 17 Elementary Schools to 106 Junior Primary and 12 Senior Primary Schools. Of these, Adamawa Division has 29 Native Administration and 37 Mission Schools; Muri 8 of each category; and Numan, 10 Native Administration and 15 Mission Schools.

The Yola Middle School moved into its double-storey building in 1949, after the first entrance examination, open to girls as well as boys, had been held in 1948. It has now been upgraded to a Provincial Secondary School. Besides the primary schools listed above, there are Teacher Training Centres at Mubi (1950), Numan, and Lassa, and girls' schools at Numan and Jimeta; the former is the oldest in the Northern Region.

The Adult Education campaign started seriously in 1952, although in Kilba District an enterprising ex-soldier had anticipated Government by running his own voluntary literacy classes. There are now more than 600 classes in Adamawa Division and about 140 in each of the other two Divisions. Simple primers have been prepared in most of the leading vernaculars.

JUDICIAL PROCEDURE

Native Courts date from one of Lord Lugard's earliest proclamations of 1900. By 1904 they had been established at Yola, Song, Girei, Namtari, Malabu, and Gurin in Yola Province, and at Gassol, Jalingo, Muri, and Lau in Muri Province. In 1911 a warrant was issued to the judicial council of Shellen and in the following year the Alkalin Numan's court was gazetted. The Northern Appeal Court of Adamawa was established in 1936 and that of the Southern Area in 1953. Regional pagan courts were started in the Mubi touring area in 1938.

In all areas the district and village headmen are encouraged to settle minor disputes by arbitration. At the other end of the judicial scale, the Lamido's court has Grade A status, with full judicial powers in all criminal and civil actions, save that no sentence of death may be carried out until it has been confirmed by the Governor.

To quote from the Resident's report:

In a province which still has a high proportion of backward people easily excited, it is not surprising that the number of homicide cases is fairly high. In 1955 the Lamido's court heard 49, and 11 such cases from Muri and Numan Divisions were heard at sessions by the Supreme Court.

The valuable contribution made by the Native Courts can be judged by the following record of cases heard in one year:

Adamawa Division had, besides the Lamido's, Chief Alkali's, and three appeal courts, twenty alkalis' and twenty tribal courts with lesser jurisdiction. These heard 7,528 criminal and 15,344 civil cases.

Muri Division had, besides the Emir's and Chief Alkali's courts, twelve courts of minor powers, which heard 1,367 criminal and 3,198 civil cases.

Numan Division had, besides its Federal and Alkali's courts, six courts of limited powers, which heard 1,876 criminal and 4,756 civil cases.

The Provincial Courts, established by Lugard in 1900 and presided over by the Resident, were abolished in 1934. Adamawa falls within the Jos Judicial Division of the Supreme Court, whose Puisne Judge goes on circuit to Yola from time to time. A Grade I Magistrate from the Jos Magisterial District holds court at Yola once or twice a year, while all Divisional Officers are appointed Grade III Magistrates with power in criminal cases to impose a maximum sentence of £25 fine or three months' imprisonment.

POLICE

From the first there has been a strong detachment of police at Yola, under a superior officer who has been known at different times as District Superintendent, Commissioner, and Assistant Superintendent of Police. In 1926, for instance, there were out-station detachments of 15 at Jalingo, 10 at Gashaka, 13 at Numan, 12 at Song, and 30 at Mubi, each with a Political Officer.

Today the provincial establishment of Nigeria Police is 2 gazetted officers, 2 inspectors, 21 N.C.O.s, and 107 rank and file. A detachment of 2 N.C.O.s and 11 constables is stationed at Mubi and another of 1 N.C.O. and 5 constables at Jalingo. The Gwoza detachment is outside Adamawa, though it comes under the Superintendent of Police, Yola. A detachment was at one time maintained at Gashaka until the Mambila area was declared 'open' in 1936, and till 1952 a small force of constables was always sent to Numan during the shipping season.

In 1953 Yola became a Motor Licensing Authority. There is a police wireless link with Maiduguri and Sokoto. Modern police quarters have just been built at Headlands Barracks, Yola.

Each Native Authority maintains its own force of constabulary, the standard of which rose greatly after 1945 with the recruitment of ex-servicemen. These N.A. forces, started in Yola in 1929 with 1 N.C.O. and 12 constables and in Muri the following year, have developed from the obsolescent *dogarai*, who were the traditional body-guards of the Fulani chiefs.

PRISONS

There are Native Administration prisons at Mubi, Yola, Jimeta, Numan, Jalingo, Jada, and Gembu, all staffed by their respective

Native Administration warder services. There is no government prison in the Province, and if it is considered undesirable to retain in a local jail a prisoner convicted by a Magistrate's Court, he is sent to Jos or Kaduna. Most District Headquarters possess a lock-up.

NATURAL RESOURCES

Adamawa, once the treasure island of ivory, is now essentially an agricultural province; in addition, it is one of the richest pastoral areas, while its fine river systems provide valuable fishing. The principal cash crops are groundnuts (nearly 14,000 tons in 1955) and cotton which, boosted only since 1951, is now approaching the 1,200-ton mark. In recent years the commercial firms have, at one time or another, also bought Niger gum, gum-arabic, shea-nuts, beeswax, benniseed, castorseed, and rama fibre; ghee was bought in Numan during the 1939–45 war. The Gongola and Yedseram valleys constitute magnificent granaries whose guinea-corn is bought by traders from as far afield as Jos, Kano, and Maiduguri, and the Benue marshland provides a celebrated dry-season corn, *maskwari*.

It is estimated that there are over 500,000 head of cattle in the Province, with an influx of a further 100,000 in the dry season. There is a considerable trade in hides and skins. Trade cattle are trekked southwards on the hoof to supply the Eastern Region with meat: in 1954 these numbered 23,640 of Nigerian origin and 27,223 of French origin. Most of the riverain tribes are industrious and skilful fishermen, and there is a profitable local trade in dried fish.

Minor industries that deserve mention are dyeing, weaving, smelting, and the localized specialities of coffee in Mambila and pigs in Numan. The *faifai* mats of Adamawa are among the finest in Northern Nigeria.

Salt was worked in two large areas of the old Muri Province. Akwana now belongs to the Wukari District of Benue Province, but there is still a centre round Bamenda, whose 'red salt' was celebrated when Barth visited Adamawa a century ago. There is a saline spring in Gashaka which is attractive to cattle; when it was reopened a few years ago, a number of charms were found nearby, said to have been placed there by Lamdo Banyo in an attempt to deny the salt-lick to the cattle across the French border.

Antimony or galena, which is widely used as a cosmetic for the eyes, was also found in worthwhile quantities in the Wase District of the former Muri Province, and small deposits of gold were located round Takum. The Northern Nigerian Lead Mines Ltd. worked the lodes in Zurak, in Muri Division, from 1928 to 1937 and exported a large tonnage of metal. When Clapperton was in Sokoto in 1824, Sultan Bello spoke of 'the gold and silver to be obtained in the hills of Yakoba (Bauchi) and Adamawa'.

Muri Province, and Yola to the east of 12°15', were gazetted as safe for prospecting in August 1903, though the Zinna and Yungur Districts were closed again in 1906.

There are veins of iron ore in several of the Adamawa hill systems, but nowhere on a scale where it would at present be worth exploitation. The Mumuye wash and smelt their magnetite sands, and the Lala, Verre, and Sukur groups are renowned for their charcoal-smelting and smithing. There is a minute deposit of coal in the Longuda hills. In 1949 a mineral survey was made of the potential deposits of the Verre and Alantika mountains.

AGRICULTURE

After the failure of the experimental farm at Bole in 1945, 2,000 acres were set aside at Kofare for a Government Farm Centre. The main objectives were to experiment with a herd of local Adamawa cattle and a flock of sheep, to carry out tests with fertilizers and manures, and to undertake variety trials with groundnuts and guinea-corn and long-term fallow experiments. It was only during the last war that an Agricultural Officer was posted to Adamawa.

Mixed farming started in 1949 with eighty ex-servicemen, all in Adamawa Division. It had its ups and downs, especially financial ones, but by 1955 there were 1,150 established mixed farmers in the Province, of whom Numan had set up 350 in four years and Muri 120 in two years. Mixed farming extension, soil conservation, and the introduction of cotton were among the roles of the Production Officers, who did such good work in their brief existence between 1952 and the present time.

The first cotton market was opened at Banjirain in 1951, when 42 tons of cotton seed were bought; there are now ten such markets in Numan Division, which bought 865 tons this year (1956), Banjiram leading with 137 tons. In Adamawa Division seven cotton markets were opened between 1952 and 1955, but they did not prove popular and they have all been closed. Seed cotton was first distributed in Muri in 1954 and proved so successful that this year purchases of cotton seed reached 311 tons.

Experiments were recently tried with mechanical rice ploughing at Yola, Hong, Uba, Balala, Gurin, and Fufore, but the cost per cleared acre proved too high. On the Mambila plateau successful trials have been carried out in coffee-growing and kola seedling plantations. In 1952 Arabica coffee was introduced from Bamenda by a far-sighted Touring Officer at Gembu; since then five small nurseries have been opened by the Native Administration, in addition to the 40 acres of coffee owned by private farmers.

Pigs are abundant, especially in Numan, but poultry improvements have been defeated by the virulence of disease. The locust plagues of the 1930's remain a disastrous landmark in the Province's agricultural history. The first post-war agricultural show was held at Jada in 1951; there are now annual shows at Jada, Yola, Kiri, Jalingo, and in Northern Adamawa. More than 5,000 bags of fertilizer are now sold each year, the majority to Kilba District.

VETERINARY

With a cattle population that is possibly as high as three-quarters of a million during the dry season, the Veterinary Department is of especial importance in Adamawa. The original scheme, mooted in 1944 when the first veterinary centre outside Yola was opened, of providing a network of inoculation camps moving from herd to herd, has been replaced, at the request of the Fulani cattle-owners, by a chain of fewer camps for longer periods. The size and success of this prophylactic campaign are shown by the fact that in 1955 121,656 cattle were treated for rinderpest and 42,077 for trypanosomiasis.

The greatest concentration of cattle is on the Mambila plateau, where over 150,000 head make over-grazing a very real danger. This plateau now carries one adult bovine per 6·3 acres per year; there are plans to channel off some herds to the Filinga plateau. Trade cattle occupy much of the care of the department. There are now inspection stations at Dorofi, Toungo, Mubi, and Sorau, and control posts at Mayo Belwa, Nguroje, Kiri, Jalingo, and Ganye. Most of the French trade cattle pass through Sorau and Mubi, while Nguroje is the biggest centre for Northern Nigerian cattle. The latest figures show that over 12,500 cattle, 13,000 goats, 3,500 sheep, and 350 pigs were slaughtered in markets throughout Adamawa last year.

At one time the Veterinary Officer used to live at Ngurore, where he ran a large immunization camp.

FORESTRY

No forest officer has ever been permanently posted to Adamawa Province, which has been guided by occasional visits from the Provincial Forest Officer, Bornu Province, and by officers on special duty. As a consequence, the gazetted forest estate is very low, only 1·43 per cent. of the total area of the Province. In 1946 1 square mile was gazetted in Jimeta and a further 21 square miles were gazetted at Namtari in 1953. A year later, after some difficult surveying, the largest forest reserve of the Province was established, that of Bagale Hill, which comprises 70 square miles. In addition to these reserves, there are 85 communal forest areas in Adamawa Division, 39 in Muri, and 12 in Numan, with a total estate of 54 square miles.

In 1955 an officer of the department undertook a reconnaissance survey of the Province, primarily to investigate reports of large areas of timber-bearing high forest in Muri and Southern Adamawa Divisions. The survey, which covered the supposed forests of Gashaka District, revealed that this type of forest had been over-estimated, although it would appear from the climatological data available and from the generous hydrological system of the area that the district could carry high forest. Survey and demarcation of possible gazetted reserves are now being undertaken.

What was originally classified as high forest is in fact good-quality Guinea savannah. The areas of high forest are confined to the rivers and streams and to valleys or ravines on hillsides. There is no evidence of any large-scale human interference with the forest areas. Minor migrations have taken place but the population seems to have been static for many years now. Remains of habitation have been found in parts of the high forest areas, which tradition explains as refuges from slaving or warring expeditions. Today a few pit-sawyers are working them.

Plantation of exotic species has not been successful, but this may be due to lack of supervision. A considerable amount of amenity planting is done by local authorities. Mubi in particular, and Zinna to a lesser extent, are threatened by a fuel scarcity as the surrounding district becomes bare of tree growth.

COMMERCIAL FIRMS

The Niger Company remained in Adamawa after it had turned over its administrative functions[1] to Government at the turn of the century. Now, as the United Africa Company of Nigeria Ltd., it has established canteens at Jimeta, Dalmare, Wafango, Micika, Hong, Little Gombi, and Mubi; Lau, Lankoviri, Kunini, Gidan Usmanu, Jen, Gassol, and Mutum Biu; Numan, Shellen, and Banjiram. New stations are about to be opened at Jalingo and Beli. The old Niger Company house-cum-canteen has progressed down-river in the past two generations, from Jimeta through Lau to Gidan Usmanu.

In the first decade of the present century the German firm of Pagenstecker set up in rivalry and were granted a first-class trading licence at Yola in 1909, but by 1911 they had closed all their factories on the Benue.

John Holt and Company were granted a certificate of occupancy at Yola in 1923 and sent up a steamer with building materials, but they were unable to afford to open until 1927, when Yola started as a branch of their Ibi venture. In 1929 it became a venture of its own. There are today canteens at Jimeta, Wuro Bokki, and Mayo Belwa (1930), Jada (1943), Little Gombi and Mubi (1946),

[1] See Chapter IV.

Dalmare (1950), Zinna (1943), Numan (1928), and Lakumna (1929). At one time there were also canteens at Jen and Gidan Usmanu, while sub-ventures were opened at Lau and Girei between 1930 and 1933.

The French firm, Société Commerciale de l'Afrique Occidentale, opened in Yola in 1950, taking over the plot of the Jos transporters, Tahir Brothers. Another canteen was opened in 1952 at Mubi, but in Adamawa it is difficult for them to develop fully as licensed buying agents without a river fleet of their own for evacuation of produce.

In 1952 Vivian, Younger, and Bond extended southwards from their Maiduguri headquarters and operated as buying agents at Mubi, Micika, and Little Gombi. These stations were closed in 1954 when the firm withdrew from Adamawa, and their Mubi canteen was temporarily taken over by A. G. Leventis and Company.

The Sudan United Mission opened a bookshop in Jimeta a few years ago, and there are now branches at Little Gombi, Song, Mayo Belwa, Jada, and Numan. In 1953 a branch of Barclays Bank, D.C.O., Ltd., was established at Jimeta, thus providing a much-needed service in the Province. Alhaji Bakari maintains a regular and expanding transport service between Yola and Jos, and 1954 saw the start of a private garage in Jimeta. At present the London and Kano Trading Company Ltd. are considering plots in the Jimeta and Numan trading layouts.

COMMUNICATIONS

The overriding need for adequate communications is reflected in nearly every annual report from Adamawa Province. Thirty years ago the Resident noted that

there is every prospect of great development and progress . . . if by road construction we can nullify the blighting effect of distances,

while a current report opens with:

'Communications are Civilisation': the need to develop road communications if Adamawa Province is not to remain backward has long been realised, but the cost and difficulties of making a good road system for the whole Province have been beyond the resources and capacity of local administrations. From Colonial Development and Welfare Funds, and more recently from the Cameroons Development Fund (a third of the Province is Trust Territory), over a million pounds have been allocated for five major roads which, when completed, will transform road communications to and within the Province. The amount required speaks for itself and matches the extent of the task. Unfortunately physical difficulties, which still keep the Province remote and large areas within it isolated, are more easily surmounted by ideas, and these are stimulating a demand for 'services' which cannot be met until the roads exist.

In the early years, communications to the Yola and Muri Provinces were orientated on the Benue river and on the Bauchi and Maiduguri caravan routes. So notable a rôle has the former played, and still plays, as Adamawa's lifeline, that a special section has been given to it in this chapter.

The first car was seen in Yola in 1922 and a few months later the Lieutenant-Governor braved the journey by road from Kombo. In 1950 a car reached the heights of Panti Sawa, and in 1955 a land-rover made the difficult journey up to Gembu from the direction of Ndu—a fine tribute to local road-making. Road development in Adamawa followed the normal pattern of the Northern Provinces, with a remarkable acceleration in the last few years which has led to Adamawa having construction work in hand on three Trunk 'A' roads simultaneously. There are now about 700 miles of Trunk 'A' road in the Province: the A 17 Numan-Gombe road has brought the railhead nearly 200 miles nearer by providing an all-season link with Jos instead of the weary 500-mile detour via Damaturu; the A 14 Yola-Takum road has penetrated the empty bush of Southern Muri and is now pushing on to the Santai river, perhaps to meet with the Eastern Region's road system or even to be linked with an all-season road in the difficult terrain of Mambila District; and work on the Uba-Madagali stretch of the strategic A 4 Bama-Bamenda road was started this year. This network is supported by some 150 miles of Trunk 'B' road, such as the Little Gombi-Garkida, Lankoviri-Lau and Numan-Mayo Belwa roads; and on to the whole the

Native Administrations have built an extensive system of feeder and produce-evacuation roads.

In an essentially mountainous province there are bound to be huge rivers to span. Especially is this so on the main north-south line of communication below Yola, where important rivers cut right across the trace to flow into the Benue. There is much bridging here, such as the crossing over the Mayo Ine at Ngurore, the Mayo Belwa (1953), Lamurde and Fan Manga bridges, and the 1,100-feet bridge over the Taraba at Beli, where the first piers for the twenty-five spans are now in.

There is a new pontoon ferry at Jimeta, where a tug is due soon. Meanwhile, the crossing can still take an hour during the height of the rainy season and at least one traveller has spent four hours while the polers gallantly struggled against the current. At Numan there is a power-assisted pontoon, and at Lau a poled ferry.

Yola airport, whose main runway was completed in 1940, now has a twice-weekly Heron service provided by the West African Airways Corporation, serving Jos and Kano. Since the inception of the Northern Region Communications Flight in 1955, airstrips have been laid down at Jalingo and Mubi.

Besides the Post Office at Jimeta, which moved into its new building in 1954, there are Post Offices at Numan and Lau. In other towns postal agencies open and close according to the ability of the staff provided by the Native Administrations.

Twice has the railway been about to penetrate Adamawa; now, after the Corporation's 1955 decision to build a line from Jos to Maiduguri, Adamawa will share with Kabba the distinction of being the only Provinces of the Northern Region without a single sleeper. In the proposed extension of the 1930's from Lafia to Bornu, Song was mooted as an important railway station. In the 1954 railway survey, the terms of reference included the examination of the economic aspects of, *inter alia*, building an additional extension of the proposed Jos-Maiduguri line from Damaturu, via Biu, to the bank of the Benue opposite Yola or Numan. A tentative alignment was Bauchi—Gombe—Kombo—Bobini—Banjiram—Kiri—Imburu—Numan, with an alternative of Gombe—Biu—Dadin Kowa—Song—Yola.

PUBLIC WORKS

Much of the energy of this department is concentrated on the vital work of road construction and maintenance, which are considered in a separate paragraph. Apart from road staff, the Public Works Department maintains mechanical staff in the provincial headquarters. Valuable work has been done since the war by the Rural Water Supplies teams in sinking cement-lined wells throughout the Province, and in the past few years the Urban Water Supplies staff have been preparing piped-water schemes for Jalingo, Yola, Numan, and Mubi. A successful windmill was erected at Jada in 1951 and others have since been put up at Gulak and Micika. The department recently laid the first tarmac road in Adamawa, in Jimeta town and the Government Residential Area, and the tarring of the Jimeta-Yola stretch will soon be completed. Yola has a large Native Authority Works Yard, which moved into its new buildings in 1954.

THE BENUE AND ITS SHIPPING

The Benue has ever been Adamawa's lifeline. There is always an aura of romance about riverain life, which in Africa is enhanced by the annual visits of old favourites of the river, boats that readily recall Sanders and his gun-boats or the Mississippi and its particular craft. Each Division has its port: Lau, Numan, Jimeta, as you move upstream; none of them is beyond the influence of the Mother of Waters.

The normal pattern of the river is a steady rise from the onset of the rains till August, when it reaches between 8 and 10 feet. Then comes the characteristic mid-August fall to between 7 and 3 feet, followed by another rise to the September peak, and the final, rapid fall in mid-October which has furrowed the brow of many a shipping agent. The mean 'high' is between 14 and 16 feet, but in 1948 the depth at Yola registered 21 feet 3 inches; the lowest 'high' in the past twenty years was 11 feet 3 inches in 1944.

The shipping season is thus confined to the three months from July (the first ships generally reach Yola in the second week), but even that period is often an uncertain and anxious one, for the August fall can overtake a fleet in full swing. In 1953 no fewer than thirteen ships of the United Africa Company were immobilized for a fortnight between Lau and Garua. In 1954 a local record was established when the stern-wheeler *Atta* delayed her departure from Yola till 29 October; in 1950 a sister-ship was less fortunate and was obliged to deposit her cargo in bond at Lau in order to reduce her draught and make Makurdi before she was stranded till the following July.

Another limiting factor is the notorious flats at Gamadio and Wuro Bokki. If these can be eliminated, the companies estimate that a fortnight could be added to each end of the shipping season at Yola, and even the Garua trade could be prolonged by an extra ten days. It was with this object of lengthening the season that a firm of Netherlands engineering consultants (Nedeco), in conjunction with an interlocking French undertaking, carried out in 1955 hydrographical and topographical investigations from Garua to Numan.

The United Africa Company run is from Burutu to Garua, about 986 miles, and this takes the big ships between three and four weeks. It is interesting to note that Rei Buba,[1] 1,022 miles up-river, featured in the company's 1939 tariff list. The present flagship is the *Lord Trenchard*, which superseded the *Colonel Ratsey* and first came up to Yola in 1950. This takes six barges, giving 2,600 tons, besides its own load of 250 tons of cargo. Other ships still on the river, with local associations, are the *Chadda*, *Adama*, *Ribago*, and *William Wallace;* while only in the last five years or so have the *Yola*, *Faro*, *Gongola*, and *Taraba* been scrapped. The bell of the stern-wheeler *Muri* (launched before 1900) now hangs in the United Africa Company's office at Lau. Most of the ships are coal-burning stern quarter-wheelers; these are gradually being converted to oil-burning, and propeller diesel-burning vessels are beginning to appear.

Most of the cargo brought up-river is for Garua, not Adamawa. Down-river trade consists almost entirely of produce evacuation: some of it has already been brought down the Gongola by the

[1] See Chapter IV.

United Africa Company's special poling barge fleet, thirty-four strong, each of 10 tons. At one time produce was also evacuated from Wafango to Numan by the Mayo Ine. These barges are also used to on-carry cargo from Yola to Garua, and again on a bad river to evacuate produce from Numan to Makurdi or Lokoja.

The United Africa Company fleet call at Gidan Usmanu, Lau, Jen, Numan, Dalmare, Jimeta, Wuro Bokki, and Garua. Gassol, on the Taraba, is due to be replaced by Shagadda on the Mayo Ranewa, and Kwata Namido, near Mutum Biu, will shortly become a port of call. In 1955 wireless links were made between Burutu, Makurdi, Yola, and Garua, and ten ships were fitted with sets. Of particular interest in the Benue history was the advent of the tug *Adama*, which in 1952 brought up the first barge train of bulk motor spirit to Garua.[1]

The John Holt fleet operates from Warri. Their tonnage is about 4,000 tons spread over ten boats. The year 1956 expects to see a new venture on the river, the *Susie* of the Compagnie de Transport et de Commerce.

CUSTOMS

At various times there have been customs posts at Mayo Belwa, Beli, Malabu, Chukol, Takum, Bakundi, Gurin, and Uba. Those at Takum and Bakundi, which had been set up in 1903 to collect the tariff of 2d. per lb. on ivory, 3d. per 10 lb. on rubber, and 2s. per 100 lb. on kola-nuts, were closed in 1907 as they were not paying their way; they were revived a few months later under new management and were finally shut down on the outbreak of war in 1914. The only station remaining is that at Yola, in the charge of an officer of the Customs and Excise Department. The Benue is an international waterway and goods destined for French territory are therefore exempt from customs dues if certified as being in transit and shipped in sealed holds.

MEDICAL

The medical work of Government dates from 1902, when a Medical Officer was posted to Yola to start a hospital there, and the Lamido placed a compound at his disposal until the new

[1] See *Nigeria Magazine*, No. 41/1953, for a full account.

building was completed. The mud buildings continued to be used till 1934, when a new 28-bed hospital was erected and 'for the first time since the British occupation, the Government Medical Officer has an operating table and a theatre for his use', as the Resident wrote in his report. There are today Government hospitals at Yola, with accommodation for over 100 patients, and at Mubi, and Mission ones at Numan and Bambur (S.U.M.), Garkida and Lassa (C.B.M.). A Rural Health Centre was opened at Sugu in 1954, run jointly by the Adamawa Native Administration and the Roman Catholic Mission.

Yola dispensary was opened in 1915. Then came those at Jada and Mayo Belwa in 1930. The 1926 dressing station at Mubi was converted into a dispensary four years later, and was closed in 1955 on the opening of the hospital there. By 1932 there were 8 dispensaries, and today Adamawa Division has 18 Native Administration and 3 Mission; Muri, 7 Native Administration ones; and Numan, 1 Native Administration and 4 Mission dispensaries. These are served by road and, in Muri Division, by river ambulance.

In 1952 the first Health Sister was posted to the Province, and a year later a Health Superintendent was appointed. Maternity and child-welfare clinics are held regularly at Yola, Mayo Belwa, Jada, Karlahi, and Girei. The Church of the Brethren Mission runs a very fine leprosarium at Garkida, which was opened in 1929 to replace the lesser centre at Yola, and the Sudan United Mission maintains a large leper colony outside Numan.

MISSIONS

There are four missions operating in Adamawa: Sudan United (Danish and American branches), Church of the Brethren (American), Cameroons Baptist (Swiss) and the Roman Catholic (Augustinian Order). Their work comprises evangelization, education and medical services.

The Sudan United Mission[1] first appeared in Muri Province when a station was opened at Wase in 1904 with the object of

[1] The Mission's Nigerian history has been recounted in *Half a Century of Grace*, J. L. Maxwell, 1954.

'evangelizing the pagan peoples of the Sudan, beginning with Adamawa and the Upper Benue'. Despite considerable friction with the Sarkin Wase, they extended their operations among the Munshi (Tiv), opening stations at Wukari in 1906 and at Ibi in 1908; their work among the Tiv was subsequently taken over by the Dutch Reformed Church.

In 1907 J. G. Burt had carried out a missionary reconnaissance in the Wurkum area, and in December 1909 three members of the South African branch of the Sudan United Mission opened a station in Mbula District, on a site slightly to the north-east of Dilli selected by K. Kumm[1] during his missionary trek from the Niger to the Nile. This station was in the charge of V. H. Hosking, but because of an attempt to develop too quickly it met with little success and was closed in 1911.

In 1913 the Danish branch arrived in Numan, where under Dr. Brönnum they opened their mission station in the following November; this has since become their headquarters in Nigeria. Though labouring under the disadvantage that no lady worker was allowed in the Yola Province, Dr. Brönnum and his two assistants embarked on a big programme among the Bachama, on whose language Dr. Brönnum soon became a recognized authority. Stations were opened at Lamurde and Shellen in 1921, at Pella in 1922, and at Dilli and Gurum in 1929.

In 1916 C. W. Guinter had been advised by the Resident that the time was not yet ripe for work in the heart of the Mumuye territory, and it was agreed that a station should instead be opened at Kona as the key to Mumuye land. In December 1923 Guinter started the mission centre at Bambur, which is now one of the Mission's big centres (American branch), and three years later the Evangelical Church took over the Wurkum area as its field. Gandole was opened in 1926, Zinna in 1932, Bambuka in 1938, and Lankoviri in 1941. The first Mumuye convert was baptized in 1940.

Meanwhile the Numan area had been going from strength to strength. A small hall of worship was erected in 1920 and by 1922 it had become an organized Church in the accepted mission sense.

[1] See Chapter VII.

With the approval of Sarkin Bachama, who had transferred his headquarters to Numan from Lamurde in 1921, about sixty children started attending a regular school. In the mid-twenties the Sudan United Mission undertook a bold experiment by opening a girls' boarding school in Numan. At first it was confined to Bachama girls only, so as to encourage Bachama families of good standing to take a pride in it, but the scheme was so successful that the school expanded and has now become one of the finest girls' schools in Northern Nigeria. In 1931 the Sudan United Mission annual conference was held at Numan and it was resolved to make Numan the Danish branch's headquarters for the whole of Nigeria. In 1939 the first lady medical officer was posted to the hospital, and ten years later the remarkable cathedral in Numan, one of the largest buildings in the Northern Region, was opened. In the same year, Miss Madsen, the mission nurse at Numan, was awarded the M.B.E. for her thirty years' service among the Bachama. The Numan hospital was rebuilt in 1951, in which year also the Mission's hospital at Bambur was opened. By 1954, the Sudan United Mission was able to claim 185 churches and 5,000 church members in Numan Division, where its record has indeed been one of praiseworthy achievement.

In 1905 the World Evangelization Company (U.S.A.) sent out two prospectors, but they did not remain in Muri. The Société des Missions Africaines de Lyons established themselves at Shendam, then in Muri Province, in 1907.

The Roman Catholic Mission did not begin work in Adamawa Province until 1940. The first mission site was secured at Sugu. The chief and people of Sugu came out about 15 miles to welcome the Fathers and to lead them in procession to the town. But even before a mission house was built the Fathers had run a First Aid Centre which was soon treating over 200 patients a day. Unfortunately the 1939 war put a stop to the supply of medicines and the Mission was unable to continue this work. An elementary school was opened in Sugu in 1941.

In the same year another mission station was opened among the Chamba, this time in Mapeo. In 1941, too, the Mission Headquarters was established at Yola, where the immigrant Catholic population was steadily growing. An elementary school was opened at Mapeo in 1942 and also a southern type school at Jimeta. No further expansion took place until 1945 when a station was opened among the Jukun at Jauro Yinu, about 6 miles from Jalingo. Schools were opened at Jauro Yinu and at Kona, which is the big town of the Jukun in Adamawa.

In 1948 two more stations were opened, one at Bare, 10 miles north of Numan, and the other at Kaya Gulak, a Marghi settlement in Madagali District. In 1950 a station was opened among the Higi at Bazza. During the serious cerebro-spinal epidemics of 1949 and 1950 the Fathers took charge of a number of specially erected isolation camps. An elementary school proved so successful in Bazza that in 1954 the Mission decided to build a Senior Primary boarding school in the village. In 1955 two more stations were opened, one at Yakoko, in the Zinna District of Muri Division, and the other at Mucella, a Fali town about 10 miles north of Mubi.

Missionary Sisters of the Franciscan Order of the Divine Maternity came to the Mission in 1950. They have taken charge of the Health and Maternity Centre of Adamawa N.A. at Sugu, and one Sister works in the Government Hospital at Yola. The Sisters also run an Adult Women's Education class. The class work is done in the convent grounds, but the Sisters spend their evenings visiting the compounds and giving help and guidance to the women.

The Roman Catholic Mission has enjoyed a splendid record during its brief history in Adamawa Province and its achievements were justly recognized by the recent promotion of the senior Father to the coveted position of Prefect Apostolic of Yola.

The Church of the Brethren Mission, an American enterprise, operates in Northern Adamawa. Its headquarters are at Garkida, where a school was opened in 1923, and where there is now a substantial colony of adherents grouped round the hospital, leprosarium, and school. Another hospital is run by this mission at Lassa, and there are stations at Gulak, Mubi (1954), and Uba (1955). It is unfortunate that illness has prevented the Church of the Brethren Mission leader, Dr. H. S. Kulp, whose knowledge of the Northern Adamawa peoples is extensive, from drafting notes on the valuable part his Mission has played in the history of the Province.

At Warwar, in Mambila District, the Cameroons Baptist Mission opened a station in 1939. At first its extra-mural concern was solely with agriculture, but a school and station have now been started. 'Ice-cream hill' is affectionately recalled by many Touring Officers.

A province with the marked pagan pattern of Adamawa offers great opportunity to missionary enterprise. On account of the unquestionable social and political advantages offered by Christianity and Islam, many pagans accept conversion and its attendant benefits. Contact with the adherents of either faith tends to modify profoundly their social organization, for a state of suspended pagan animation has proved incompatible with modern life, and acceptance of one or other religion looms large as a key to the wide world that lies beyond the hamlet. The following quotation from the *Gazetteer of Plateau Province*, itself another rich missionary field, admirably describes some of the strains and stresses in the mind of the potential catechist:

Monogamy and the greater performance of the Christian marriage bond are the principal stumbling blocks. The polygamy of paganism is an institution which is based on social economies, and the arithmetical impossibility for all to be polygamists may have been the cause of the relative unpermanence of its marriage bonds. Paganism cannot be said to be dying hard, because it is not yet ailing. Moreover, it probably will not ail easily, as its nature is not sufficiently highly strung to make it sensitive to infections. While the Christian and Mohammedan religions are primarily concerned with man's spiritual welfare and his condition in a future life, paganism is concerned intimately and in great detail with man's material welfare in this world and pays little or no attention to his condition in a future world. It is certainly concerned with the supernatural and the next world, but only in so far as they affect the materialities of this natural world. The how and when of its innumerable rites are known to everyone, but the why and wherefore are usually known only to the hierarchy. For the multitude paganism means action, not thought.

IX

HISTORY OF ADAMAWA DIVISION

ADAMAWA DIVISION, conterminous with the Emirate, today consists of those portions of the old kingdom of Adamawa that were assigned to the British under the Conventions of 1902 and 1907, based on the dichotomous Anglo-German Agreements of 1886 and 1893. In addition, it contains those Trust Territory areas which, originally part of old Adamawa, were returned to it by the 1922 Mandate from the League of Nations and are now administered as an integral part of it both for reasons of political convenience and because of ties of traditional allegiance.

The Emirate consists of 18,558 square miles, contained within a strip of country extending nearly 400 miles south and west from the Bornu boundary to that of the Southern Cameroons. On the north it marches with the Dikwa and Bornu Emirates, on the north-west with the Biu Division of Bornu Province, on the west with Numan and Muri Divisions of Adamawa Province, and on the south with the Wukari Division of Benue Province and the Nkambe Division of Bamenda Province; on the east it is continuously bounded by the French Cameroons. The 1952 decennial census gave a population of 799,150, of whom 63 per cent. were pagans and 34 per cent. Muslims.

HEADQUARTERS

The Emir of Adamawa is known as the Lamido, which is the Fulani word for 'ruler'. At first the meaning of the title was restricted to 'being governor of', since it was granted to a lieutenant of the Sokoto empire, but the word quickly took on the nuance of absolute sovereignty. The full title of *Lamido Fumbina* or *Amiru Yemen*, meaning Lord of the South, was conferred on Modibbo Adama, from whom the Emirate takes its name, by the Sultan of

Sokoto during the *jihad* at the beginning of the nineteenth century. Adamawa, however, was not quite identical with Fumbina, for it properly denoted only those areas of the great southern (i.e. from Sokoto) districts that had been conquered by the Fulani. From his headquarters town of Yola (population 8,500) the Lamido administers through District Heads his districts, which are all that is left of his ancestors' far-flung domains that covered 40,000 square miles from Marua to Ngaundere and from Lere to Mayo Ine.

The name Yola derives from the augmentative form of the Fulani word *yolde* and means a village on a rise or slight eminence. Its origin has also been ascribed, falsely, to the royal quarter of Kano. The first capital was Gurin, whence Adama moved in 1830 to Ribadu as a better base for his operations against the riverain Bata. On account of its insalubrity he transferred to Jobolio in 1839 and finally, in 1841, to Yola. Though the marshes rendered a walled defence unnecessary, the site was more suitable as a war-base against the Verre and Bata tribes than as an agreeable capital town.[1]

THE FULANI CONQUEST

This account is given, with reservations, for what it is worth. In the absence of written records the assessment of nomadic migrations must remain largely conjectural. As an hypothesis it may be accepted provisionally, pending that more detailed research which, backed by sound scholarship and linguistic analysis, may confirm or disprove it.

Of the early penetration of Adamawa by the Fulani mention has already been made. There is reflected their gradual tendency to abandon the purely pastoral way of life, coupled with an increasing interest in the politics of the pagan tribes among whom they found themselves, their eventual partial conversion to Islam, and their participation in the Holy War, in the course of which they subjugated the majority of those tribes. It may be noted *en passant* that, though the Fulani brought with them vast herds of fine cattle, they did not actually introduce cattle to Adamawa, where a breed of *muturu* dwarf cattle already existed.

[1] See Appendix A.

The Yola royal family, which is of the Ba'en clan, preserves the tradition that its ancestors were driven out of the Damaturu neighbourhood by the Kanuri in the fourteenth century and entered Adamawa by the Yedseram valley. It seems that the main penetration, however, did not occur till the eighteenth century, though there were advance parties in Bornu and Bauchi during the fifteenth century and some Fulani had reached Baghirmi by about 1550.

Two main branches are distinguished in this stream of migration. The first consisted of the Wolarbe, the Ba'en, and several smaller clans, while the Ilaga'en constituted the bulk of the second. The fission appears to have taken place after the foundation of settlements in the Upper Yedseram valley by both sections. The Wolarbe and the Ba'en, with some of the Ilaga'en, kept to the western slopes of the Mandara mountains after they had spread through the Marghi lands, whereas the remainder of the Ilaga'en, with the Mbewe'en and Gara'en, turned eastwards through the mountains and penetrated the basin of the River Kebi before settling around Marua.

The Mandara empire—later the most powerful and highly organized enemy that the Emirs of Adamawa had to face—was hostile to the Fulani long before the *jihad* and blocked their approach round the northern tip of the Mandara hills. Thus the eastern movement of the Ilaga'en could not be achieved until they had reached a point well south of the Mandara territories— probably from Mubi, itself a settlement of this clan, through the narrow Ba'a valley which is the only practicable opening in the 70-mile mountain barrier that separates the basin of the Kebi from those of the Yedseram and Kilengi rivers.

The western branch of the migration continued south-westwards, crossing the Yedseram and Kilengi watershed and so entering the basin of the Benue. For some time its southern front paused in the highly organized kingdom of Kilba on terms dictated by the tribal chief, and a great deal of intermarriage seems to have taken place, the effects of which are still discernible in the physical characteristics of a people otherwise indistinguishable from the southern Marghi. Thence the expansion pushed on into the

Benue valley proper, where its immediate range was limited by the Verre hills to the south and to the west by the intractable hostility of the tribes occupying the Gongola valley and the Mumuye plateau. Eastwards from this barrier the Benue lowlands were occupied by centralized Bata principalities, with whom the Fulani came to terms.

By the end of the eighteenth century the immigrants were established in numbers throughout the Bata territory. The whole of this region, watered by the Benue and its tributaries and rich in large marshes, fertile cotton soil, and good grazing pastures, was dotted with growing Fulani settlements, each under an *Ardo*, a title originally given to chiefs owing allegiance direct to the Lamido; nowadays it has lost its meaning of family leader, though it still retains among the settled Fulani an archaic suggestion of respectability and blue blood. These settlements remained in a state of subservience to the pagan chiefs until the time of the Fulani crusade. Furthermore, the eastern and western branches were once more in contact: the former had reached the Benue by way of the Kebi and Tiel valleys and settled in some strength in the Bata state of Demsa, near Garua, while the latter, passing eastwards along the south bank of the Benue, had crossed the River Faro into Bundang, another Bata state.

As the Fulani influence with the indigenous chiefs increased, often by way of intermarriage, subservience became distasteful to the immigrants, particularly when emphasized by the insistence of the Bata kings on their *droit de seigneur*. Such a demand in about 1803 by the chief of Bundang was, according to legend, the occasion of the first direct step towards the establishment of the Fulani supremacy in Adamawa. Ardo Jobdi, head of the Wolarbe around Song, slew his daughter rather than yield her up, then turned and killed the chieftain lest he demand again what had been refused beyond recall. His deed was the signal for war and the Wolarbe withdrew to the Verre hills where, under Ardo Haman, they entrenched themselves at Gurin Hosere. A pagan force from Song attacked them but was repelled. The Verre, however, afraid that they might be drawn into the quarrel, refused to allow the Fulani to remain, and in 1804 the latter moved down to the plains and camped on the west bank of the Faro on the site of what was later to become Gurin town.

ADAMA: 1806–48

In this first battle perished Ardo Hassana, a Ba'ajo noble. His son Adama, fancifully said to be a great-grandson of Jobo Rum, a Persian, returned to his people at Weltunde near Guriga in the following year after a period of travel and study in Bornu, under Mallam Kiari of Kukawa, and in Sokoto, during which he had perfected the learning and piety that won for him the title of *Modibbo*. Adama brought the news that Usman dan Fodio had declared a *jihad* against the heathen. Many of the local Fulani had already embraced Islam, and Adama persuaded the various clans to combine and follow the crusading example of Sokoto. A mission was sent to Usman dan Fodio, the Commander of the Faithful, to request his sanction and support for the *jihad* in the east. The party included Adama and Kokomi, the Bata chief who, having seen that the Fulani must become the dominant power, had thrown in his lot with theirs. By his foresight Kokomi secured the confirmation of his office for himself and his descendants, and also the title of Magaji, with authority over all the riverain Bata later subjugated by the Fulani, and a monopoly of ferry rights, while his whole clan was granted immunity from enslavement and taxation.

The Shehu received the mission favourably and gave a flag to Ardo Boronga of the Wolarbe, the senior clan-chief, whom the delegates had nominated as their leader in the Holy War when Adama declared that he preferred to abstain from secular command. The grant of the flag and the commission which it signified were conditional upon the sending of a yearly deputation to Sokoto with a regular quota of slaves: the latter presented no difficulty, but the idea of a recurrent pilgrimage involving over a month's journey was disagreeable to the Adamawa delegates, who determined, in Adama's absence, that the conditions attached to the commission should be disregarded. This dishonesty came to the ears of Adama, the leading spiritual force of the party, and indignant at such perfidy he reported it to the Sultan at a public audience.

Usman dan Fodio recalled the mission and publicly took back the flag. He then presented a new flag to Adama:

When you return tell them this is what Shehu gave you. Say also that I accept their greetings. Bid them place their hands in yours; whoever gives his hand to you, joins hands with me. Tell them I greet them. Make flags for them like this that I have given you, and give them the flags, with the orders I have laid upon you. You are the envoy; whatsoever they desire let them tell it you, then do you come and tell me.[1]

As a special mark of favour and honour, the Shehu is said to have unwound Adama's turban and crowned him with a fez from his own head. In his letter of appointment he conferred on Adama the title of *Lamido Fumbina*, with a firman to propagate the faith from the Nile to the Bight of Biafra, and allowed him to recruit Fulani volunteers (Toronkawa) in Sokoto. Their ranks were swelled by Hausa mercenaries, fired by the prospect of slaving, and Adama thus acquired a nucleus for the Adamawa army which he was to raise on his return. In fact, Adama never adopted the title of Lamido, for he was always—and still is—known as Modibbo, the learned one.

It is interesting to see to what extent Usman dan Fodio's instructions to carry the Holy War to the far south were carried out. Barth records that Ardo Sambo of Chamba

made himself extremely famous by his daring and distant expeditions, and more especially that to the Ibo country and to Mbafu, through which he has succeeded in extending not only the influence but even the dominion of the conquerors, in a certain degree, as far as the Bight of Benin.

In the event it was this Bamum Sultanate of Fumban that marked the southerly limit of Adamawa's crusade, and the check is described in a recent travelogue:

The Fulani stormed Fumban hill and they drove the Bamum out into the obliterating grassfields. The victorious cavalry, whose animals with their dilated nostrils and flag tails the Bamum had never seen before, trooped northwards to fetch their flocks and womenfolk to settle in

[1] I have made generous use in this chapter of the Fulani manuscripts collected by the Yola school staff and later published under the title of *Stories of Old Adamawa*, 1935.

Fumban. In their absence, runs the Bamum tradition, the defeated tribe returned and dug the trench and ran up the earth wall which now runs like a snake along eighteen miles of the contoured hills of Fumban. Next dry season the Fulani returned. Enraged, they charged the hills. The horses would not face the ditch and wall. Some were left with broken legs, others were killed by chance spears. The skulls of these outlandish animals were cleaned and dried, and with the skull of the Fulani commander they were laid away in the Sultan's Treasury, where they are to this day.

Adama arrived back in Gurin in 1806. He initiated his campaign by sacking the neighbouring Bata towns of Pema, Turuwa, and Tepe. Another tradition maintains that he obeyed the commands of Dan Fodio and waited three years before undertaking any conquest; this was in contrast to the zeal of Buba Yero of Gombe, whose conquests of the Yungur, Lala, and Hona areas were taken away from him by Dan Fodio, as a punishment for his precipitancy, and handed to Adama. For the next forty-two years Adama was occupied with extending his conquests and subduing rebellious vassal-governors of his provinces as he gradually carved out the kingdom of Adamawa.

Demsa. The Fulani of Demsa, the capital of the most powerful of the Bata states, had at first held aloof from the *jihad*, but in 1810 they appealed to Adama for help against the exactions of the local Bata chief, Yideng, who was demanding a heavy tribute. Adama sent a force under Ardo Haman, who took Demsa, routed the Bata army, and was appointed governor of the territory. He made his headquarters at Shebowa on the south bank of the Benue, later moving to Garua Lainde and finally to modern Garua. Not long after this, Ardo Haman rebelled against the Lamido and was defeated and captured.

Mandara. About 1820 the old hostility between the Fulani and Bukama, Sultan of Mandara, broke out afresh, and in 1823 the combined forces of Mandara and Bornu, supported by the Arab escort of the Oudney-Clapperton-Denham mission, were defeated by the Fulani at Masfel, a village some 40 miles east of Madagali. The Mandara army rallied and, in a battle soon afterwards at Isa Habe, the Fulani clan called the Gara'en was almost exterminated. Adama, who in his youth had herded his father's cattle in the Mandara country round Waloji and thus was well acquainted with the terrain, hastened to the scene in person, defeated Bukama at Guidder, about 60 miles south-east of Mubi, and occupied the Mandara capital, Dolo. Bukama escaped to Dikwa, and Adama, finding himself too weak to hold such an advanced position as Dolo, sacked the town and withdrew. By this campaign he added to his kingdom the western Mandara districts of Mubi, Moda, Micika, and Uba.

Kilba. About the same period, Ardo Dau of the Wolarbe clan obtained a hold over the Kilba, partly by force and partly by diplomacy. The hill villages were never entirely subdued, but a *modus vivendi* was established which enabled Fulani and Kilba to trade at the border market of Bila Kilba, where many a Kilba public malefactor was disposed of by sale as a slave.

Holma. This, too, was added to Adama's kingdom by peaceful means when one of the Fulani leaders married the daughter of Dimitelli, the pagan chief. The son of this alliance, Ardo Dembo, succeeded to the chieftainship, and the rich volcanic soil was settled with slave farms. The Holma chiefs were notably loyal to the Emirs of Yola.

Malabu and Song. In the early 1830's Adama undertook an expedition in the north which resulted in the conquest of the Njirai-Bata districts of Malabu and Zummo occupying the watershed of the Kilengi and Tiel rivers immediately north of the Benue. In 1838 he turned west and established the province of Song as an advanced base from which to attack the Lala tribes of the eastern escarpment of the Gongola-Hawal valley. On these pagans Adama made little impression and once suffered defeat. During the Song campaign the Fulani losses in men and cattle were considerable, due, it is said, to the unhealthiness of the area.

Bata. With the final move of his headquarters to Yola, Adama was able in the 1840's to press home his campaigns against the Verre and Bata tribes. At Namtari on the Mayo Ine he established an outpost against the Bata, now entrenched at New Demsa, while posts at Beti, Sebore, and Nyibango encircled the Verre hills. Beti is noteworthy as being the sole camp in charge of a Hausa, namely Bapawo, Sarkin Zamfara, one of the volunteers who had followed Adama from Sokoto; the village today bears his name. The raids against the Bata were rarely more than hurried slave-raids, as these pagans were mounted. Riding bareback, with cuts across the horse's back to help them keep their seat, they were admirable mounted spearmen and as often as not were a match for the heavy cavalry of the Fulani.

While Adama fought against the Bata and attacked the Marghi and Mandara territories in the north, his lieutenants extended the Fulani dominion to the south and east.

Laro. Leaving the pagans, expelled from the plains south-west of Gurin, in their Alantika fastnesses, an expedition of the Wolarbe clan under Ardo Hamman Joda and Ardo Sammatu pushed farther south up the valley of the River Deo, a western tributary of the Faro, and built a fortified camp at Laro on an ideal ridge overlooking the river.

Koncha and Banyo. In 1835 Ardo Sammatu's son, Hamman Gabdo Dandi, led an expedition from Laro against the Kotopo and took their stronghold of Koncha. Modibbo Adama was so pleased at this advance that he granted Dandi the governorship of the new territories and as much more as he could annex. Dandi, elated by such an honour, advanced up the River Deo in the following year and attacked Banyo, the capital of the Wute tribe, and about 190 miles from Yola. He routed the Wute army and that of the Tikar (Mambila) pagans, who had come to its assistance, in a pitched battle at Sambo Labbo in about 1840. Ardo Dandi now established himself at Banyo and, finding that the superior strength of the Bamum pagans at Fumban forestalled any further southward extension of his domains, turned his attention to the Mambila, Chamba, and Jukun tribes of the highlands to the west of Banyo. After a long struggle he overcame the pagans of Gashaka, whither he moved his headquarters shortly before his death in about 1872, leaving his sons in charge of Koncha and Banyo as well as Gashaka.

Tibati. Meanwhile the Wolarbe force under Ardo Jobdi and Ardo Hamman Sambo had overrun the Chamba settlements along the River Faro and, following its valley southwards, had conquered the Manna, Woka, Tinger, Gabin, and eastern Kotopo tribes. Hamman Sambo settled at Tibati, of which he was appointed governor by Adama.

Ngaundere. Ardo Jobdi pushed southwards into the country of the Mbum, with whom he made a treaty, and camped near Delbe, their chief town. Later a dispute arose between the Fulani and the Mbum, whereupon Jobdi denounced the treaty, attacked and burned Delbe, and founded on its ashes the modern town of Ngaundere. From this base, with his neighbours of Tibati and Rei, he made war on the surrounding tribes with such success that he soon became one of the most powerful Fulani governors. He died suddenly on the occasion of a visit to Adama at his war-camp at Bundang, and it is said that the Emir procured one of Jobdi's concubines to poison him. Whether this is true or not, the later history of the Ngaundere, Tibati, and Rei governorates indicates that Adama's distrust of the rising power of their unholy alliance was not ill-founded.

Rei. In the early days of the *jihad* one Ardo Yajo, son of Ardo Bondi from Melle and cousin of the Sultan of Sokoto, passed through the Mandara country from Bornu and, reaching the upper waters of the Benue, settled on the edge of the Dama and Laka territories, where he was appointed lieutenant by Adama and given a flag. Yajo died soon afterwards and was succeeded by his son Jidda, who made his headquarters on the banks of the River Rei and entered into a treaty with the Dama chief, cementing this by the marriage of the latter's daughter to his son, Buba Jirum. Despite this treaty, the Dama were soon reduced to serfdom. Jidda then extended his conquests into the Laka and Baya country and consolidated his position by allying himself with the governors of Tibati and Ngaundere. A climax came when he called on the governors of the minor provinces of Balda, Njarendi, and Wuro Mayo to throw off their allegiance to Adama and acknowledge himself as suzerain; at the same time he sent an embassy to Sokoto with a large present of slaves and a request for the recognition of his independence of Yola. This appeal was refused; at the Sultan's orders, Jidda returned his allegiance to Adama.

In the following spring, according to custom, Adama ordered Jidda to send a force to take part in the annual slave-raid on the

Namji pagans. No contingent from Rei appeared, the raid failed, and Adama retired defeated. Immediately Jidda demonstrated that he could succeed where Adama had failed; he attacked the Namji with his own forces and captured a number of slaves, some of whom he tauntingly dispatched to Yola. He was soon summoned thither himself to explain his conduct to the Emir, who made a show of accepting the proffered apologies but in fact planned to procure Jidda's death by drowning on his way back from Yola. Hearing of this plot, Jidda, on his departure, dressed his brother Umaru in the blue gown which he himself habitually wore and sent him to take his own place in the canoe; as Jidda had anticipated, an upset was staged and his brother was drowned. The same night Jidda fled overland to his capital; the revolt of Rei was on.

Jidda's first rising was easily put down by Adama, who punished his rebellious henchmen by taking all his territory north of the River Shina and giving it to Ardo Bibeme. The second uprising was disastrous, for Adama actually entered Rei, deposed Jidda, and appointed his son Shehu governor in his stead. Yet no sooner had Adama left Rei than Jidda rallied his remaining forces and retook his capital, Shehu being killed in the assault. Adama hurried back but was unable to recapture the town. Thereafter he was obliged to tolerate the virtual independence of Rei, the successive chiefs of which nevertheless continued to recognize the spiritual leadership of the Emirs of Yola and to furnish in normal years nearly the whole of the annual tribute of slaves payable by Yola to Sokoto.

Chamba. A similar bid for independence was made in 1842 by Ardo Amadu, governor of Chamba, who sent a magnificent present of slaves and merchandise direct to Sultan Atiku of Sokoto. Contrary to precedent, Atiku granted him a separate flag of office, whereupon Adama, despite his advanced years, decided to retire to Mecca for the pilgrimage. He set out from Yola with a very large following, but before he had reached the limits of his territory he was overtaken by messengers bearing the news of Atiku's death and a petition from all his vassal chiefs, except the governor of Chamba, begging him not to desert them. Adama at once summoned his recalcitrant vassal to a meeting at Beka, 10 miles south of Gurin. It is said that this meeting took place before the greatest host of horse and foot ever assembled in Adamawa. Amadu did public obeisance and was ordered to return his flag and commission in person to Sokoto.

In 1848 Modibbo Adama died in his bed at the age of seventy-seven. His piety is still revered in Yola, and is enhanced by contrast with the ostentatious behaviour of Sanda and later Lamidos. It is said that at his death Adama left only his Koran, his simple clothes, and one female slave. He had the reputation of being a man of great learning and much energy, and as a leader was bold and able. In disposition he is said to have been mild to a fault, though inflexible once his mind was made up. He was by preference a scholar and saint rather than a warrior, universally respected and even beloved by his people. He made no less than eleven pilgrimages to Sokoto. At his death he ruled over an empire twice the size of Wales, stretching from Banyo in the south to Marua in the north and in breadth from Lere to the Mayo Ine.

Of Adama's wives, Yaseba bore him two sons, who were said to have been excluded from the succession because one night their mother kept Adama waiting outside her hut in the rain; Astajam was the mother of Lawal, Sanda, and Mansur. Yara, said to be a Marghi concubine given to him by Yaseba, bore Zubeiru and Bobo Ahmadu. It is remarkable that Adama was succeeded by his four sons in turn, three of them in accordance with his dying testament of 'La-U-Zu'. Adama had altogether eleven sons and four daughters.

LAWAL: 1848-72

It was the destiny of Lawal—his real name was Hamman—to consolidate the empire his father had carved out. His reign was largely occupied with wars against the Fali of Mubi, the tribes of Lere and the Logone valley, and the Bata of Bagale hill, while much of his energies were expended in dealing with the turbulence of his governors, especially those of the southern provinces. He founded the fiefs of Girei and Namtari which, like his father's Gurin, have remained as traditional appointments of the Lamido, conferred as a personal reward.

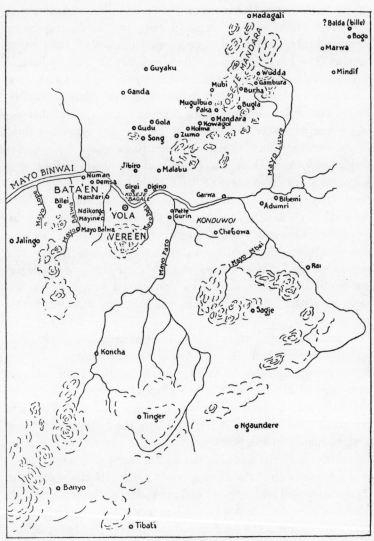

From 'Stories of Old Adamawa' by R. M. East

ADAMAWA IN THE NINETEENTH CENTURY

Fali. Lawal's Mubi campaign was successful. The Fali either retired to the mountains or submitted to the Fulani and accepted a precarious status midway between serfs and feudal tributaries; some embraced Islam and were granted the fiefs of their native villages. The Lere expedition added fresh territory, and Mundang was made the headquarters of a new province under Lawal's son by a Lere concubine, Sulei. In his raids into Marghi country, Lawal came into conflict with the Shehu of Bornu, a fact that was to affect so adversely Barth's visit to Yola in 1851 when he offered Lawal his unfortunate credentials from Kukawa.

Madagali. Ardo Dadi, who had founded a Fulani settlement at Rumirgo a few miles north of the Marghi town of Madagali, had been succeeded by his son Hamman Jidda, to whom Modibbo Adama had given a flag. In about 1854 he resigned in favour of his son Bakari who, much to the chagrin of the elder son Buba Ciuto, was recognized by the Lamido as Ardo. In 1858 Buba Ciuto persuaded the Lamido to give him the stewardship of Madagali, but twelve years later, after a violent quarrel with Yola, he was again displaced by Bakari. Bakari was killed by the Germans in 1901.

Bagale. The Bata stronghold in the Bagale hills opposite Yola had, under their chief Geloya, resisted assault for many years, but it was eventually betrayed in 1853 by one of its women, another concubine of Lawal. She secured admittance by pretending that she had escaped from her master's harem and wished to take refuge with her relatives. A few days later the Fulani forces made a night march to the point nearest to the town affording them concealment. In the morning this woman set fire to some houses at the opposite side; the Bata garrison rushed to that quarter to repel a supposed raiding party and the Fulani captured the stronghold almost without opposition. Thus was Lawal able to fulfil the promise he made when he marched out of Yola that he would not return from his war-camp until Bagale had been stormed. To quote from a Fulani chronicler:

Lamido Lauwal had reigned for three years when he decided to make war on Bagale. He collected his forces, and went and encamped round the foot of the hill. He said, 'Listen, my people, to what I say. I am

Lauwal, Death or Glory!' He remained two years, and the women-folk kept on sending out dried meat from the town. For this reason they gave his camp the name 'Takkande'. Every morning they would go out to fight until the sun had passed its zenith at the time of afternoon prayer, then they would return to the camp for the night. They beat the drums at the crack of dawn; the foot-soldiers took up their shields and weapons; the horsemen put on their chain armour and coats of mail, their girdles and their helmets, they slung their swords round their shoulders, took their spears in their hands, and went out to fight.

It was at this time that the village of Girei was founded, after the Bata menace had been scotched.

Tibati. Against his insubordinate governors Lawal was less successful. Jidda of Rei refused to take the oath of allegiance, though he continued to send deputations and the annual quota of slaves. Ardo Hamidu of Tibati broke his fealty by making war on the neighbouring provinces of Banyo and Ngaundere. Lawal put down this revolt, but the governors of Banyo and Ngaundere, rescued from Hamidu's attacks, promptly repudiated their allegiance to the Emir, though they abstained from active rebellion. Hamidu himself gave no further trouble, but on his death his son Buba seized the chieftainship of Tibati and proclaimed his independence. Lawal crushed this rebellion and exiled Buba, appointing in his place Hamman Lamu, another son of Hamidu. A few years later, however, he too revolted, and this time Lawal was unable to re-establish his suzerainty over Tibati, which remained independent of Yola till 1899, when the Germans took control of it.

Lawal died in 1872, at the age of seventy-five. Barth described him thus:

The governor was very simply dressed and had nothing remarkable in his appearance, while his face, which was half-covered by a somewhat dirty shawl, had an indifferent expression.

Today in Yola, Lawal is often regarded as the *beau idéal* of the Fulani administrator: warrior, scholar, and religious ascetic. He enforced a strict censorship of moral conduct and even of dress, for makers and wearers of short garments were severely punished, and whistling, guitar-playing, and smoking or snuff-taking were

absolutely forbidden. He founded many schools with the help of
Adama Gana (held by many to have been a fellow-student and
friend of Adama and known as Modibbo Adama the lesser; but
claimed by others to have been Adama Aganna, chief of Bundang,
whom Lawal had captured), who is revered as a saint and is buried
in Yola mosque.

SANDA: 1872–90

The succession was claimed by two of Modibbo Adama's sons,
Sanda and Hamidu, each of whom sent a deputation to Sokoto;
the Sultan decided in favour of Hamidu, but as he died before
the emissaries returned to Yola, Sanda obtained the Sultan's
commission.

The new Emir was weak, and the provincial governors were
quick to take advantage. Buba Jirum, who had succeeded Jidda
at Rei, demanded the return of the territory of which his father had
been deprived by Adama as a punishment for rebellion, and the
case was referred to Sokoto. The Sultan ordered the disputed lands
to be restored on payment of 1,000 slaves each to himself and to
the Emir and of 100 to the Yerima, or heir-apparent, of Yola. The
dispute was settled on these terms, and the fact that all three
payments were promptly made suggests that Rei's claim to independence had never been substantiated. Ngaundere and Banyo
remained in revolt throughout Sanda's reign, while in the north
Buba Ciuto, whom Lawal had exiled from Madagali, defied the
Emir until his defeat and capture in the Gulak campaign.

There were other insurrections which Sanda was unable to
suppress. The Tirgele tribe revolted and regained their freedom
by defeating the Emir's troops; the Fali got out of hand; and the
Fulani hold over the Lere pagans slackened considerably. Another
uprising occurred at Moda, headed by Ardo Hamman, grandson of the first Moda governor, Ardo Sambo, who had migrated
from Chad. Sanda also led a dismal campaign, in co-operation
with the Emir of Muri, against the Lala and Kilba tribes.

Sanda died in 1890. Indolent by nature, preferring ease and the
delights of his harem to the active affairs of state—from which he
at one time tried to abdicate in favour of his son Iya (later the
sixth Lamido)—his reign was unfortunate for Adamawa. It was

while Sanda was ruling at Yola that the Royal Niger Company
first appeared on the scene.[1]

A Fulani manuscript relates:

When Sanda was dying, he commanded all his slaves to come and
encircle his house after his death and tell the people to bury him there
and not take him anywhere else. So the slaves encircled his house, and
when he was dead they said he was to be buried there, and even started
to dig his grave. Then one came and filled it in, saying: 'Cease this
folly of yours; take him up and carry him to the tomb of his father, so
that he too may receive his father's blessing.' Then they took him up
and carried him to Modibbo's house and buried him there.

ZUBEIRU: 1890–1901[2]

Zubeiru was a man of very different character. He at once set
about reforming abuses which had flourished in his brother's
reign. A strict moral and social code was enforced; Lawal's
sumptuary laws were repealed; professional dancers were banished;
and corruption amongst the officers of state was severely punished.
These measures naturally excited much hostility among his
subordinates, who are said to have made several attempts to
poison the Emir.

Having set his capital in order, Zubeiru next turned his attention
to the provinces. Of his zest for campaigning, a Fulani relates:

Lauwal Zubeiru was a very keen crusader and was always making
preparations with a view to war. On account of his love of crusading
men used to cry out against him, 'Alas! Month after month the people
have been in a state of war. When are they going to stop?' Whenever
they came back from an expedition, and before the people had dispersed,
he had a proclamation made that they were to get ready and make every
effort, for he was not sitting down.

But his military skill was offset by his impetuosity which on
many occasions brought him near to disaster. His first campaign,
against the Fali, was successful. His second, against the Mundang
pagans, was less so, for in the course of the fighting he lost his son
Sadu who was captured and tortured to death. Against the
Binder pagans Zubeiru achieved little, and his expedition against
the Marghi suffered a reverse at Bazza. Subsequently he was able

[1] See Chapter IV.   [2] See above, pp. 55–64.

to make a triumphant progress as far as the River Logone, and in later campaigns he reduced the Marghi and Mundang to nominal submission. Mubi state also caused some trouble, and Zubeiru appointed a new chief, Ardo Isa. Isa, however, was driven out by Ardo Jobdi, who seems to have been left to enjoy the chieftainship he had seized. There is a tradition in Yola that on one or two of his campaigns Zubeiru used the two cannon given to him by Mizon,[1] carrying them on camels, but that the gunfire was never really effective.

Hayatu. One of the most serious rebellions that Zubeiru had to face was that of Hayatu, an exiled scion of the royal house of Sokoto. He settled in Yola for some years. During his stay he is said to have bought only bridles in exchange for everything he possessed—for such was his ruling passion; even Lamido Sanda's farewell present he sold for more bridles. Hayatu left Yola to settle at Marua, where Sali was the chief. There he built up a large following, founded the town of Balda, and began to attack Marua. Sanda had been too weak to intervene, but now Zubeiru led an army against him and the two forces met near Marua. It is said that two days before the battle the Sarkin Katsina, who was senior captain of the Hausa troops from Yola, made the last of many appeals to Zubeiru to avoid this conflict, for he deemed it shameful and irreligious that a son of Modibbo Adama should join battle with so near a kinsman of the Sultan. Zubeiru refused, whereupon Sarkin Katsina withdrew and, assembling the other Hausa commanders, made public intercession that he might not himself be permitted to see the day of such internecine strife. His prayer was granted; that same night he fell sick and died next day on the eve of the engagement. The battle was counted the most disastrous since the beginning of the *jihad.* Hayatu's army totally defeated that of Zubeiru, which had to retire in disorder; but meanwhile the Fulani of Marua had fallen on Hayatu's camp and destroyed it, carrying off women, slaves, and beasts of burden. Deprived of transport and supplies, Hayatu was unable to follow up his victory, and retreated northwards. Fulani chroniclers hold that neither party gained any advantage, Zubeiru's losses in the field—including

[1] See Chapter IV.

his brother Aliyu and much of the flower of Yola's youth—and in prestige being offset by the destruction of Hayatu's camp and by his retreat. Hayatu was later killed when fighting Rabeh near Dikwa.

Zubeiru was successful in dealing with the insubordinate governors of Ngaundere, Tinger, and Banyo. The first two submitted after chastisement and continued in office, but the governor of Banyo proved so irreconcilable that he was deposed and his son Umaru was appointed in his stead. This Umaru showed himself both loyal and capable, and undertook to act for the Emir in dealing with Sambo, his uncle, who had seized the walled town of Gashaka and established himself there as a paramount chief in defiance of both Banyo and Yola. Umaru attacked Gashaka, captured Sambo and his three sons, and sent them to Yola, whence Sambo was banished to Madagali. Umaru reigned at Banyo till 2 February 1902, when he was killed after stabbing the German D.O., Oberleutnant Nolte. Zubeiru also forced the governors of Rei and Tibati to resume the annual tribute of slaves, which had been interrupted, but they never really resumed their allegiance.

It was with Zubeiru that the Royal Niger Company came into such severe conflict at Yola. One of the Company's executive officers has left an account of the Emir's character:

He was not only *mallam* by name but a highly educated scholar of the Mohammedan school . . . He was continually at war with the surrounding pagan tribes and, while sometimes successful when he caught a number of slaves who mostly went as tribute to Sokoto, frequently he came off second best . . . During the whole of this period I can say that one man saved the situation time and again: that was the Emir's Majindadi, Arkal. He nursed the Emir and acted the go-between for years until he was killed by pagans on one of the Emir's mad raids. The Emir, with all his faults, was a real ruler, but I think during the last years of his career he was more or less mad. I was told that over-study during his youth had affected him before he became Emir.

Zubeiru was a man of great bravery, personal strength, and energy, gifted with much astuteness and a sense of almost harsh discipline, and at times a fanatical Moslem. He would, for instance, enslave dark men, angrily denying that they could be Fulani; his reign was marked by many slave-raids, at Dakka, Mubi, Uba,

Hildi, Marua, Ga'anda, Demsa, and the greatest of all, Goila; and it was his intolerance and hatred towards the infidel Europeans that brought about his eventual overthrow. He executed as an example one of his own nephews who had indulged in robbery on the Yola-Banyo road, and he caused to be amputated in Yola market-place the foot of a grandson of Modibbo Adama for a similar offence. It was to this constant severity that his critics ascribed the several calamities of his reign, such as the great cattle sickness of 1891, the locust plague, the menace of Rabeh, and the invasion of the British. Mizon was told that Zubeiru had a chronic illness and that once a fortnight he used to spend a whole day shut up alone. Local belief was that he suffered from epileptic fits—one is reminded of Macdonald's comment that 'fits of temper seem to be hereditary in the Emirs of Yola'—which the Fulani considered a sign of possession by the devil. It was even said that the Sultan of Sokoto had been so displeased by the accession of the epileptic Zubeiru that he had sent, for his coronation, a black gown and turban instead of the white ones traditional for a royal investiture.

BOBO AHMADU: 1901-9

After the defeat and flight of Zubeiru, the succession passed to Bobo Ahmadu. Soured by the loss of territory and prestige consequent upon the 1907 International Boundary Convention, he became intractable and in 1909 was deposed for misrule and exiled to Lokoja, but on account of his old age he was allowed to return to Yola, where he died in 1916. Boyd Alexander, who was passing through Yola in 1910, retails several instances of misbehaviour which led to the Lamido's conviction of extortion and worse among the Verre and Malabu pagans, and describes him thus:

He possessed an inordinate love for amassing money, the accomplishing of which was rendered easy by his power and position, while his commanding presence helped him in no small degree to further this end. Dark-skinned, tall and stoutly built, and with white beard flowing from the chin, we can picture him surrounded by some hundreds of richly gowned horsemen, riding into the country to visit his towns, where he would demand without payment double the amount of food required for his men, and then order the remainder to be sent with him. The chief of a town named Zuma had the best house and compound made

ready for his royal master. The bed upon which he was to recline and
the floor as well were spread with costly gowns. In the centre of the bed
shone a heap of silver, while at the head and foot knelt two young
virgins ready to receive him.

IYA: 1909–10

Iya proved weak and hopelessly extravagant, and after only
eighteen months as Lamido he abdicated. He died in 1920.

ABBA: 1910–24

Abba, who was Lamido during the delicate years of the
Cameroons campaign and the division of the mandated territory,
showed considerable ability and was awarded the C.B.E. for his
services. He died in 1924.

MUHAMMADU BELLO: 1924–8

Muhammadu Bello, better known to the Yola Fulani as Maigari,
had been District Head of Nassarawo before his appointment as
Lamido and had been noted for his loyalty to the Germans up to
the time of their evacuation from German Adamawa. He died in
1928, after several months of ill-health.

MUSTAFA: 1928–46

Muhammadu Mustafa, a great-grandson of Modibbo Adama,
was only twenty-eight when he succeeded to the throne. His reign
was one of the more notable ones, and his generous character is
still recalled. He was an enthusiastic horse-owner and a keen polo
player, and it is in these interests that the equine badge of the
Native Authority Police has its origin; those constables who
joined during Mustafa's reign are rightly proud of their badge of
office.

AHMADU: 1946–53

Ahmadu's reign is perhaps too recent to be properly set in
perspective, yet it does not seem that it will make its mark among
Yola's happier days. In him the less desirable Fulani traits out-
weighed the finest features of his race, and with his eventual
removal there were an appreciable slackening in the tension and a
welcome improvement in the atmosphere of the Emirate Council.
Lamido Ahmadu must share the credit for the success of the

1949 Visiting Mission of the United Nations Trusteeship Council, who were greatly impressed by the quasi-durbar he arranged in Yola. The official U.N.O. report was enthusiastic about the prince and his pageantry:

The colorful [*sic*] receptions which the Lamido gave in honour of the Mission will always remain outstanding in the memory of the members of the visiting Mission . . . Riding on colorfully-adorned horses, surrounded by some twenty or thirty footmen carrying ceremonial weapons or playing drums, flutes and horns, the chiefs, one after another, would extend their greetings by first raising their right fists, then dismounting from their horses, and finally kneeling in front of the Lamido . . . Every chief was a knight in shining armour, every woman an adornment with her colorful attire, and every child a gala participant in the whole joyous affair. Over that tumultuous parade presided the Lamido, a tall, young and handsome man, whose white robes added to his impressive dignity as he watched his people and received their homage with imperturbable eyes. His princely bearing was matched by his perfect courtesy. His eminent position did not detract from his kindness to his guests.

In 1951 Ahmadu accompanied the Emir of Gombe on a six weeks' tour of Europe, during which he visited Oxford, Ascot, and Paris. But the glory of his 1949 performance had begun to tarnish; all that glisters is not necessarily gold, and those in closer and more constant touch with the Emirate administration than an ephemeral mission were disturbed by the evident backsliding. Measures taken in 1952 to try to improve Ahmadu's administration and his personal conduct, by placing him under the surveillance of the traditional Council of Selectors, were unsuccessful. His character proved to be too warped and inflexible to change; his inability to work with his councillors continued; he failed to regain the confidence of responsible people in the Emirate, and matters came to a head in June 1953, with a rowdy, organized demonstration against the Council. Ahmadu abdicated and has since been living at Biu, a little too near to Adamawa for the comfort of the present Lamido and Council.

ALIYU: 1953–

Aliyu Mustafa was recognized as the eleventh Lamido of Adamawa on 26 July 1953, and was installed by His Excellency the Governor in January 1955.[1] He had previously been Supervisor of the Native Authority Police for eight years, having received training with the Nigeria Police Force at Kaduna, Enugu, and Lagos. Remembering a long history of maladministration and corruption, the Council of Selectors insisted on a comprehensive list of conditions before they offered the office to the candidate of their choice. In such a youthful Lamido, much will depend on the soundness of his selection of councillors and on their moral calibre.

GENEALOGICAL TREE OF THE LAMIDOS OF ADAMAWA

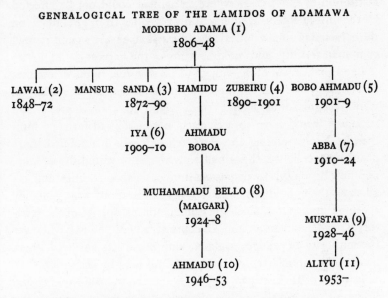

PRE-BRITISH FORMS OF AUTHORITY

The pagans before the Fulani conquest were grouped in tribal kingdoms, of which traces can be found even among tribes where today the largest definable unit is a small group of hamlets. The typical form of such kingdoms was probably a loose confederation of villages, which would become most effective in war. The king might be at once priest and war-chief, though generally there was a tendency to separate these offices. The priest-chief would be the fundamental bond uniting the tribal kingdom: his orders for the times of sowing and harvesting would be accepted, though it

[1] For a very full account see the Hausa pamphlet *Ranar Tabbatad da Lamido*, published by the Northern Region Literacy Agency, Zaria, 1955.

is doubtful whether they could have been enforced except by the sanction of unpopularity whereby the community might ascribe a calamity to the intransigeance of an individual. In regard to crime it is unlikely that any offence was regarded as being the affair of the community as a whole, save perhaps witchcraft among the Kilba, who used to sell their public nuisances to the Fulani as slaves; even homicide would concern the principals and their relatives only. The priest-chief would be required to advise on restitution in those cases where settlement could not be effected by the village elders. He derived his revenues from gifts made on the occasion of such arbitrations, offerings to ensure a good rainfall or human fertility, and the first-fruits of the harvest.

Land tenure would be subject to prescriptive rights of families and villages. Certain groups, for instance among the Marghi, were recognized as having prior claim to certain areas, and strangers would have to seek their permission to farm or hunt therein. Except among the Bata, whose chiefs maintained more positive sovereignty, the tribal lands were not vested in the king, nor had he power to dispossess individuals or families and re-allocate their holdings, though his arbitration was generally accepted in disputes, since the rainfall and prosperity of the territory were dependent on him. In contrast, among the Fali wherever the authority of village headmen and elders has survived, there has been an annual redistribution of land held by the group.

In most of these pagan kingdoms the chieftainship was vested in one or two 'royal' families, descendants of the leader who first brought the tribe into the country and carried with him the sacred emblems of the rain-cult. In some of the older villages the ancestry of the priest-chief has been traced back to pre-Fulani days, as many as ten generations being recalled.

The effect of the Fulani penetration was to dismember these kingdoms. With some the invaders made treaties, others were converted to Islam, while many withdrew to the sanctuary of the hills. In a few cases a Fulani governor of tact and character acquired some personal influence with his pagan subjects, more especially if he had married the daughters of important local chiefs or had himself been born of such a union.

Land tenure under the Fulani was feudal, and all rights were vested in the local chief subject to appeal to the Emir. Barth notes how

... the dominion of the Fulbe is generally centred in single settlements, which are of various descriptions, comprising not only large towns, where a numerous host of these intruders and a powerful chief reside, but also more private settlements, such as country seats of governors, *ribado*; seats of mere petty chiefs or *joro*; farm villages or *uro*; and slave villages or *rumde*.

Pagan lands in the plains were held on a compromise: the Fulani refrained from harrying the farmers on the understanding that the pagans allowed cattle to graze unmolested up to the foot of the hills and in the broader valleys during the dry season. In their own hills pagan lands continued to be held on the old system, modified by the disintegration of the tribal kingdoms; failing the arbitration of the central priest-chief the farm boundaries were now determined by annual war between neighbouring villages, with a subsequent truce as soon as the rains really set in before it was too late for further sowing. Standing crops seem to have been immune from such disputes.

The Fulani village headships were vested in the patriarchal manner, in most cases in families. In slave villages the appointment would be made by the owner. He usually installed a trusted slave or freedman as overseer, whose stewardship might in time become hereditary. The governorships, from which are derived many of the present Districts, fell into three categories: a pagan chief as vassal of the Emir; a lieutenant of Modibbo Adama, or a conquering Fulani chief recognized by the Emir as hereditary ruler; or an Emir's individual nominee for a specific appointment.

The remaining pagans followed their original succession of chiefs in older villages where members of their ruling houses were available, while in newer settlements the founder's family provided the chiefs. In the older communities the five or six principal elders hold hereditary titles, and without their consent the village chief is powerless to act. An office of great importance in the village organization of many pagans, particularly in Northern Adamawa, is that of the smith.

THE DEVELOPMENT OF PRESENT-DAY ADMINISTRATION

In comparison with most of the Northern Provinces the administrative development of Adamawa was retarded, though since the start of the 1946 Ten-Year Development Plan the province can proudly claim a success equal to that of any sister province. There were three specific reasons for this slow start, which must be borne in mind when considering the history of Adamawa. First, the direct set-back caused by the Cameroons campaign of the 1914–18 war; secondly, the diversity of the primitive pagan tribes who make up two-thirds of the province; and thirdly, its inaccessibility, internal as well as external: not till the mid-thirties was Adamawa connected by a would-be all-season road and as late as 1950 the touring centre of Gembu was a minimum of eighteen days' trek away from its Divisional Head-quarters. Even today Yola remains a terminus rather than a junction.

By 1911 the Administration had so far extended its control over the remote tribes of Yola Province that it was possible for the Lamido to tour among them. Various devices for better government had been tried, just as the original Fulani administration had taken different forms in different areas. In 1909 the province was reorganized in five Divisions, designed to suit supervisory touring rather than with regard to political or tribal boundaries—the fifth Division, for instance, contained the heterogeneous population of four districts of Adamawa Emirate and five independent pagan tribes. This unnatural arrangement soon ended, and in 1912 all the pagan tribes within the borders of the emirate were placed in charge of *kalifaen*, or Fulani guardians, who were supposed to act through tribal authorities. This system, too, proved a failure and was abandoned in 1913. The First World War brought new territory and new administrative problems. For a while experiments were made with a Southern Cameroons Division, and then in 1926 came the great reorganization of all the Northern Provinces, from which emerged Adamawa Province.

For the past thirty years the administrative set-up of Adamawa Division has centred on Yola, with a Senior District Officer in charge of the Division, and on touring areas, each with an Assistant District Officer. In the Northern Trust Territory (headquarters Mubi) and the Southern Trust Territory (headquarters Gembu) there has been an A.D.O. for most of the time, but the filling of the Central Districts (headquarters Song or Gombi) and the Belwa-Chamba area (headquarters Jada) has been at the mercy of the fluctuating staff establishment. This administrative policy may be traced to His Honour's minute of 1920 in which he expressed his disapproval of creating separate Divisions within an emirate, since a permanent Divisional Headquarters 'must render the supposed control of the Emir in his Emirate quite illusory'. He therefore urged that in a big straggling emirate like Adamawa there must be 'political officers on tour for months at a time, making their temporary headquarters at convenient centres, but returning regularly to Yola'.

The Lamido's Council has expanded through the years and is now widely representative. It has recently become one of the first Native Authority Councils in the Northern Region to introduce an elected element. The new composition of the Council is thus:

The Lamido.
Three traditional Fulani title-holders: the Waziri, the Galadima, and one Fulani district head nominated from among themselves.
Three traditional non-Fulani title-holders: the Til of Kilba, the Gubo of Yungur, and one Chamba chief nominated from among themselves.
Six Councillors, nominated by the Native Authority.
Six Councillors, elected by the Outer Council from among themselves.
Personal appointments of Alhaji Muhammadu Ribadu, M.B.E., Federal Minister of Mines and Power, and the Native Treasurer.

Since 1953 the Emirate Outer Council, consisting of about 100 elected and nominated members, has met twice a year. At the end of 1955, instruments were published under the Native Authority Law (1954), creating elected Town Councils for Yola, Jimeta, and Mubi, though for some years these councils had been working well on less grandiose lines. District Councils are active, and the more progressive ones are beginning to raise a sort of local rate; Village Councils remain embryonic.

X

HISTORY OF MURI DIVISION

GENERAL

MURI DIVISION today comprises the Emirate of Muri, known earlier as the Hammaruwa kingdom, and the independent pagan district of Zinna. These are the remnants of the old Muri Province which had existed from the British occupation in 1900 down to the reorganization of the Northern Provinces in 1926. At that time the Ibi and Shendam areas were within the jurisdiction of Muri Province.

The Division consists of 11,014 square miles, is almost square in shape and comprises a generous slice of territory on both sides of the River Benue. To the north-east it marches with Numan Division, to the north with the Gombe and Bauchi Divisions of Bauchi Province, to the west momentarily with the Pankshin and at length with the Lowland Divisions of Plateau Province, and to the south with the Wukari Division of Benue Province. The eastern boundary marches with Adamawa Division throughout. The 1952 decennial census gave a population of 260,288, of whom 78 per cent. were pagans and 21 per cent. Muslims. The distribution of this population is very uneven, the density in the predominantly pagan districts of Zinna, Mumuye, and Wurkum greatly exceeding that of the rest of the Division.

HEADQUARTERS

The Emir of Muri rules over the Emirate, which covers the whole of the Division apart from the Zinna District which, under its own chief, is a Native Authority subordinate to the Muri Native Authority. There are ten other districts in the Division, each under a District Head.

The headquarters of the Division is Jalingo (population 4,166), a name derived from the Fulani word for a war-camp, which was Jalingo's origin in the campaigns against the Kona and Mumuye

pagans. Jalingo, however, has not always been the capital of the
Division. From the pre-British days the kingdom of Hammaruwa
was centred on the town of Muri, on the north bank, until 1893
when it was superseded by Jalingo. The Niger Company agent
visited it two years later, and wrote of it:

The camp itself is a settlement of, I should think, 1,000 people, built in
a circle with four gates at the N. S. E. W. aspects respectively. A high
mud wall surrounds the whole place with loopholes for guns about
every two feet . . . Contrary to the usual custom, the houses are not
packed together, each house having a small farm attached, this being in
the event of siege.

In keeping with their policy of penetration by the rivers, the
British made the first headquarters of Muri Province at Ibi, then
transferred it to Gassol in 1903, and again, in 1905, to Amar.
Meanwhile the Muri Divisional Headquarters followed the Emir
of Muri as he moved his court from Lau to Mutum Biu in 1910
and finally to Jalingo in 1917. Lugard noted that, as the Benue
formed the main artery of the province, it was advisable to balance
the administrative posts on its bank with a corresponding station
in the interior; hence Wase formed a would-be hill station for
Amar, Jalingo for Lau, and Wukari for Ibi, these being the three
Divisional Headquarters of the old Muri Province.

THE FULANI CONQUEST

The first aggressive contact of the Fulani with the pagan tribes
of Muri occurred at the end of the eighteenth century, when
Buba Yero of Gombe, anticipating the declaration of the *jihad* by
Usman dan Fodio, conquered the tribes of the Gongola valley.
He ravaged Yungur, Song, and Holma, and defeated the Fali
pagans at Bulmi. Here he received orders from the Sultan of
Sokoto, who, incensed at his general's precipitate campaign,
commanded him to return at once to Gombe; and it was on his
way back that he marched through the country of the Wurkum
tribe.

HAMMAN RUWA: 1817–33

Buba Yero's younger brother, Hamman Ruwa, remained
behind on the western edge of the Wurkum territory, and when

the *jihad* was declared in 1804 he waged war in this area as a general in the army of his brother who had been appointed Emir of Gombe. Buba Yero failed in his ambition to rule the Muri Fulani. By 1817 Hamman Ruwa had overrun the greater part of the present Emirate of Muri, except Wase and Bakundi, and was appointed governor of his conquests. For many years he followed his elder brother and went in his train to do homage at Sokoto.

In 1833 Buba Yero, who was then about eighty, was anxious to secure the succession of his son Koiranga to the Gombe throne. Fearing that the people would choose Hamman Ruwa, the natural heir, he summoned him and his eldest son, Bose, to a conference at Gombe. As soon as they arrived he had them executed on the pretext that they were scheming for the secession of Muri from Gombe. The people of Muri thereupon appealed to the Sultan for their independence, and he gave the deputation a flag to take to Hamman, the eldest surviving son of Hamman Ruwa. Finding popular opinion against him, Hamman retired in favour of his brother Ibrahim.

IBRAHIM: 1833–48

Little is recorded of Ibrahim's reign. About 1836 he became insane for a brief period, during which Hamman acted as regent. In 1848 he again went mad; he was deposed and was succeeded by his elder brother Hamman.

HAMMAN: 1848–61

Hamman's reign was troubled by internal dissensions. Shortly after his election he had to deal with trouble between his son Burba and his nephew Hamadu, the son of the murdered Bose and founder of Gassol town on the banks of the River Taraba. Burba, who had settled near Wurio, accused Hamadu of misappropriating tribute in transit from Donga and Wukari to his father at Muri. The Emir, fearing open warfare, placed the two leaders under arrest in the capital and put garrisons at Wurio and Sendirde under trusted slaves to prevent an outbreak of trouble. Hamadu escaped and returned to Gassol. Two years later the

Emir, during a visit to Sendirde, was attacked and wounded by Hamadu and his followers while riding on the Taraba sands. Burba, who was in the Emir's retinue, asked to be allowed to exact vengeance, but the Emir refused and returned meekly to Muri. Hamadu immediately captured Sendirde, and Burba left his father in dudgeon and re-established himself near Wurio. This weakness over Gassol brought the Emir into disrepute with the Muri Fulani, who accused him of insanity and degeneracy, and of caring only for the pleasures of female company. He was deposed in 1861 and died at Mayo Ranewa.

It was during the first year of Hamman's reign that his slave Kuso attacked and overcame the Jibu stronghold at the junction of the Donga with the Benue. The Jibu fled south to the Wurbo country, where they founded the town of Beli, on the Taraba. About the same time two other slaves, Bula and Aliyu, founded settlements at Ibi and Bantaji, which were thus added to the Emirate; Ibi, dating from 1855, became an advanced post for the *bayin Fulani* or Muri slave bands.

Baikie, who visited Muri during Hamman's reign, has left the following description:

Hammaruwa is a powerful Pulo province, tributary to the Sultan at Sokoto, and considered but little inferior to Adamawa. It comprises a considerable extent of country, on both sides of the river, extending from Kororofa and Bautshi or Baushi to Adamawa. Prior to its occupation by the Fulatas, this country was occupied by various independent races, the Muri being on the north, and several races speaking dialects of Djuku on the south. Different tribes still remain in a state of semi-independence on the confines of Adamawa, and to the eastward along the river, they are all heathens, and are considered very barbarous. Several countries pay annual tribute to Hammaruwa, among which are Wukari, as having been conquered by the brother or uncle of the present Sultan, and Zhibu, as a Pulo dependency. The tribute consists chiefly of slaves, and the amount varies according to the success met with in their annual predatory excursions. In what they look on as a productive year, Wukari sends from thirty-five to forty slaves, carried off mostly from the Mitshis, or from the barbarous natives living beyond Kororofa.

Muri he describes as a large town, measuring two miles by one and a quarter, but carrying a population of only 8,000.

HAMADU: 1861–9

After the deposition of Hamman, the people chose his rival, Hamadu of Gassol, and as the representative of the Sultan of Sokoto was opportunely in Muri at the time, the appointment was ratified without delay. Hamadu lived part of the time in Muri, where his son Umaru Sanda took charge during his absence, and part of the time in Gassol, Sendirde, and Wurio, in each of which he placed a son in command. His cousin and old enemy, Burba, retired southwards and founded Bakundi. The Wurbo pagans were then living in a village built on piles in a lake close to the site of Bakundi, but when this tribe, together with the fugitive Jibu pagans at Beli, agreed to follow Burba, he broke up this village. It is said to have been built about 1800 to protect the Wurbo against raids from the Chamba.

BURBA: 1869–73

On the death of Hamadu, the Sultan of Sokoto directed that Abubakr, a son of Hamman Ruwa, should be appointed Emir, but the people refused to accept him and chose the rebel Burba instead. Burba's first act was the arrest of the three eldest sons of the late Emir, who had come to Muri as claimants to the throne. They escaped and raised the standard of revolt at Gassol and Wurio. Burba himself attacked Gassol, while another force was dispatched under the Kaigama to subdue Wurio. Both enterprises were successful at the time, but four years later Gassol again revolted and before Burba could organize a punitive expedition he became insane and was deposed. He later recovered his sanity and returned to his old home at Bakundi, where he remained as an independent ruler, paying tribute direct to Sokoto, till his death in 1892.

ABUBAKR: 1873

Burba was succeeded by Abubakr, the original nominee of Sokoto. He died within seven months of his appointment and was succeeded by his son.

MUHAMMADU NYA: 1874-96

Muhammadu Nya, an able and energetic Emir, first established friendly relations with Burba at Bakundi; both parties agreed to live in amity and to combine, if necessary, against the house of Hamadu. Thus secure against Gassol, the Emir set about extending his dominions. He undertook no less than four campaigns against the Tiv, penetrating as far as Katsina Ala, which he sacked and burned. He found himself unable to hold his Tiv conquests and withdrew his garrisons.

The next campaign was against the Jukun stronghold of Kona. The original Jukun settlement of Kuro, some 5 miles north of modern Kona, had been sacked by Hamman Ruwa, and when smallpox followed on this catastrophe the Jukun left and built Kona under their chief Agungwa. They paid tribute to Muri in the shape of slaves, food, and labour. During Nya's reign the Jukun slaves managed to escape. They assembled at Zonko, a town about 16 miles south of Jalingo, today in ruins. Nya collected his army, crossed the Benue, and camped at Hosere Bolere, to the south-west of what is now Jalingo. Meanwhile Agungwa gathered a force of Bachama and Mumuye pagans and placed this reinforced Kona contingent under a Demsa Bachama named Panabuguri. This general, before setting out for the attack on Zonko, swore a vinic oath, with his head bowed to the earth in homage to the chief of Kona, that he would bring in the Emir of Muri dead or alive.

The pagan force fell on the Fulani camp, but much of their ferocious energy was dissipated in shooting at each other from the opposite directions of attack, so that the Muri troops were able to escape with only a few casualties. The Emir rallied his men and cornered the jubilant pagans in a marsh, where many were slain, among them Panabuguri. A younger brother of Agungwa, named Dau, declared that he would seize the Emir dead or alive and thereby prove the superiority of a Jukun over a Bachama oath. He charged the Emir's party, threw two spears at Nya, but missed him. The Emir, on learning that this was the brother of the Kona chief, drew his sword, cut his horse's tethering rope, set his horse at Dau, drove him back into the bog, and dispatched him with a spear.

This war with the Kona pagans continued for the next four years, until Agungwa sent his messenger, Fokuru, to the Sultan of Sokoto with a promise to follow the Emir of Muri and to pay an annual tribute of 100 slaves. In 1892 Agungwa's successor, Yinu, led another uprising, which the Emir put down with the assistance of the adventurer Mizon, breaking the town with the French cannon. From this war-camp at Jalingo the Emir later undertook a number of raids against the Mumuye plains settlements, but he made little impression on their hill villages.

Mockler-Ferryman has recorded how, after Burba had reconciled himself with Sokoto,

. . . a few years later Nya, in his turn, offended, and the Sultan of Sokotu, wishing to reinstate Barba as Emir of Muri, summoned him to repair to Sokotu. Barba, however declined, saying that, having been wrongly deposed, he refused to be at the beck and call of Sokotu. The Sultan thereupon ordered Nya to appear before him at his capital so that he might publicly reprimand him; but Nya openly defied him, knowing well that the distance was too great for him to suffer at the hands of the suzerain and, if the worst came to the worst, he could claim the protection of the Royal Niger Company, with whom he had contracted an offensive and defensive alliance.

It was during Muhammadu Nya's reign that the Royal Niger Company first appeared on the Muri scene; their relations with the Emirate have already been outlined.[1]

HASSAN: 1897–1903

On the death of Muhammadu Nya his son Hassan returned to Jalingo from Mutum Biu, where he had settled in 1895 after his defeat at Yola Mbodewa when Nya had sought to make him Yerima of Gassol. Though his father had supplied him with rifles and about fifty cartridges, the Gassol army had waited till all the cartridges had been exuberantly fired off and then they advanced on the town and forced Hassan back to Mutum Biu. It is said that his younger brother, Muhammadu (Hamman) Mafindi, had refused to be nominated, probably because of his exiguous follow-

[1] See Chapter IV.

ing. However, emboldened by a delay in the Sultan's recognition
of his brother, Muhammadu Mafindi joined forces with Abubakr
of Wurio in an attempt to seize the power and divide the kingdom.
The Emir scattered their armies at Wuzu, the port of Muri.

A report from L. H. Moseley, the Royal Niger Company agent
on the Upper Benue at this period, reveals the delicate position
of Hassan:

The Emir's messengers have arrived here with the following message—
Sokoto messengers have arrived, Al Hassan Emir of Muri is the only
man recognised by Sokoto. He is to call all his followers, viz. Gassol,
Wurio, Sendirde, Bakundi, etc., and to publicly read this letter to them.
Those who refuse to recognise him he is to punish with the aid of the
Sarikin Fada of Sokoto . . . Wurio also sent to say Sokoto had sent a
friendly message to him. This, however, was a mere salutation and, I
think, intended to smooth matters in face of the Muri letter. Wurio
considers he is the proper person to be Emir of Muri and his present
feeling towards Hassan is very bitter . . . Hassan has not at present
quite the authority his father had, and is considerably troubled by his
brother, now Yerima.

He goes on to add:

It is worthy of record that this Emir Hassan on more than one occasion
—in 1896 and 1900—in circumstances of the basest treachery, made
successful enslaving scoops of those of the Kona people who had preferred to live in exile after the reduction of their town by Mizon and of
some of the Mumuye who followed them.

Hassan died at Jalingo in 1903, shortly before the High Commissioner approved his deposition for slave dealing.

MUHAMMADU MAFINDI: 1903-53

After his defeat at Muzu in 1897, Muhammadu Mafindi took
refuge with Abubakr in Wurio until 1899, when the Royal Niger
Company put him to flight after a company of troops entered
Wurio in order to arrest the two leaders, who were suspected of
aggravating the tension between the Emir and the Taraba chiefs.
Travelling through Bakundi and the Dakka country, Muhammadu
Mafindi arrived at Zubeiru's court at Yola and offered his services.
He was given Mayo Belwa as his residence, to control the Mumuye

with whom he had considerable influence. (It may be added here, in parenthesis, that when Muhammadu Mafindi died in 1953, the Mumuye spoke of the passing of their *babban dodo*.) After the fall of Zubeiru in 1901, Muhammadu Mafindi was the first to tender his submission and, continuing to play his cards well, he later escorted Dr. Cargill and Captain Ruxton through the Mumuye country to Jalingo, where a truce was patched up between him and his brother the Emir. It was agreed that Muhammadu Mafindi should henceforth live at Bamga, in Yola Province.

Immediately on hearing of his brother's death, Muhammadu Mafindi hurried to Jalingo. Tradition has it that for three days he sat in silent prayer in the middle of the mosque, conspicuous to all but conversing with none, until the Council of Selectors became so anxious about the meaning of this unusual behaviour that they elected him Emir. Muhammadu Mafindi informed the Resident that he had seized the throne, and a fortnight later he was installed at Lau.

The reign of Muhammadu Mafindi is one of the most remarkable among those of any emirs in the Northern Region, and it was amid widespread rejoicing that in 1953 this grand old gentleman completed his golden jubilee, only a few months, alas, before his death at the age of eighty-four. Spanning thus the whole lifetime of modern Northern Nigeria, the Emir inevitably felt towards the end that events were moving faster than he would have liked. He was created a C.B.E. in 1931 and in 1946 was awarded the C.M.G. for his notable services.

MUHAMMADU TUKUR: 1953–

District Head of Jalingo Habe District since 1912 and of Wurkum District since its inception, this younger—in such a longeval family the term can only be relative—brother of Muhammadu Mafindi was chosen by the Council of Selectors after a lengthy and thorough deliberation. The death of his predecessor marked the end of an age and it now became possible to introduce into the Emirate certain reforms and development projects which it would have been indelicate to have urged during the closing years of Muhammadu Mafindi's reign.

GENEALOGICAL TREE OF THE EMIRS OF MURI

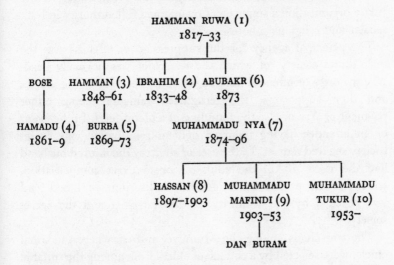

HAMMAN RUWA (1)
1817–33

BOSE   HAMMAN (3)   IBRAHIM (2)   ABUBAKR (6)
        1848–61   1833–48   1873

HAMADU (4)   BURBA (5)   MUHAMMADU NYA (7)
1861–9   1869–73   1874–96

HASSAN (8)   MUHAMMADU   MUHAMMADU
1897–1903   MAFINDI (9)   TUKUR (10)
                1903–53   1953–

DAN BURAM

PRE-BRITISH FORMS OF AUTHORITY

It seems clear that before the Fulani conquest Jukun influence was widespread, and even the Mumuye and Chamba units were largely influenced by the Jukun organization, though many groups, such as the Mumuye and Wurkum, retained a much looser form of government. Land was held by local groups, not by individuals, but in some tribes the authority of the group was concentrated in the local chief, who would be responsible for the allocation of farm-lands to adult males.

Among the Mumuye there appears to have been an early division of the two aspects of a chiefly presence. This cleavage separates the offices of priest-chief and war-chief. The former has no executive power and is concerned principally with the rain-cult. The latter is the executive authority, though he retains certain religious functions, especially those associated with the *dodo* activities of men's secret societies and youths' initiation rites, the maintenance of which was essential to the discharge of his primary duties as secular and war-chief.

In the Chamba-influenced group the war-chief was not so

clearly separated from the priest; if there was a divided authority, the war-leader remained the deputy of the fetish-chief. In the Jukun organization a single chief maintained full authority in both secular and religious spheres.

The principal agency for the suppression of offences was the male secret society, of which the war-chief was normally head. The majority of offences were regarded as personal to the parties and their supporters, the recognized remedies being either payment of *diya* or else the founding of a blood-feud. In the event of an offender having incurred general reprobation, the secret society secured redress. In the case of adultery the injured husband had the right to kill the adulterer or to exact compensation, whichever he preferred. In general, indiscriminate blood-feud was checked by the authority of the war-chief and the secret society.

The war-chiefs among the Mumuye, and elsewhere the tribal chiefs, were selected by a council of elders from among the suitable male members of the royal family, and succession was patrilineal. The choice of rain-makers and purely religious heads depended more on the wishes of the previous incumbent, who alone was capable of initiating a future successor into his mystic art—the Mumuye rain-making cult, for instance, has descended from father to son for many generations. Nevertheless, the formal approval of the assembled minor priest-chiefs of the villages was necessary before a new rain-maker could assume office, an approval secured only on his passing severe tests to probe his knowledge of the ritual.

Under the Fulani the tribal organization of the southern kingdoms persisted, though Kororofa had in fact been broken up before the arrival of the Fulani and Kona remained as the sole survival of the old Jukun empire. Naturally, such tolerance was subject to the payment of tribute from the tribes which had come to terms; for those who had not, raiding was inevitable. The Fulani did not aim at 'administration', in our sense of the word, among these tribes, for they found the coherence of tribal organization and the spread of Islam incompatible. In the areas in which the Fulani power was firmly established, such as Muri, Jalingo,

Mutum Biu, Bakundi, and Gassol, there were alkalis' courts administering the Maliki code.

Up to the time of the British occupation the organization of the Fulani was above all military, perhaps not so very different from the feudal system obtaining in England in the period immediately following the Norman conquest. This was due not only to the wars waged by successive emirs against the pagans but also to their struggles against rebellious relatives. The inhabitants of the principal towns lived on the proceeds of their raids and left agriculture to the slaves; cattle was their main peaceful interest. Their settlements were widely scattered and there was plenty of farm-land available.

THE DEVELOPMENT OF PRESENT-DAY ADMINISTRATION

The evolution of Muri Division's administrative set-up must first of all be studied in its proper context, that of the former Muri Province, which retained much of the original form of the temporary Upper Benue Province of 1900. On the reorganization of the provinces of the Protectorate, the Muri Emirate became part of the Province of that name, though all claims to suzerainty west of the Donga were definitely disallowed and Bakundi, Gassol, and Wurio were treated as independent units. By 1904 Muri Province consisted of three Divisions: Lau, which was co-extensive with the Emirate and was renamed Muri Division in 1915; Amar, which was absorbed into Ibi Division in 1910 when the station was abandoned; and Ibi, which after the First World War was split into two, the Ibi and Shendam Divisions.

Though the history of these last two Divisions now rightly belongs to that of Benue and Plateau Provinces, mention should be made in passing of two events. One was the Mahdi rising of 1916 in the Donga District of Ibi Division, when a pagan of Nukko, called *Mairigan Karfi* or the 'invulnerable one', raided the surrounding villages and eventually attacked the town of Donga. He was wounded when quite close to it and retired. The Resident, J. M. Fremantle, followed him up with twenty police and captured him, thus scotching what might have developed into a serious rising. He was convicted on a charge of murder and executed at

Nukko in 1917. The other incident concerns the wild Montol
pagans of Shendam Division, a cannibal tribe against whom
numerous punitive patrols were undertaken throughout the first
decade of the century. In 1916 the Montols suddenly attacked and
killed F. E. Maltby, A.D.O., and his unarmed party, among whom
were several chiefs of neighbouring friendly tribes.

To turn to the history of the present Muri Division, Bakundi
and Gassol were incorporated in the Emirate in 1907 and two years
later Wurio resumed its old allegiance. The Mumuye country,
which had been first traversed by G. N. Barclay, with a patrol
under Captain Baker, from Yola in 1901-2, was 'opened up' in
1909, and in 1914 was merged with Kona District and absorbed
into the Emirate, though for some years there was a large number
of patrols in the Zinna and Yakoko areas. Zinna, whose chief was
murdered at Sensidong in 1932, became a subordinate Native
Authority in 1947. The Wurkum tribes, who had defeated the
Muri Fulani at Gwonu in about 1850, also required several patrols
before district administration could be extended to them in 1914.

In the same period further changes were initiated which have
moulded the present administrative organization. The original
districts of Jalingo Fulbe and Jalingo Habe were administered
by the Emir himself until he moved to Mutum Biu in 1910. In
1916 Jalingo Habe was added to the Balassa and Gwamu sections
to form Wurkum District, and three years later Jalingo Fulbe
District was split up by incorporating the western portion as far
as the Mayo Ranewa into Mutum Biu District, creating Lau
District out of the north-eastern area, and leaving the rest to
become the new Jalingo District under the Emir's eldest son,
Muhammadu, with the title of Dan Buram. In 1913 the Sansanni
District of Ibi Division was transferred to Muri and put under
Gassol District, while the Kam District along the Cameroons
border was brought under Bakundi District in 1914.

Wase, transferred to Adamawa from Plateau Province in 1926
as an independent emirate, was incorporated into Muri Emirate in
1928 upon the conviction of its chief for tax embezzlement. It was
returned to Plateau Province in 1946. Reference has been made
earlier to other temporary changes in the Divisional administration

consequent on the capture of the German Cameroons,[1] to the 1926 dismemberment of Muri Province,[2] and to the excision of Gashaka in 1924.[3] The southern half of the Zinna and Mumuye Districts remained a declared unsettled area until 1954.

Divisional Headquarters, which have remained at Jalingo since 1917 despite the fact that the nearest telegraph office is 32 miles away at Lau, consist normally of the Divisional Officer with one A.D.O., who during the years before the Second World War was posted primarily for touring among the Mumuye; since the Karim Lamido riot of 1954 the emphasis has shifted to the Wurkum area.

The Emir's Council, in which is included the paramount chief of Zinna, follows the novel pattern of Advisory Councils, and its composition is still in the process of expansion. There has been an Outer Council since 1953, and District Councils function satisfactorily.

[1] Chapter VIB.   Chapter VIII.   [3] Chapter VIB.

XI

HISTORY OF NUMAN DIVISION

GENERAL

NUMAN DIVISION, the only non-emirate division in Adamawa Province, has emerged from a congeries of independent pagan districts which were administered, with divers additions and excisions, sometimes as a Division and sometimes as a district of the old Yola Province. Though the title of Numan Division dates from 1912, its modern formation did not properly crystallize until the 1926 reorganization of the Northern Provinces.

The Division consists of 2,214 square miles, centred upon the confluence of the Benue and Gongola rivers, and carries a population estimated at 121,438 during the 1952 decennial census. In the area south of the Benue the divisional boundary marches with Adamawa Division; north of the Benue, the boundary to the east again runs with that of Adamawa, then as it curves westwards it merges into the lower Hawal valley to form a narrow enclave abutting on the Biu Division of Bornu Province, and finally drops back to the Benue, with its western frontier fringing the Gombe Division of Bauchi Province and Muri Division.

The competence, industry, and intelligence of the Bachama and Bata who make up about half the population; their longer and closer contact with European sophistication; the monopoly by the Sudan United Mission of the Division's educational and medical activities till the last decade and its consequent influence; the smallness of the area that has allowed of closer administrative supervision during the formative years—these have all combined to provide an educated, efficient, and self-reliant Native Administration which has earned its people the respected title, shared with the Tiv of Benue Province, of the Ibos of the North. The mission influence has always been strong in Numan Division—for instance, even in 1955 all medical work was in their hands and there was no

N.A. dispensary—and the Christians total over 12 per cent. of the population, while Muslims account for less than a quarter.

HEADQUARTERS

The Numan Federation of paramount chiefs has its new Native Administration offices at Numan. The town was originally an important wooding station of the Royal Niger Company and later a hulk was stationed offshore. In 1903 a small force of troops was based permanently on Numan and thereby founded the modern administrative headquarters. This was extended in 1913 when the Bachama evacuated the present Government Residential Area and moved to the new town a mile to the west. In 1921 it superseded Lamurde as the District Headquarters of Bachama District when Mbi, defying all taboos, crossed the Benue and built his palace there. Its present population is 7,198. Numan has remained a busy shipping centre for the Benue commercial fleets.

BATA AND BACHAMA

The Bata and Bachama are subdivisions of a single tribe. According to one tradition, they were driven out from the neighbourhood of Sokoto by mounted invaders. Another account relates that the tribe once lived in Gobir until a dispute about precedence arose between the daughter of their chief, Jaro Falami, and the daughter of the chief of Gobir, and in consequence they left Gobir and migrated by way of Zim and Maifoni to the region of Garua.

It has been established that after the fall of the Jukun empire the Bata invaded the Benue valley from the Mandara highlands. Some of them turned west and founded the Jira settlements of Song, Malabu, and Zummo, others headed south and founded Demsa Poa near the original site of Garua. When the Fulani drove them from their capital in about 1810, the Bata royal family fled westwards, and despite stands at Dasin, Dogire (the site of Yola station), Ngurore, and Mayo Wono, were eventually forced to establish themselves in a backwater of the Benue, where they founded Demsa Mosu. From here they spread as far as Numan, whence they ejected the Jenjo, and to the south over the Mayo Ine and Mayo Belwa deltas.

Not long after the foundation of the new Demsa the division of the tribe took place (see above, p. 17). The following is the story of the rupture, as told by one of the most famous Bachama chiefs, Hamma Mbi:

The first chief of Bachama and the chief of Demsa were brothers, of the same father and mother; both of them were children of Taginaya. They were Degbiri, also called Atingno Jejumse (Lord of the Seat of Power) or Bitti Paromo (white) from Lamurde, and Pani, also called Jaro (black), from Demsa. They were parted thus: A slave of Demsa sought a slave of Lamurde. Lamurde said, 'This is not to be borne', and he killed the slave. Then Demsa said, 'If I leave my brother unchecked he will one day supplant me.' Then he proposed a hunt, and gave orders to the men that during the hunt they should kill Degbiri. But his younger sister, Borobittikin, overheard his talk and warned Lamurde, saying, 'Do not go hunting, for our brother intends to kill you. Let us escape across the Benue.' Then Demsa went hunting, and Lamurde and Borobittikin entered the chief's house and took away the royal ornaments, the elephant-tusk horns and the sacred emblems, and escaped over the Benue. Demsa followed them but they were already on the other side. Then Demsa cried, 'Go your ways,' and he cast his turban out over the water to Lamurde, saying, 'We have parted, for if I were to come and drink of the water of the Benue I must surely die.' But Lamurde said, 'If I wish I will come and drink the water of the Benue, and I will cross it. You, Demsa, depart, and henceforth hold only Demsa; continue to steal the cattle of the Fulani, for that is the limit of your power.' So Lamurde took all and left Demsa with nothing but Demsa.

The Demsa narrators naturally prefer another conclusion:

Demsa cast his turban across the river and Atingno caught it. Then Demsa drew his knife and severed the turban, saying, 'Henceforth you must dwell on the north bank and I on the south bank, neither of us must look on the other's face nor on the River Benue. Your part shall be to sit at home, slave of the shrines; mine shall be the hunt and the battle and war against our Fulani foes.'

There is a supplementary tradition that when Atingno was crossing the Benue he dropped the sacred pot of the rain-cult, and that this pot was later recovered and taken to the shrine of Nzeanzo at Farei, a village half-way between Numan and Demsa. In reward for her services to Atingno, Borobittikin was made chief of the village of Dimuso, since when this village head has traditionally been appointed from among the female relatives of the chief of Bachama.

During the 1850's a Bata called Maikwada from Jungum, southeast of Gurin, founded a rival kingdom at Numan. He defeated the Yola Fulani at Billi, in which battle he captured Gachekon, one of Lamido Lawal's concubines, who carried with her charms given to Lawal by the Sultan of Sokoto. It was during Maikwada's reign that Baikie reached Jen, and it is said that Maikwada hurried thither in order to enlist the European's help against the Fulani; but Baikie had not tarried at Jen.[1] Maikwada died in a fight with the Waka, who up to a few years ago still preserved his head; his body is buried in Numan.

The following is a list of the Bata and Bachama chiefs since the secession:

Bata	Bachama
Palangye (founded new Demsa)	Bittiparomo (founded Lamurde)
Tiluke	Sunganukuda
Gwe Gwe (1856)	Nzelbamato
Tara	Gamsa (1853)
Samba	Mangawa (1874)
Kauyang	Bagwism (1891)
Panti	Njeldumso (1900)
Jomoi (pensioned 1921)	Jero (killed by police in 1910 revolt)
Teneke (deposed 1934)	Pafratso (deposed 1921)
Jalo (died 1955)	Mbi (moved from Lamurde to Numan, 1921; died in Yola hospital, 1941)
Enoch Swade (1955)	Ngbale (1942)

MBULA

Their tradition is that the god Nzeanzo[2] brought them down the Benue in an iron canoe, together with the Bata and Tikar tribes. Another legend claims that they stem from the area of Rei or Ngaundere. A third version derives them from Mundang, and a fourth from Mboi near Song. The last-named, which tells how

[1] See Chapter III. [2] See Appendix D.

the Mbula travelled overland to their present home by way of
Tambo in Girei District, accords with the traditions of their
Yungur and Njirai neighbours who say that they drove the Mbula
south-west with their own advance.

With the permission of the Bata, the Mbula settled on their
present lands. After the break in the Bata tribe, the section of the
Mbula which lived on the south bank of the Benue was in nominal
subjection to Demsa, and that living on the north bank to Bachama.
The most important dignitary in the tribe was originally the priest
of the cult at Bwozo, who, though venerated by all groups, cannot
be described as a tribal priest-chief since he exercised no positive
control outside his own village. The tribe did not recognize even
nominal subordination to the secular authority of a single chief
till 1896, in which year the Royal Niger Company's agent engaged
Safam, village head of Mbula, to be purveyor of fuel to the
Company and gave him a letter of appointment; from this distinction, interpreted as a warranty of the Company's support,
Safam gradually extended his influence over the tribe.

The following is an account by a chief of Mbula of their
conflict with the Fulani:

We men of Mbula once had a war with the King of Yola, Muhammadu
Lawal; the reason of it was this. It was our custom to go against the
Fulani of Mayo Belwa to drive off their cattle and take them back to
Mbula that we might have meat. One day these Fulani made complaint
of us to the King of Yola, who said to them: 'If you hear that the heathen
of Mbula are coming to attack you, then send the word of it that I may
come and help you.' They answered that it was good. Now at that time
a certain Mbula man called Geno Chidaya went to Yola country, and
near Namtari fell in with a Fulani, who captured Geno and brought him
to the King of Yola. The king said, 'Geno, Geno, is it you that God has
brought hither?' And Geno said, 'Yes, it is I, O King.' Then Muhammadu
Lawal said, 'Geno, what is your expectation?' And Geno answered, 'I
know that you will kill me.' But Muhammadu Lawal said, 'I will not
kill you, you shall go back to Mbula.' And he brought gowns and gave
them to Geno and other gifts besides, and he said, 'I desire that we
make a covenant, Geno. When you hear that Mboima, Chief of Mbula,
is preparing war against the Fulani, you are to send word of it to me.'
Geno answered, 'Very good,' and he went home to Mbula, where he
became Muhammadu Lawal's spy. Now one day Mboima brewed beer

and assembled his people and said to them, 'Let us drink this beer, and then we will go up against the Fulani.' They answered that it was good. This was in the year 1870. On the day that we went out to war Geno sent word to Muhammadu Lawal. Then Muhammadu Lawal set forth with his men; he left Yola two hours after noon and he camped at the river Mayo Ine. On our side the war captains were three: Mai-Kwada, Mboima and Faneitako, of whom you would say 'they are the begetters of war'. Now Muhammadu Lawal set forth from the river Mayo Ine after dark and travelled all night to Chukkol of Mayo Belwa. There we came upon him and did battle with the Fulani for two days. And in that battle Mai-Kwada and Mboima escaped death but narrowly at the hands of the men of Yola.

The following is a list of the chiefs of Mbula:

Boima (1894)

Safam, 'Mai-Takarda' (1896)

Lena (deposed 1918)

Isa (deposed 1928)

Usmanu (resigned 1943)

Kwaston (1944)

Biyapo (1944)

KANAKURU AND LONGUDA

The proper name for the tribe occupying the eastern slope of the Ga'anda valley is Dera, but these people are more commonly known by the nickname of Kanakuru, which derives from the first Hausa traders who came into contact with the Dera and heard their morning salutation of *kanakuru kanadingding*. Of the three subdivisions of the tribe, the Dera and Jera are mainly centred round Shani and Gasi in Bornu Province, while the Shellen group predominates in the Numan district of that name. This section settled first at Mada, but as a result of friction with their Shani kinsmen they moved south to the region of Kanakuru on the west bank of the Gongola, while a few of them crossed the river and established themselves among the Binna of Yungur District.

The following is a list of the chiefs of Shellen, whose hereditary title is *Amna*:

Lumbu (founded Lakumna)

Mollubi (1804)

Tungadera (founded Shellen *c.* 1844)

Kupta

Samboina

Jauwan

Mijibona (1909)

Jomun (1924, resigned 1941)

Halilu (deposed 1950)

Jangbarata (died 1955)

Isa (1955)

At some time during the eighteenth century, after the founding of Lakumna, the Longuda tribe, which had lived on and around the western escarpment, began to penetrate into the plains, and with the permission of the Kanakuru settled first around a low hill a few miles north-west of Lakumna. This new colony was called Gweo, later Guyuk, and has remained the political centre of the plains Longuda, in opposition to the spiritual influence of Dukul, the escarpment village of the hereditary rain-cult. From Guyuk they spread over the whole plain and eventually ousted the Kanakuru, who retired across the Gongola and established their headquarters at Shellen, directly opposite Lakumna.

About the turn of the eighteenth century Buba Yero, first Emir of Gombe, invaded the Gongola valley. The Longuda tradition is that they themselves were the main object of attack; that Buba Yero, whose mother was a Kanakuru, enlisted the services of his pagan cousins against the Longuda towns of Bobini and Mada; that though he sacked them both he suffered heavy losses, and that he finally turned upon his allies, whom he accused of lukewarm support, and drove them out of their town of Lakumna. Tradition adds that the Longuda prepared an ambush for the Fulani army at Kombo as they were retiring on Gombe but that Buba Yero successfully evaded it.

While there is little historical evidence to support this, it is certain that Buba did attack the Kanakuru. He was unsuccessful in 1792, but in 1798 he overran the whole of the Gongola valley south of Nafada, and it was on this occasion that Bobini and Mada were sacked. Whatever part was actually played by the Longuda in these campaigns, they were never again molested by the Fulani. Furthermore, they escaped the attack made on Shellen by a Bornu force in 1888, and for the first two decades of the British occupation they so maintained their reputation for intractability that as late as 1924 an official publication was describing them as

a wild timid people, who have the power of summoning death to their release by apparently being able to die if they will themselves to do so, and have therefore never been enslaved . . . The men are cannibals and eat their own dead, besides murdering strangers for meat. Their weapons are bows and arrows, spears, and slings with which they have an effective range at a distance of from 250–300 yards.

The rain-priest of Dukul exercised considerable spiritual influence over the Longuda and could impose fines for a breach of morality throughout the tribe; he was also consulted about the auspices of undertaking war. Amongst the secular village leaders the chief of Guyuk was regarded as senior and he acted as the mouthpiece of the Dukul rain-maker amongst the plains Longuda. The special influence of Guyuk persisted after that village had entered into friendly relations with Shellen and had adopted the Kanakuru system of chieftainship. A settlement was achieved in 1929, when the northern section of the tribe was reorganized into two groups under Dukul and Guyuk respectively, subject to the chief of Shellen. At the same time the spiritual supremacy of Dukul over the whole tribe was officially recognized.

The Longuda continued to respect the superior culture of the Kanakuru in spite of having dispossessed them of their territory on the west bank. During the nineteenth century there was extensive intermarriage, and by the end of that period a member of the Shellen ruling family, usually the heir apparent, regularly held the headship of Guyuk. It seems probable that much of the respect felt for the Shellen dynasty by the plains Longuda was due to their admiration for the unusual office of central war-chief, hereditary, secular, and magico-religious, a phenomenon unknown to the Longuda tribe.

LALA

This name is applied to a number of clans inhabiting the high tableland in the angle of the Hawal and Gongola rivers. Their origin is obscure, but they appear to have adopted the Jukun *tsafi* and to have acted as intermediaries between Wukari and Biu; the annual present from Biu was forwarded by the Lala, with their own, to Bachama, who sent both on to Wukari. The Lala, though attacked by the Gombe Fulani and nominally part of the Song governorate, were never overcome by the Fulani, and Lamido Sanda's later invasion was reduced to a rout.

PIRI

The Piri, who are probably related to the Tangale tribes, inhabit the hills north of Lamurde. They long enjoyed the reputation of cannibals, and in 1906 invited the white man to visit them in order to see how his flesh tasted. A resettlement scheme was started among them in 1951. Their hilltop village of Pwa is still finely walled and boasts a remarkable cave.

With the Libu, the Lala and Piri tribes have remained a shy and retiring people.

KIRI

This area contains both the remnants of the western Kanakuru and the old settlement of the Kiti'en Fulani who have remained unconverted to Islam.

PRE-BRITISH FORMS OF AUTHORITY

Before the advent of the British, two-thirds of what is now Numan Division were controlled by the tribal kingdoms of Bachama, Bata, and Shellen, while among the remainder—the Mbula, Longuda, Piri, and Lala—there was no secular authority higher than the village headman. The organization of the three kingdoms was very similar: the chief's government exercised authority for the purposes of war and fertility magic, but interfered very little in village affairs except in cases of homicide or disputes too serious for the local headman to adjust.

Among the Bachama, the most highly organized of the three, the headmen of many important villages were members of the king's family or court. In addition to its civil head, each village also had a *kasalla* or war-leader, to whom the king sent direct when he wished to raise a military levy.

The chief's revenue was derived from tribute paid in gowns, goats, grain, and fish by his Bachama villages and in cattle by the nomadic Fulani. He was also entitled to a share of the meat of all large animals killed within his tribal territory, and a special official was responsible for collecting this royal perquisite. All fishing rights were vested in the chief, who would lease them to individuals or groups on surrender of half the gross catch. The penalty for homicide was decapitation; if a murderer found sanctuary at one of two special shrines, he could leave it with impunity after ten days, but he was thenceforward reckoned as a slave of the cult, and should he fail to make regular votive offerings he would be executed. The duty of vengeance rested with the uterine relatives of the deceased, primarily with the sister's son who, if the murderer himself was not available, would endeavour to kill one of his family, preferably on the sister's side.

Minor crimes which the local chief and elders had been unable to settle were referred to the priests of the tribal cults. Witchcraft was punishable with death and all the uterine relatives of the accused—except the children, unless the witch were a woman— were sold into slavery and their property was confiscated. Land was vested in the chief, who delegated his authority to his local chiefs. If a farm was deserted for more than a year it reverted to the chief for reallocation, and the man to whom a farm was so reallotted would make a nominal present to the chief. The chiefs of Bachama were selected from among the suitable members of the royal family by a certain lineage which resided at the village of Hadio.

In Demsa and Shellen conditions were similar to those in Bachama, but less formalized: Demsa's village organization was never really stable because of its constant war with the Fulani, while Shellen, with its farm settlements thinly scattered through the Gongola bush, lacked the compactness of the Bachama villages built along the Benue banks. The rule of the Shellen chiefs seems to have been more directly patriarchal, if less developed, than that of the Bachama, and the royal prerogatives in regard to land tenure were very emphatic.

Among the Mbula, conditions were different owing to the lack of tribal chiefs with secular powers, and the villages remained mutually independent. Homicide was normally followed by a vendetta, and witchcraft alone was regarded as the affair of the whole community, the punishment being burning in a bundle of roof-thatch.

The succession to the headship of the river villages was normally hereditary. Inland among the Libu a different system prevailed, where the chief was also rain-maker and where the office of king-maker survived. Failure to produce adequate rain entailed a fine of one cow, which was eaten by the people. In 1928 a chief of Libu was so fined, but retired from office rather than pay; in consequence the village was greatly distressed in the following year by the lack of a genuine rain-maker chief and when the new farming season began they agreed to waive the fine. The chief was induced to resume office, for apparently nobody else could fill his place while he was still alive.

The Longuda had a more elaborate tribal organization, though they never had a central secular chief. The chief of Guyuk had no personal authority outside his own village, for the spiritual headship was vested in the priest-chief of Dukul. In addition to the powers of arbitration normally held by priest-chiefs, the Dukul rain-maker also exercised supervision over morals. This discipline he could tighten by the appointment of a temporary official, known as *kwandarite*, to any village that had lapsed into laxity. The duty of this moral censor promoted him above the village head during his two years of office, and he was empowered to inflict fines for both public and private offences, particularly theft and wife-beating. At the end of his term, the fines were taken to Dukul, where the priest-chief divided them into three portions: one for the *kwandarite*, one for the village concerned, and one for himself. The office of censor was then suspended until the conduct of the village should again require special correction.

The Longuda customs in regard to offences against persons and property showed a considerable development of social conscience. In the case of homicide the procedure combined the kindred ideas of blood vengeance and compensation with a third and more advanced idea, that of reconciliation for the benefit of the community. The murderer had at once to go into exile. Meanwhile the head of his family sent apologies and ceremonial gifts of nominal value to the chief of the dead man's local group, requesting him to act as intermediary with the matrilineal relatives of the deceased. These men relieved their feelings by a formal raid on the murderer's group, who would offer no resistance even when their property was seized. Later the deceased's family might accept substantial compensation in live-stock and eventually become so far reconciled as to agree to the return of the homicide from exile.

Chárges of witchcraft were determined by reference to one or other of two shrines both outside Longuda territory. If the accused was found to be innocent, he was entitled to damages from his traducer; if he was declared guilty, his punishment was complete ostracism.

THE DEVELOPMENT OF PRESENT-DAY ADMINISTRATION

In 1901 patrols were sent from Yola to clear the roads on both banks of the Benue which had been closed by the Bachama below Numan, and in the following year heavy opposition was met at Banjiram when a military force tried to open up the Gongola valley. On their way back from Kwa the force was met near Numan by Jaro, son of the recalcitrant Bachama chief, Njeldumso. Jaro offered to displace his father and to rule the Bachama in accordance with the wishes of Government. His offer was accepted, but in 1903 Njeldumso, despite his age and blindness, raised the Bachama and ousted his son; the force sent to deal with this rebellion marked the beginning of administrative headquarters in this area.

For the first few years Numan was the headquarters of the Independent Pagan Division of Yola Province. It lost Waja, Tangale, Longuda, and Piri Districts to Bauchi Province and Bura District to Bornu Province in 1907, and in 1908 it changed its title when Yola Province split into three Divisions: South Benue (headquarters Yola), North Benue (headquarters Pella), and Gongola Division (headquarters Numan). A year later there was a further reorganization of Yola into five Divisions, among which Number IV Division comprised Lala, Yungur, and Shellen Districts with headquarters at Gudu and Shellen, and Number V Division combined the Fulani districts of Mayo Faran and Mayo Belwa with the pagan districts of Bachama, Mbula, Bata, Waka, Yakoko, Mumuye, and Chamba, with headquarters at Numan and Chukol.

There was another change in 1910, when the headquarters of

Number IV Division were moved to Pirambi and Song was included in the Division. In 1911 Longuda and Piri were handed back to Yola Province, and next year the Independent Pagan Division was resurrected, taking in modern Numan with Yungur, Yendam Waka, Zinna, Mumuye, and Chamba. In September 1912 the title was changed to Numan Division.

After the First World War further changes were necessary in Yola Province, and three divisions were authorized: Number I, with its headquarters at Song, comprised the 7,540 square miles north of the Benue; Number II, with its headquarters at Sugu, comprised the 7,000 square miles south of the Benue; and Number III consisted of the 3,017 square miles of the independent pagan districts in the Gongola-Benue area. Lala District was added to Numan Division in 1921, but three years later the Division was reorganized. The Lala-Hona Districts were made into Shellen Division, with its headquarters at Shellen, and this included Garkida, the Hona-Bura District, Yungur, Lala, Longuda, Kanakuru, and the Shani enclave. Numan Division meanwhile was compensated by receiving Gurumpawo and Yebbi. In the great reshuffle of 1926, Numan Division took on more or less its present shape, with the Shellen, Bata, Bachama, and Mbula Districts forming its area. Shellen, which had begun to emerge as a responsible unit under its chief Mijibona, remained a Division from 1924 until 1926 and retained its own Native Treasury till 1951.

Such a constant shuffling of the administrative cards was bound to have an unsettling influence on these independent tribes, and a number of patrols had to operate in the Division during the years which followed on those of the occupation. In 1910 the chief of Bachama resisted a police patrol sent to depose him for his instigation of highway robbery and he was killed in the firing that ensued. Later an outbreak of lawlessness at Kwa necessitated another patrol. During the First World War the inevitable shortage of staff precluded adequate touring and there were several set-backs to the progress of the Division. The Longuda resumed their head-hunting practices, some Bata villagers attacked their chief and had to be brought to order, and in 1918 the Piri, who had been assessed for the first time in the previous year, attacked the District Officer. The 1921 Billi patrol in support of the chief of Demsa was the last occasion on which the use of armed force was necessary in the Division.

For a while the administration of the Division was effected through the mutually independent chiefs of Shellen, Bachama, Bata, and Mbula, each of whom was directly responsible to the Divisional Officer. In 1936 the last three combined their resources in a loose federation, each tribe retaining its local autonomy, while the Longuda remained subservient to Shellen. In 1951 there was constituted a single Native Authority for the whole Division, known as the Council of the Numan Federation. This council consisted of the four classified chiefs, the President of the Longuda Council, and eight other members; the office of president of the Numan Federation rotated monthly among the chiefs of Bata, Bachama, Mbula, Shellen, and Longuda. An Outer or Advisory Council, with official and elected members was constituted in 1952. In 1955 the Numan Federation Native Authority was remodelled to include seven *ex-officio* members (the chiefs of Bata, Bachama, Mbula, and Shellen, and the village-heads of Guyuk, Kiri, and Longuda), three personal appointments, and one nominated member from each of the five District Councils. Each chief spends a month in Numan, in turn, to represent the Native Authority between the full meetings of the Council.

XII

LEAVES FROM THE PROVINCIAL DIARY

ADAMAWA PROVINCE came into being in 1926. An outline of the history of the earlier Yola and Muri Provinces during the first twenty-five years of Government has already been given: the occupation and pacification, the development of administration, the Cameroons campaign, the assumption of mandated territory. From the 1926 reorganization of the Northern Provinces the history of Adamawa falls less readily into periods; and as this coincides with the creation of Adamawa Province, the date is a convenient one from which to start a summary of those events, year by year, which have not already been recorded elsewhere in these pages. It must be emphasized that this is not a catalogue of the principal occurrences, but a note of events, major or minor, that have failed to gain a mention in previous chapters. Wherever possible the exact words of the Annual Report have been used.

1926

The Province had, in its four Divisions, 'A' company of the 2nd Nigeria Regiment as well as a strong detachment of police in view of its numerous unsettled areas.

There was an outbreak of lawlessness in Muri District, where a Fulani was murdered and a government rest-house burnt down. The Tuku tribe made a treacherous attack on their Political Officer. Both these incidents necessitated a patrol.

The hill tribes of the northern mandated areas were still trading in slaves.

A full programme of six main roads aimed to nullify the blighting effect of distance.

1927

Moda and Michika districts were amalgamated as Cubunawa. Five of the twenty-seven district heads in Adamawa Emirate were deposed. The whole of Numan Division's previous unsettled areas declared open.

Two aeroplanes from Maiduguri landed at Yola.

There were serious epidemics of pneumonia and smallpox, with over 5,200 deaths, 1,562 of which were in Wurkum District.

Galena prospectors were active near Zurak in Muri.

1928

An outbreak of crime and lawlessness in Song District was brought to an end by a public execution in the area, which had a far-reaching deterrent effect. Two murderers of a Hausa trader in Numan were also publicly executed in Bachama District.

For the first time there was no patrol anywhere in Adamawa Emirate, nor any case of homicide in Wurkum District.

There was a marked expansion in produce buying throughout the Province, but disease among goats hindered the start of skin purchases.

1929

Seven district heads were deposed for peculation.

Lala and Hona districts amalgamated as Ga'anda.

N.A. leper settlement at Jimeta closed.

Elementary schools opened at Yola, Jimeta, and Gurin, making a total of seven with those already started at Mubi, Mayo Belwa, Jada, and Girei.

Reorganization of Sorau, Vokna, Maiha, and Marghi Districts.

1930

There were several hostile incidents in the Northern Mandated area, partly attributed to the disturbing effects of the locust plagues which were believed by many to portend the passing of British rule.

Namberu District was merged with Nassarawo.

The chief rain-maker of the Mumuye was persuaded to accept the headship of this District, hitherto administered by the Emir direct.

Schools closed at Jada and Wase, opened at Song, Malabu, Ribadu, and Mutum Biu.

A sudden fall of 50 per cent. in the price of groundnuts halted the economic progress of the Province. Corn, however, was cheaper in Yola than at any time since 1910.

Mr. C. C. Nylander, chief clerk, left Yola after twenty-five years' service there as Resident's clerk.

1931

Hausa introduced in schools as the language of instruction.

The slump had settled; groundnuts bought at only £5 a ton, yet foodstuffs were cheaper than they had ever been before.

Adamawa N.A. continued to employ a seconded Roads Engineer.

Severe locust plague.

1932

A police patrol was necessary in Zinna after the murder of the district head, Zainvoro, who was shot in the dark by a poisoned arrow.

Zummo and Wafango Districts amalgamated.

For the first time a district head could safely tour in any part of the mandated areas.

Three Chamba boys sent to Toro to be trained as the first pagan teachers.

1933

Groundnuts reduced to £2 10s. a ton and shea-nuts were refused by the firms.

After two successive bumper harvests there was a glut of corn, and poor rains and the continuation of the locust plague made it a sorry year for farmers.

Fulani to continue as the medium of instruction up to the end of Class II.

1934

A year memorable for its economic misfortunes, and general tax to the value of over £4,300 had to be remitted.

Outbreaks of discontent in the Chamba and Mubi areas.

The Emir of Muri celebrated his thirty-first year on the throne by undertaking the pilgrimage to Mecca by car.

Recurrence of head-hunting in Bachama District.

Benniseed distributed to farmers as an experiment.

Fulani re-established as the medium of instruction in schools.

Adult education classes started.

1935

The year marked a return towards prosperity and administrative progress. Groundnuts bought at nearly £6 a ton. Commercial interest revived in Adamawa gums.

A minor affray on the Maiha border.

Jimeta waterside settlement amalgamated with Yola under the Galadima. Goila and Betti Districts abolished.

An outbreak of head-hunting among the Mumuye, who had heard rumours that the death penalty had been abolished. Lamido persuaded to hear complaints daily *coram populo*.

Pagan and female education at a standstill.

1936

Formation of courts and councils approved among the Marghi and Higi groups. Tribal courts established among the Longuda and Lala. An additional magistracy approved for the Mumuye area of Muri Division.

The first course held for Koranic teachers. Class opened in Mubi to train scribes for pagan courts and councils.

Telephonic communication between Yola town and the Government station established. Jimeta Post Office removed to within the Government station. R.W.A.F.F. company finally withdrawn from Adamawa.

First agricultural show of the Province.

1937

Yungur District reorganized under a chief and council.

Koma tribe of the Alantika hills paid their full tax for the first time.

Kwojji District in Muri Division reorganized.

Epidemic of cerebro-spinal meningitis caused nearly 1,000 deaths.

Sleeping-sickness survey carried out in much of the Province.

Veterinary Laboratory opened in Yola to produce and store anti-rinderpest serum.

Silver lead-mining venture closed in Muri.

1938

A year of declining trade and economic disappointments, consequent on Adamawa's reliance on the groundnut crop, the price of which fell to £2 10s. a ton.

The Chamba federation of Yebbi, Gurumpawo, Binyeri, Sugu, and Nassarawo established.

Patrol necessary in the Alantika hills after a Koma had refused to submit to his trial by ordeal and disturbances had occurred.

Road communications remained in their infancy.

Experiments made to introduce shea-nuts, ginger, benniseed, and ghee as alternative crops.

A bumper harvest of corn, yams, and rice.

1939

Groundnuts raised to £4 13s. 4d. a ton.

Dissolution of Mandara District.

Police action required in Gashaka to forestall a *coup d'état* by the ex-district head.

Work started on the Mayo Ine bridge at Ngurore.

Aerodrome constructed at Yola.

Recruiting campaign brought in over 400 applicants during the first week.

1940

Alarm in Mugulvu, near Mubi, when on collapse of metropolitan France the Fulani village head spread the rumour of an impending German reoccupation of the Northern Cameroons.

Mandara District divided into Madagali and Cubunawa districts.

Gashaka District divided into Gashaka and Mambila districts.

The vicious Jukun cult of Mam declared illegal by Order-in-Council.

2,000 deaths in Zinna District from an epidemic of measles-cum-pneumonia.

School closed at Kwojji, one opened at Belel.

End of Mubi special pagan class for scribes.

Completion of concrete pile bridge over Mayo Ine brought all-season link between Yola and Numan.

Little Gombi laid out as headquarters of Ga'anda District.

Local volunteer defence force raised in Yola.

Twenty-four people killed and partially eaten by a leopard in Gureshi village, near Shellen.

14,216 tons of groundnuts purchased.

1941

A Fulani district head appointed to Mumuye District.

A full pioneer company of 500 men raised in Yola.

Lamido undertook a six-weeks' tour on horseback of all districts north of the Benue.

School opened at Bakundi.

The hot season was generally recognized as one of the unpleasantest on record.

50,000 lb. of a new export, anaphe silk, purchased in North Benue districts.

1942

Corn requisitioning necessary to provide food for local labour in Yola and Jimeta.

First Numan N.A. school opened. New schools started at Micika and Lamurde (Mubi).

Resident Minister for West Africa, Lord Swinton, visited Yola R.A.F. detachment.

Kiri village headship reverted from a Fulani to a Kanakuru family.

His Excellency's visit to Jalingo was the first ever paid by a Governor to that town.

Reappearance of local cloths brought about by rationed sales of textiles in canteens.

1943

Groundnut campaign, with an administrative officer in full-time charge, aimed at 30,000 tons.

Rubber production in Gashaka and Dakka resuscitated.

Provincial Development and Welfare Board constituted.

Clarified butter fat produced in Yola and Kabbawa.

Jos-Yola mail lorry service inaugurated.

Unsuccessful police patrol in Alantika mountains to arrest a long-wanted criminal.

A sugar-crusher installed at Yola and Jalingo to help meet the demand for sugar.

1944

Scant rains totalled only 28 inches against the average 39 inches.

On the dismissal of district head of Zinna, the Divisional Officer, Muri, was appointed as the Native Authority.

Adamawa Law School opened with nine *muftai* and eight Koranic teachers.

Bole experimental farm laid out, with 15 acres.

Armed police escort under Assistant Superintendent necessary in Northern Touring Area to enforce collection of fines imposed after an inter-village fight.

Boys' Brigade started at Numan by the Sudan United Mission.

Groundnut buying stations opened at Mubi and Micika.

The Resident's original draft annual report was blown overboard when he was touring on the Benue.

1945

The 4,000th Adamawa man recruited into the R.W.A.F.F.

First tour by Resident or Lamido to Gashaka and Mambila districts.

Fulani appointed to take care of Kwojji Federation in the absence of agreement among the Pantis.

Fifty-two casualties in a Wurkum inter-village fight.

Severe outbreak of cerebro-spinal meningitis caused 3,969 deaths in Muri Division.

1945 tax assessment exceeded that of 1939 by 112 per cent.

Sudan United Mission reopened Zinna school.

Bole experimental farm abandoned because of waterlogging, and 2,000 acres set aside at Kofare.

Oil-palm cultivation started in Gashaka and Mambila.

1946

His Excellency the Governor presented the Emir of Muri with C.M.G.

Whole top form of Yola Middle School failed for mass cheating in final examination.

Demsa town replanned by a Development Officer.

Unrest in Mubi and Cubunawa districts consequent on rumours of British withdrawal from the area.

Dispensaries built in Uba and Hong.

School opened at Jada.

Seam of coal discovered in Numan Division.

1947

Patrol sanctioned in Deli village of Verre District, whose inhabitants refused to see the Touring Officer and drove off his emissaries with arrows.

Twenty-one miles of contour banking completed at Kofare farm.

Jada replanned by Development Officer and Zinna lay-out prepared.

Investigation into danger of overstocking on Mambila plateau.

1948

An A.D.O. stationed at Zinna to implement the new status of subordinate Native Authority and to supervise the move from the old town to the newly laid out headquarters.

Yola-Kano service introduced by West African Airways Corporation.

Well-sinking programme from Colonial Development and Welfare funds started round Zinna and Mayo Belwa.

Survey of Southern Adamawa undertaken by Anglo-Oriental Nigeria staff on behalf of Cameroons Mining Corporation.

Mixed farming started in Adamawa.

1949

Shortage of food pushed crop prices up to record level.

Visit of first U.N.O. Mission, which spent only one day in the Province, at Yola.

Affrays at Kiriya and Tur in Northern Touring Area.

Jidda 'Mahdi' rising in Lala District necessitated a police patrol, which was attacked.

A road was cleared between Toungo and Serti.

Outbreak of cerebro-spinal meningitis in Numan caused 420 deaths.

First leper segregation village established at Pirkasa in Ga'anda District.

Sudan United Mission cathedral opened at Numan.

Muri Division river school scheme started.

1950

Fulani overlordship withdrawn from Kwojji Federation.

District headship of Maiha reverted to Njai family.

Hong town moved to new site.

Superphosphate distributed to Ga'anda, Kilba, and Yola districts.

Establishment of baboon-killing teams north of Benue.

Withdrawal of special exclusive prospecting licences held by the Cameroons Mining Corporation over Adamawa Trust Territory.

Serious outbreak of cerebro-spinal meningitis limited by excellent work of Medical Field Unit with only 604 deaths out of 7,056 reported cases.

Sleeping-sickness survey of Bakundi revealed incidence of 1·2 per cent.

1951

Groundnuts bought at £35 a ton.

The new U.A.C. diesel *Général le Clerc* named at Garua by the High Commissioner for the French Cameroons and a Minister from Paris.

Agitation by the Kilba, Chamba, and riverain Bata for secession from Adamawa Emirate.

Piri resettlement scheme started.

New district headquarters at Hong, Karlahi, and Mayo Nguli.

Five members elected to the new Northern House of Assembly.

M. Muhammadu Ribadu appointed a Central Minister and awarded the M.B.E.

Hospitals at Yola, Numan, Garkida, and Lassa expanded.

New Middle School completed at Yola.

Work started on the Numan-Gombe trunk road.

1952

Production officers and a Health Sister first posted to the Province.

Lamido's Council broadened from six to fourteen members, and for the first time there were non-Fulani members and representation from outside Yola.

The administration of Madagali and Mambila districts broke down.

Numan Federal Court upgraded and several tribal courts established in Northern Adamawa.

Groundnuts purchased totalled the record of 14,219 tons.

Introduction of petrol supplies by tanker barges to Garua.

Tractor ploughing disappointing in the pilot scheme near Yola.

Coffee introduced on the Mambila plateau.

Adult literacy campaign greatly extended.

Yola hospital extended to 100 beds.

The fiery passage of a meteor distinguished 13 November; it was seen from Yola, Jalingo, Jada, and Bamenda, but its fall was unmarked.

1953

Redistribution of portfolios within the Lamido's Council and the appointment of a Secretary to the Native Authority. Two commoners appointed to the Council. The Chief Alkali now remains outside the N.A. executive and Council.

Disturbances in Madagali District and a brief, pungent riot at Mubi.

Friction in Kilba District continued, and in Mayo Belwa there was a large financial scandal.

Reorganization of Muri Division's executive N.A. staff.

Opening of Mayo Belwa bridge and that over the Yedseram at Mubi.

Native courts opened in Mambila and a southern appeal court established.

A record of 16,735 tons of groundnuts purchased.

Tsetse-fly clearing scheme undertaken at Kiri.

New Police Barracks started at Yola.

1954

Serious disturbance at Karim Lamido, in which the police were forced to open fire.

Kunini-Jen road constructed.

Adamawa Native Administration's Central Office reorganized, with resident councillors each holding a departmental portfolio, and a Secretary appointed to the Native Administration.

The uneconomic districts of Namtari, Zummo, and Yendam Waka amalgamated with their neighbours.

Bata District Council reorganized as Chief and Council instead of a sole Native Authority.

Numan Federal centre completed.

First piles driven of the Taraba bridge at Beli.

New headquarters laid out for Dakka District at Sabon Gari.

Mubi-Bukulo road built by Adamawa Native Authority.

Government hospital opened at Mubi.

Permits to operate for all expatriate missionaries introduced.

Trading layout approved for Little Gombi and Hong.

Third-class staff of office presented to the chief of Zinna.

1955

His Excellency the Governor installed the Lamido of Adamawa and the Emir of Muri.

The first non-Fulani appointed as Councillor with portfolio in Adamawa Native Authority.

Kilba and Mubi district councils imposed their own local rate in addition to general tax.

A Kirim, the son of a Wurkum chief, appointed to Muri N.A. Council.

Jalingo N.A. headquarters offices rebuilt and finally laid out.

Kildasu-Mutum Biu all-season link with the Yola-Wukari trunk road built.

Third-class staffs of office returned to the Numan chiefs.

Divisional offices closed down and correspondence now addressed direct to Native Authorities.

Petrol rocketed to 5s. 9d. a gallon, a handicap to any development.

New power station (A.C.) opened to replace 1938 (D.C.) one.

New Gulak laid out to replace Madagali as district headquarters.

Severe epidemic of dysentery, especially in Song, Chamba, and Dakka; 400 deaths in Chamba.

XIII

VALEDICTION

ADAMAWA can hold her own with any Province of Northern Nigeria for the variety and splendour of her scenery. The rolling grasslands or steep-sided canyons of the Mambila plateau and the fertile plains of the Gongola and Yedseram valleys; the remarkable indigenous stone architecture of the Cubunawa hill villages and the unique paved causeway from Sukur's summit; the broad sweep of her many rivers; the grotesque monoliths along the frontier escarpment of the Northern Cameroons, 'natural towers and battlements giving individuality to each one', and the granite crags and pinnacles of the Mumuye massif . . . indeed, in the strange beauty of her highlands and the breath-taking abruptness of her rugged peaks, Adamawa may justly claim to be second to none in Nigeria and to share that imaginative and evocative description of the Jos plateau, where 'groups of hills rise in majestic masses, which when seen from a distance deserve the name of mountains'.

As becomes a Province with an international history, tributes have been lavished on Adamawa's scenic beauty by French, German, and British travellers alike. Lenfant declared that 'Yola est le pays des souvenirs, c'est la région fertile et pittoresque à laquelle le rude paysage environnant donne une poésie captivante, empreinte d'un charme singulier.' Bauer was equally eloquent: 'Die Berge treten wieder näher an den Fluss heran und sind von entzückender Mannigfaltigheit. Sie atmen in ihrer zerklüfteten Zerissenheit eine wilde Romantik.' Even the prosaic task of a Boundary Commission inspired the praise: 'While allowing for all the hardships and discomforts inseparable from mountaineering in the tropics, there still remains that indescribable glamour which is always associated with a mountainous frontier. A natural borderland lies among these long blue ranges with their sharp-pointed peaks and untrodden valleys, among great silent open spaces.'

Nor is Adamawa's charm confined to her magnificent scenery. In the mysterious origin of the Fulani or the traditions of the many and fascinating pagan tribes there remains, even today, much that is unknown. To both the amateur historian and the professional anthropologist this treasure-trove of unrecorded knowledge offers a rich reward, not the least part of which is a sympathetic understanding of Barth's cry—'the country after which I had been panting so long'.

Though it would be wishful thinking to claim that 'a visit to the Province would itself be sufficient return for the expense and toil of getting there from Europe', those who have been fortunate enough to visit Adamawa will have experienced the enchantment of its landscape and of its people. An officer who has been posted to Adamawa rarely fails to succumb to its spell; on leaving it he will, for many a month in his enforced exile, pine for what Barth described as 'the beautiful green of the plain against the dark colour of the mountains and the clear sunny sky'—his memory of picturesque Adamawa.

ADAMAWA BIBLIOGRAPHY

As mentioned in the Preface, extensive use has been made throughout this book of *The Gazetteer of Yola Province* (1927), *The Gazetteer of Muri Province* (1922), and an undated typescript draft history of Adamawa Province, probably written about 1930. Another source that has furnished material for nearly every chapter has been the Provincial Reports from 1901 to 1955, especially for Chapters VIII–XII.

Chapters III and VII have their sources documented as footnotes, in the hope that this will encourage further reading of these interesting chronicles, most of which have never been quoted before and many of which are here translated for the first time.

As might be expected, there is a wealth of German material on Adamawa, much of it lying uncatalogued in rather heavy geographical magazines. Particularly rewarding are the volumes between 1900 and 1914 of *Deutsches Kolonialblatt, Mitteilungen aus den Deutschen Schutzgebieten, Globus,* and *Geographische Mitteilungen.* French geographical journals, too, have much of value on the shared peoples of the Cameroons: *Etudes Camerounaises* is a first-rate publication, and L'Institut Français d'Afrique Noire (I.F.A.N.) publishes some valuable *mémoires* and a *Bulletin.* The bibliographies under 'Cameroons' in the libraries of the Royal Empire Society, Royal Geographical Society, and Ecole Coloniale, Paris, are extensive but not exhaustive.

The following works will be found useful:

CHAPTER I

D. A. Bannerman. *The Birds of Tropical West Africa,* vol. I, 1930, to vol. VIII, 1951.

G. L. Bates. *Handbook of the Birds of West Africa.* 1930.

K. M. Buchanan and J. C. Pugh. *Land and People in Nigeria.* 1955.

A. A. Culien. 'Adamawa Province', *Nigeria,* No. 19. 1939.

J. M. Dalziel. Notes on the Botanical Resources of Yola Province, *Kew Bulletin.* 1910.

— *The Useful Plants of West Tropical Africa.* 1937.

J. D. Falconer. *The Geology and Geography of Northern Nigeria.* 1911.

J. Hutchinson and J. M. Dalziel. *The Flora of West Tropical Africa.* 1928.

H. V. Lely. *The Useful Trees of Northern Nigeria.* 1925.

C. T. Quinn-Young and T. Herdman. *Geography of Nigeria* (2nd ed.). 1954.

D. R. Rosevear. *Checklist and Atlas of Nigerian Mammals.* 1953.

R. E. Sharland. 'Birds on the Benue River', *Nigerian Field*, vol. XVII. April 1953.

Anonymous. 'Over the Hills to Yola', *Nigeria*, No. 29. 1948.

Annual Report on the Cameroons under United Kingdom Administration.

CHAPTER II

R. L. Baker and M. Zubeiru Yola. 'The Higis of Bazza Clan', *Nigeria*, No. 47. 1955.

R. Brandt. *Nomades du Soleil.* 1956.

J. G. Davies. *The Biu Book*, privately published in Zaria. 1956.

E. S. Fegan. 'Some Notes on the Bachama', *Journal of the African Society*, vol. XXIX. 1929–30.

A. H. M. Kirk-Greene. 'On Swearing', *Africa*, vol. XXV. 1955.

— 'Festival at Farei', *Nigeria*, No. 45. 1954.

— 'Tax and Travel Among the Hill-Tribes of Northern Adamawa', *Africa*, vol. XXVI. 1956.

— 'A Lala Initiation Ceremony', *Man.* January 1957.

A. Léger. 'Notes sur le Mariage chez les Païens du Nord-Cameroun', *Africa*, vol. VIII. 1935.

B. Lembezat. 'Kirdi, les Populations paiennes du Nord-Cameroun', *Bulletin de l'I.F.A.N.* 1950.

H. Marquardsen. 'Beobachtungen über die Heiden im nördlichen Adamawa', *Globus*, vol. 92. 1907.

C. K. Meek. *The Northern Tribes of Nigeria.* 1925.

— *Tribal Studies in Northern Nigeria.* 1931.

D. A. Percival. 'Notes on the Count of a Pagan Tribe in West Africa', *Journal of the Royal Statistical Society.* 1938.

F. Rehfisch. Unpublished thesis (1955) on the Mambila Tribe, in University of London Library.

F. H. Ruxton. 'Notes on the Tribes of the Muri Province', *Journal of the African Society*, vol. VII. 1908.

G. Schneider. 'Mambila Album', *Nigerian Field*, vol. XX. July 1955.

D. Stenning. Unpublished thesis (1954) on the Nomadic Fulani of Northern Nigeria, in Colonial Office Library.

L. Tauxier. *Mœurs et histoire des Peuls.* 1937; reviews many other theories on the Fulani.

C. L. Temple. *Notes on the Tribes . . . of the Northern Provinces of Nigeria*, 2nd ed. 1922.

A. J. N. Tremearne. *The Niger and the West Sudan.* 1910.

C. Vicars Boyle. 'Notes on the Yola Fulanis', *Journal of the African Society*, vol. X. 1910.

Many of the sources quoted in Chapters III and VII contain incidental ethnological information.

CHAPTER IV

A. N. Cook. *British Enterprise in Nigeria*. 1943; valuable bibliography.
W. Geary. *Nigeria Under British Rule*, Chapter VII. 1927.
A. F. Mockler-Ferryman. *Up the Niger*. 1892.
L. H. Moseley. 'Regions of the Benue', *Royal Geographical Journal*, vol. XIV. 1899.
Memoirs of the Royal Niger Company officers quoted in *The Muri Gazetteer*, 1922, and in Provincial files.
Press articles and reports of Annual General Meetings of the Royal Niger Company, 1885–1900, in *The Times* and *Les Débats*.

CHAPTER V

Lady Lugard. *A Tropical Dependency*. 1906
A. F. Mockler-Ferryman. *British Nigeria*. 1902.
— *Imperial Africa*. Vol. I. *British West Africa*. 1898.
C. W. J. Orr. *The Making of Northern Nigeria*. 1911.
Annual Reports of Northern Nigeria, 1900–11.

CHAPTER VI

H. Dominik. *Sechs Kriegs–und Friedensjahre in den deutschen Tropen*. 1901.
— *Vom Atlantik zum Tschadsee*. 1908.
J. Ferrandi. *La Conquête du Cameroun Nord*. 1928.
E. H. Gorges. *The Great War in West Africa*. 1930.
R. R. Kucynski. *The Cameroons and Togoland: A Demographic Study*. 1939; fully documented.
M. D. W. Jeffreys. 'Banyo: A Local Historical Note', *Nigerian Field*, vol. XVIII. April 1953.
F. J. Moberly. *History of the Great War: Military Operations in Togoland and the Cameroons, 1914–1916*. 1931.
H. R. Rudin. *Germans in the Cameroons*. 1938; useful bibliography.
K. Suren. *Garua: Kampf um Kamerun*. 1934.

CHAPTERS IX–XI

Additional sources, especially on the local Fulani conquest, include:
J. A. Burdon. 'The Fulani Emirates of Northern Nigeria', *Geographical Journal*, vol. XXIV, 1904
— *Historical notes on certain Emirates and tribes* (Nigeria, Northern Provinces). 1909.
R. M. East. *Stories of Old Adamawa*. 1935.
J. C. Froelich. 'Le commandement et l'organisation sociale chez les Foulbé de l'Adamaoua', *Etudes Camerounaises*. 1954.

S. J. Hogben. *The Muhammadan Emirates of Nigeria.* 1929.

A. H. M. Kirk-Greene. History of Madagali District (unpublished MS., Provincial Office, Yola).

— 'Ali Maidoki's Last Patrol', *West African Review.* December 1955.

P. F. Lacroix. 'Matériaux pour servir à l'histoire des Peul de l'Adamawa', *Etudes Camerounaises.* 1952.

F. Strümpell. 'Die Geschichte Adamawas nach mündlichen Überlieferungen, von einem ehemaligen Kaiserlichen Residenten', *Mitteilungen der geographischen Gesellschaft in Hamburg,* vol. XXVI. 1912.

APPENDIX A

THE HISTORY OF PROVINCIAL HEADQUARTERS

YOLA, the capital town of the Fulani kingdom of Fumbina from 1841 onwards, has, allied to its adjacent *sabon gari* and port of Jimeta, remained the Provincial headquarters first of Yola and later of Adamawa Provinces; but only just, for its suitability has frequently been doubted. Many an officer posted to Yola has wondered why headquarters have never been moved to one of Adamawa's healthier stations: the saga is worth relating in some detail.

It is not clear at what point the Royal Niger Company[1] first anchored their hulk, but it seems probable, from the evidence of foreign travellers on the Benue, that it was not far from the present Residency bluff.[2]

There was a subsidiary anchorage a little upstream of the Residency escarpment, according to Mockler-Ferryman[3] in 1889:

We lay close under the left bank of the river, where a rugged range of low hills, covered with granite boulders and trees, obscures the view of the town . . . Yola itself lies three miles or more from the anchorage.

Jimeta was a small village where the Provincial Office now stands; it had sprung up round the Company's factory and in 1912 was moved to its present site.

From the days of the Company the long ridge overlooking Yola town, now known as the area of the Old Station, was used for European travellers, though Sir Claude Macdonald envisaged a hill station on the top of Bagale hill:

On the right bank the slopes of a magnificent group of mountains come almost down to the water, where we decided in the future the European traders would establish their sanatorium, some thousands of feet above the plain.

[1] Chapter IV.
[2] I am indebted to G. L. Baker of the United Africa Co., Yola, who has so generously placed his knowledge of the Benue and the Niger Company era at my disposal, for an interesting discovery made after I had left Yola. There are still visible the remains of a stone causeway (built later, of course) from the waterside below Lovers' Leap to above high-water mark. Local history declares this to have been the spot where the first Company ships tied up and where subsequently the temporary godown and salt store were erected when a clerk was left ashore to trade during the dry season.
[3] For authors quoted here, see Chapters III and VII.

Passarge describes how his 1893 party landed from a rowing boat:

The path lead steeply between sandstone rocks up the forty metre high hill that formed the bank. On top a grassy plateau unfolded, on which lay Kassa, the sojourning-place of the German expedition.

After the battle of Yola on 2 September 1901, the troops were withdrawn to this bluff overlooking the Yola swamp. They were quartered by the baobab trees which now shade the government cemetery, while Captain Baker built his O.C. Troops' house immediately to the west of this (the plinth is still visible) and a fort was erected at the south-west extremity of the ridge. For the first year or so, according to G. N. Barclay's report in which he asked for one of the new wooden bungalows to be sent up from Lokoja, the Residency was 'a few mud huts[1] in Yola near the marsh'. A new Residency was built in 1902 on a site at the Bagale end of the ridge, though some years later it was rebuilt on the site between the cemetery and the shell of the former O.C. Troops' house.

Living conditions were cramped in those days, and Lugard's pre-fabricated, wooden, three-roomed bungalows, sent out from England in parts ready to be erected on concrete stilts, were the acme of comfort. Indeed, regulations had to be issued to govern the allocation of these new quarters; Gazette Notice No. 147 of 1903 reads:

When one bungalow is erected at an outstation, two rooms will be allocated to the Resident and one to the Medical Officer. When a second house is erected, it will be occupied by the Assistant Resident, District Superintendent of Police, and Revenue Officer. When a third house is erected the Resident will have a house to himself and the other four officers will share the two houses between them.

The concrete piles of the two Yola bungalows remain at the eastern end of the ridge; inhabitable examples of these Lugard prefabs still exist in Lokoja and Bida.[2]

For the situation in 1904 Lugard's report is illuminating:

The Civil Station, with its two newly-erected wooden bungalows, is some 3 miles from the landing place. It is situated on the top of a plateau, some 200 feet above the river. Nearly three-quarters of a mile distant, overlooking the dreary swamp which lies between the foot of the plateau and the city, are the military lines. The water of this swamp is bad and is said to produce guinea-worm. The Civil Station obtains its supply from

[1] There is a photograph of this zana-matted, flag-staffed compound in H. Dominik's memoirs.

[2] The interior of the old Residency at Bida, which I occupied in 1955, has not changed from the 1902 photographs of it on p. 198 of *A Resident's Wife in Nigeria*, by Mrs. Larymore; only in dignity has the exterior altered.

the Benue, and it has to be carried up a steep path half a mile in length. As permanent houses had already been erected early in the year, I did not examine any alternative site. The plateau is probably the healthier situation, but the distance alike from the landing place and the water, and the inaccessibility of the native city, are serious drawbacks. The regrettable friction between civil and military officers at Yola has doubtless been due in large part to the absurd system of living apart, and corresponding by letter. Henceforth, the military officers will share the bungalows with the Civil Staff, and we laid out a plan to include all buildings and military and police barracks. The so-called 'fort' and the native huts occupied by the military officers are of no value.

Boyd Alexander has left a good description of the layout of the Provincial Headquarters in his 1909 diary:

The manager of the Niger Company gave me a small house to stay in, as the barracks are two and a half miles away from the Company. Of all the stations I have visited in this country I do not think I have seen a less happily chosen site if utility is the thing considered. Placed 2½ miles from the only anchorage, it has not even the advantage of being in touch with Yola. It is situated at the end of a rise of ground that falls abruptly on the north-east and south to the river level, where in the rainy season a vast marsh separates it from the town of Yola. Close to the Niger Company is the village of Gimeta, dirty and ill laid out. It is a Hausa and Fulani settlement under a Hausa chief. To my mind the right position for the barracks would have been a slight prominence, rich in shady baobab trees, that lies to the left of the road towards the present barracks, and about a quarter of an hour's walk from Gimeta . . . If anything can be said for the position of the station it is the view towards the north-east, and this is magnificent.

Nor was the official attitude towards the siting of the station altogether approbatory. In 1909 the station, which had gradually moved from the south-south-west of the ridge to the north-north-east end, consisted of the Resident, two Assistant Residents, Medical Officer, O.C. Troops, and the D.S.P. Besides the Resident's bungalow there were the two wooden bungalows of the 1904 report, one two-roomed stone house and a three-roomed stone Provincial Office, the hospital, jail and store, and a poor telegraph office which earned the following stricture: 'I understand that Foreman B—— did this work and he should, unless he can give some satisfactory explanation, not return to the country.' Specie was kept in a cash tank and mint boxes stood out in the open chained to a tree. The Resident reviewed the plight of his headquarters to support his request to the High Commissioner that the station should be withdrawn to 'the ridge overlooking the Benue and within three-quarters of a mile of the landing wharf', and supported his case with complaints about mosquitoes, sandflies, distance from the landing stage, heat from

the rocks, and the mutual proximity of the quarters which had forced
some officers to build their own mud huts far from the madding crowd
of their colleagues. Though the Resident's mosquito house was adequate,
that of his assistant was too small to admit even a bed, and it was therefore used as a food safe.

In 1911 the Resident wrote that he did not consider the new site along
the ridge to be an improvement, though two bungalows had been built
on it; the swamp still sent its mosquitoes into the station, and at the
Residency the sandflies were so vicious that he was 'obliged to put up a
sandfly-proof erection like a large meat-safe covered with cotton cloth.
This is very hot to live in by day but it is the only place I can sit in to
have meals, etc.' He added a special plea that the new Residency should
contain proper accommodation for visitors in view of the fact that high
German officials had often to be entertained when they were on their
way to Garua. The whole layout, covering a length of over 3 miles,
was described as 'unfortunate . . . makes social relations a penance
rather than a pleasure'. In reply to this complaint about the distance
between the sites, His Excellency commented that officers should be
encouraged to use their horses for 'their daily avocations'.

By 1917 this dissatisfaction had crystallized into a request to move
the Provincial headquarters away from Yola. The Resident recommended
Song, Zummo, or Wuro De. The Emir preferred Girei, Mayo Ine or
Namtari, or Garua should it be returned to Adamawa after the war;
while other places advocated by the Emir were Bibeme between the
Benue and the Mayo Kebbi, Gashiga, Mayo Tiel, Gelomba, and Bundang,
all in what is now French Cameroons! The Emir pressed his claim for a
move by declaring that Modibbo Adama had never intended Yola as a
permanent capital; it had been but a base against the Bata, and Adama
had been about to move to Namtari when Rei had erupted in the east.
The Resident eventually wrote that he had 'suggested that the terminus
of the railway should be Song, and here I think could be found suitable
ground for the new headquarters'. This move to the Song area was
approved by the Governor. A site was selected at Solumchi, about
3 miles north of Song, and plans were made to leave one A.D.O. at
Yola as his *pied-à-terre* during the height of the rains.

In the following year Lugard, who had just completed the transfer
of the capital from Zungeru to Kaduna, visited Yola and, drawing on
his Kaduna experience, decided that first of all a detachment of the
W.A.F.F. should move to Song in 1919 as a trial. It was possible that
Koncha and Gashaka would be handed over to the British under
mandate, in which case Mayo Faran[1] would be a favourable site for the
new headquarters. The Emir himself again urged a move in 1920,

[1] Is this perhaps the reason why this puny village figures in so many maps of
Nigeria in encyclopaedias, etc., when bigger towns do not?

after a friend had died in Yola and his own son, back from the school for chiefs' sons at Kano, 'was noticed to slacken owing to the peculiar enervating effect of Yola air'. Both the Resident and the Lamido recommended Girei as 'a delightful headquarters', but this was turned down. The W.A.F.F. detachment returned to Yola in 1921; the Song project was held in abeyance until the eastern railway extension from Port Harcourt had been settled, as it would clearly affect the siting of the headquarters; and in Yola the station was moved to yet another portion of the ridge, known as New Site, south of the present Residency, where the 1915 fort had been.

Migeod, visiting Yola in 1922, describes this new layout:

The present station of Yola is on a plateau 220 feet above the river. The station had two previous sites, both of which had to be abandoned on account of the sandflies. Even in the new station some of the bungalows, especially those near the cliff on the up-river side, are scarcely habitable. . . . There are not many trees on the plateau, and all water has to be carried a mile up from the river.

He was in Yola a year later:

I found the station greatly improved. It is, of course, comparatively new, the old one having been near Yola town. A motor road has been made to Yola town and a racecourse was being begun; a few sandy places require careful driving over. Sandflies are still the great drawback to the station. When there is an east wind they come up in clouds from the river.

Oakley, too, was stationed in Yola at this period and has written about the change in site.

Except for the [1925] Residency, which was partly built of brick, the houses were all built of mud, with very thick walls and roofed with a thatch of jungle grass . . . Under the supervision of the Resident I was put on to build a new Provincial Office and a Native Hospital . . . The station carpenter made the doors and windows, and an engineer came five hundred miles up-river to put a 'tin' roof on . . . The station, on the face of it, was no place for a woman. Situated on the bank of a large river, close to a swamp, only 600 feet above sea-level and about the same distance in miles direct from the coast, it could hardly be called salubrious. Yet in spite of the sandflies, in spite of the mosquitoes and other *poochies*, the two women who were there during my sojourn liked it and vied with a friendly rivalry in entertaining the less fortunate men. Both were interested in the life of the country and in their men's work, and one paid the supreme sacrifice through her devotion.

Not till 1926 did the question of evacuating Yola re-emerge. The Resident now added a new argument, the annual disaster by lightning to the W.A.F.F. lines along the ridge jutting out over the Benue, and suggested a move to the Verre hills. He described the houses to the Governor, Sir Hugh Clifford, as the type where 'the inhabitants live in the verandahs, and the bats and white ants in the one room of the house'.

A rest-camp of three houses was accordingly built at Bai, 2,500 feet up in the Verre hills, in 1928, and a road was opened as far as Cholli; but as there was still a 10-mile trek on to Bai, the place could not be considered suitable as a headquarters town. Further suggestions were then put forward: the Bagale plateau, which would be near Yola and might be on the Kombo-Kilba-Mubi branch line of the Maiduguri-Yola railway; the Numan-Mumuye area, high and cool; Kunini or even lofty Panti Sawa and Mika; and Pella. His Excellency, however, now refused to consider any station to the north of the Benue. Meanwhile, the Director of the Medical and Sanitary Service condemned yet another proposed layout in Yola.

The game continued in 1929 with the dispatch of a company of troops to try out Mayo Faran and take a series of meteorological readings. Its average temperature of 92° in February, compared to the 100° of 'the Edge of Beyond, Devil's Island atmosphere of Yola', was encouraging, and a further reconnaissance was made round Numan, Chukol, Alkali Manga, and Dapanti. The Resident now favoured a site east of the Mayo Belwa, but there was the trouble of communications: 'the more I consider the matter, the more difficult does it seem to combine the Provincial Headquarters with those of the Emirate of Adamawa'.

His Honour the Lieutenant-Governor visited Yola in August 1929 and gave his approval for a three-months' trial move to Mayo Faran in the following hot season. He may not have been altogether uninfluenced by this minute from his Secretary for Native Affairs, a previous Resident of Yola:

I have visited numerous stations in Nigeria during 23 years and I have no hesitation whatever in saying Yola is the hottest station I know. I take no account of temperature readings. I go by what I feel. In no other part of Nigeria have I been kept awake by heat, though my bed was thirty yards from the house and I had nothing but a towel round my waist. The sheets and pillows were so hot that I had to throw water on them at intervals. In no other station have I suffered from prickly heat and nowhere else have sandflies been such a pest. One puts up with the hot season in other stations because it is over in six weeks, but at Yola I have known it to begin half-way through January and last till June, with a return in October and November. The only pleasant month is August, which is always the time when Governors and Lieutenant-Governors go there, and that is why the station was not moved long ago. If only someone would motor from Jos to Yola in April and stay there a few days on the hill and not in a stern-wheeler with electric fans and iced drinks, there would be no further argument.

His Excellency declared in 1930 that this twenty-year vacillation must come to an end. By now the current Resident was favouring Panti Sawa, despite opposition from the D.O. Muri Division, who advocated Zinna, and from other officers who preferred Jereng, Mubi, and Kurunyi near Pella. A committee consisting of the Resident, the Senior Health Officer, and a Water Engineer reported that, though Numan alone had an adequate water supply, they were unable to support the siting of Provincial Headquarters outside the biggest Emirate of the Province and were therefore in favour of retaining Yola, provided that radically improved living conditions were created. With this view His Honour concurred.

A new site along the Yola-Numan road was sought and in 1931 final approval was given for a layout along the northern slope of the Jimeta ridge which caught the prevailing breeze. But this was the period of the great economic slump: the Resident was informed that the financial situation precluded the sanction of the approved expenditure, but at the same time he was asked for a reconsideration of the case for a move to Song in view of the proposed Lafia-Chad railway extension which would cross the Gongola at Kiri. His Honour was in favour of a site on the Gombe-Pella plateau somewhere within the Mubi-Song-Garkida triangle, but if the water supply was difficult there he would be prepared to consider Song as an alternative, rather than Binyeri or Yungur which had been put forward.

His Excellency was prepared to approve the transfer to Song in 1932; but now the Lamido objected to leaving his traditional town of Yola, and His Honour—the very gentleman who had written the masterly 1929 minute on Yola's pestilential heat—commented that 'all this is a heavy price to pay for a lower night temperature'.

The move, however, had His Excellency's sanction, and it went forward in the advance proposals for the 1933 budget. His Honour informed the Governor that, on reflexion, he was quite unable to support the choice of Song: it had not been proved any healthier than Yola; the R.W.A.F.F. detachment was now being withdrawn from Yola which meant that there was no further need to heed the Inspector-General who had disturbed even Downing Street with his insistence for a move; the economic position did not justify the extraordinary expenditure of £40,000; the decision not to extend the railway towards Adamawa removed the main call for a new headquarters town north of the Benue; and if the day came when Government could afford to construct a railway in Adamawa, then it would certainly be able to afford a new Provincial headquarters.

And so Yola remained. Yet another new layout, where the houses would be double-storied or raised off the ground, was selected along the high ground towards the site of the present Roman Catholic Mission and the aerodrome. When His Excellency Sir Bernard Bourdillon visited Yola in 1936 he thought this layout would cause the houses to be too close; and when he learned that the residents were not too keen on losing their view over the Benue without being nearer the canteens or finding a much healthier climate, he decided to drop the scheme. The station has since developed on the forward slope of its original bluff, and to compensate for its trying climate it was among the first to enjoy the amenities of modern urbanization. By 1937 electric light and a pipe-borne water supply were installed, and work was started on seven new double-storied houses and the Provincial Office. Today Yola is, perversely enough, expanding towards its former site on the Old Station ridge.

APPENDIX B

A NOTE ON THE FULANI LANGUAGE

ADAMAWA is the sole province of Northern Nigeria where Fulfulde, the language of the Fulani, still obtains as the *lingua franca*. The Adamawa dialect, as opposed to the western or Sokoto dialect, is not only the current language among the town Fulani but is also the medium of intercourse with the many pagan tribes. Thus a knowledge of Fulfulde is the key to knowing the peoples of Adamawa.

It has been suggested that the language[1] belongs to the West Atlantic section of the Sudanic family, but its philological history is as much a subject of doubt and controversy as is the origin[2] of the Fulani themselves. There are, of course, several dialects of Fulfulde, but with the constant coining of new words and the creeping influence of the more widely spoken Hausa, the Yola Fulfulde is becoming steadily more corrupt.

Some variations, such as *hosugo* and *ho'ugo*, may rank as pure Fulani (*Fulfulde lamnde*), but others should properly be classified as *kambarire*, pidgin-Fulani or the Fulfulde spoken by strangers. Typical of the impurities gaining ground are *o vi* instead of *o wi'i*, and *leddi* rather than *lesdi*. Taylor[3] quotes the 1950 preference for *sei a waddana yam puru* instead of the earlier generation's correct syntax of *sei a waddanammi puru* to translate 'bring me the grey horse', and sums up this change by saying:

The Fulani language today is in process of being simplified, for the younger generation of students appear to be adopting forms of their language as spoken by foreigners and illiterates (*kambarire*) to the exclusion of the older forms which were in current use thirty years ago by those who were well versed in the niceties of their own language and had not been influenced by such a grammatically-simple language as English!

The significance of many place-names in Adamawa is revealed when the Fulfulde terms are translated. Among the more common villages are:

Bantaje   = silk cotton trees
Bawo Hosere = behind the hill

[1] See J. H. Greenberg, *Studies in African Linguistic Classification*, 1955, pp. 24–32; also Westermann and Bryan, *The Languages of West Africa*, 1952, p. 19.

[2] For a summary of theories, see *Mœurs et histoire des Peuls*, L. Tauxier, 1937.

[3] *A Grammar of the Adamawa Dialect of the Fulani Language*, F. W. Taylor, revised edition 1953. See also his companion volumes on Fulfulde.

Futu Dou	= Futu on top
Futu Les	= Futu below
Gassol	= a settlement, a 'dug' place with a moat or wall
Jarendi	= village on a sandbank
Jalingo	= superior town, war-camp
Lamurde	= place of ruling, capital
Luggere	= village in a hollow
Mayo	= river
Mayo Belwa	= black river
Mayo Chudde	= river of quilted armour for horses
Mayo Lope	= muddy river
Mayo Nguli	= river of heat
Mayo Ranewa	= white river
Mayo Ine	= to swim the river
Namtari	= cockpit, outpost
Nasarawo	= town of victory
Ngurore	= village in ruins
Nyibango	= newly built
Ribadu	= outpost
Sebore	= small water spring
Toungo	= village with a view
Wafango	= village by a river
Wuro	= place, town
Wuro Bokki	= place of the baobab
Wuro Manga	= the large village
Wuro Petel	= the small village
Yola	= village on rising ground
Yolde	= open place above level of countryside

APPENDIX C

THE FAREI FESTIVAL OF NUMAN DIVISION[1]

THE tribes of Bachama, Bata, and Mbula share the cult of Nzeanzo, who is their principal god. His shrine is at Farei, a small village a few miles east of Numan, where each year the main festival of the cult is held. Before describing this festival it will be helpful to give a short account of Nzeanzo himself. The name means 'the boy who is not a boy', and many of his daring feats as a child follow the usual mythological pattern of exceptional astuteness and heroic exploits. His mother was Venin, who is worshipped at the Farei festival on the first day, the Day of Mourning. From his miraculous birth—impatient to be born, he emerged from his mother's thigh when she refused to deliver him before his time in the normal way—to his uncertain end, his life is full of legendary tales, many of them familiar in one form or another. Such, for example, is the Pandora-like story of the flies. Nzeanzo, disgusted at the everlasting nuisance of the flies, captured them all and hid them in a calabash. When, despite his warnings, his brothers curiously lifted the calabash to peer in, the flies swarmed out and have ever since plagued mankind—of which there is ample evidence at Demsa today!

The cult of Nzeanzo is supervised by a lineage at Farei, the head of which is known as the Kisami or high priest. He holds his post for two years only, but the post always remains in the same family. The other two important officials, Nzo Bellato, the orator, and Nzo Duato, who is responsible for preparing the food offered to Nzeanzo and for brewing the beer, are not changed. Nzo Duato is also the custodian of Kisami's hut and of his eventual funeral rites. The medium of Nzeanzo is a priestess known as Mbamto. Unlike many mediums, she does not communicate with the god 'in a state of possession, blind, deaf and anaesthetic'—to quote Joyce Carey in another context—nor does she interpret the wishes of Nzeanzo in an unknown or secret tongue but in Bata language. This important position is always held by a virgin, whom Nzeanzo visits nightly when he emerges from his shrine in the bush outside Farei, supposedly to converse and to sleep with his wife, Mbamto. She lives in a compound in the village of Farei in which a fire is kept burning all night, and to the innermost hut of which she alone, as the god's wife, has access. To Nzeanzo's shrine the Bachama, Bata, and Mbula are wont to resort to present their troubles and their propitiatory gifts of beer and fowls, and the Kisami acts as an intermediary between the suppliants and Mbamto, who communicates the god's replies.

[1] Reproduced with permission from 'Festival at Farei', *Nigeria*, No. 45, 1954.

But it is in May or early June that Farei leaps into prominence, when the cult holds its annual festival which is attended by thousands of people from all over the Division. The festival has a threefold significance: it commemorates the death of Venin, the mother of Nzeanzo; it lauds the god himself; and it marks the beginning of the planting season. Though neighbouring villages may have been sowing for several weeks, the people of Farei will not plant their first corn until after the festival. About three weeks before the rites are due to begin Kisami visits Lamurde, the spiritual home of the Bachama on the north bank of the Benue, to announce the approach of the festival. The chief of Bachama must give him a number of gifts: *daddawar kifi*, which is a kind of fish soup of the same genus as *bouillabaisse*; eight spear-shafts, eight rolls of dark blue cloth, and eight iron bars, one for each important Bata and Bachama chief; and a quantity of the celebrated red Muri salt. From the Mbula, each village will offer every kind of guinea-corn in white calabashes when they see the gifts of the other two tribes. A few days later the chief of Bachama must make presents to Mbamto, nominally a length of dark cloth for her to wear at the forthcoming festival and some fish soup. On the occasion that we are describing the Kisami came and abused the chief of Bachama in the middle of the festival, saying that the fish offered was insufficient; and Mbamto sent another member of the lineage to say that she did not think much of this year's gift of cloth! A day or two before the ceremony another official, the messenger Nzekano Kpaken, comes to inform the chief and his people of the exact dates of the festival. In recent years an accretionary tradition has emerged, whereby the Kisami reminds the Divisional Officer that it is 'customary' for him to offer a roll of calico for the priest's dancing trousers: there would appear to be no authority in history for this custom, which is nevertheless honoured in both the breech and the observance.

Another change that has occurred during the past decade or so concerns the presence of the chiefs. Formerly the chiefs of Bachama and Bata did not attend the festival: Meek gives as the reason that, though the term priest-king would be inappropriate, they were none the less regarded as being sons of the god. Now, however, it is usual for both of them to be present at the festival. This change may have its reason in a matter of protocol, the Sarkin Bachama (who now lives at Numan, the Divisional Headquarters, and not at the tribal capital of Lamurde) considering it diplomatic to accompany the Divisional Officer on such an important ceremony; or it may, in the words of a Bachama greybeard, be because 'Bachama and Bata no longer fight among themselves, so that their chiefs may now be seen together'. The chief of Mbula has always been present, as the Mbula people are held to have been appointed by Nzeanzo as his special slaves.

The Farei festival occupies three days, each with its own programme of ritual. The first day is, if one may be permitted the metaphor, a private showing for members only: the chief of Bachama always impresses on the D.O. that *ba kowa da kowa zai je yau ba* (admission is by invitation only). In the morning the people made a pilgrimage to Nzeanzo's shrine, squatting respectfully on their heels. All were stripped to the waist and bareheaded, a fact that caused one sophisticated, renegade Bachama to declare that he would not attend since he had been taught at school to feel ashamed at being seen without his shirt!

The elders each carried a hoe. The ceremony started with Nzo Bellato rising and striking three furrows in the ground with his hoe. Then the younger men seized the hoes from the elders and began to hoe along a path that led to the village, the old men dancing behind them in a measured one-step as the drums began to beat. It was noteworthy that the men were hoeing forwards, not in the usual direction of backwards. When they were quite a way from the shrine, the leader of the young men ceremonially broke his hoe, amid a climax of drum-beating, and placed the fragments in a small mound that they had heaped up. This symbolized the vigorous effort required to hoe the farm of a king (Nzeanzo) which can but end in a broken hoe. Slowly they all danced back to the shrine, where they were greeted by the Kisami, who danced alone round the fetish-staves of Nzeanzo, a group of brass-headed staffs planted in the ground before the shrine. Mbamto then appeared and danced by herself into the shrine, the ritual one-step taught to her by Nzo Duato.

While the younger men enjoyed bouts of wrestling, the women grouped themselves into a band of about two hundred and began slowly to march up and down in a clear patch of ground, chanting in a melancholy monotone that illustrated the lugubrious emphasis of the first day, mourning for the death of Venin, the god's mother, by those of her sex. This solemn and funeral counter-marching by the women, many of whom showed signs of hysterical possession, went on for several hours. The *leit-motiv* of their song was that they were the horses of Nzeanzo and as such had to parade in slow time since a god requires unhurried dignity in all things. When the sun reached its height there was a pause in the ceremonies at the shrine until about four o'clock, when the women resumed their solemn procession, this time in the wrestling arena near the village. The rites of the first day concluded with a dance by all the men, led by the Kisami and his kinsmen, towards the house of Mbamto, who herself appeared at the tail of the dance.

It is the second day that is, at least for the mass of spectators who throng Farei, the most important and the most colourful. Then the somewhat sombre atmosphere of the previous day's mourning at the shrine is replaced by one of gaiety and entertainment, all taking place in the village itself. From early morning a market was active, drawing hundreds of visitors from neighbouring villages and districts. Shortly after midday the performance was continued with wrestling bouts in a dip of ground beyond Farei that provided a natural arena. As each village group of *samari* or young men arrived, the men would parade round the arena in single file, marching in step with a jaunty, rolling, challenging stride, to show the other villages that they had come to fight. Then they sat down and watched the other bands announce their arrival. On one side of the hollow squatted the men from the Bachama villages of Numan, Imbruru, and Kedemin, and opposite them waited the Mbula men. In the centre stood a group of *Balagwe* (not more than one from each village), who act as policemen to ensure fair play and to keep the crowds back. This they did by swinging in their hands long ropes, now and again clearing a space where the curious had pushed too far forward, or cracking their ropes, like a ringmaster, at some imprudent sightseer. From both sides men began to saunter into the middle and squat down, each waiting for an opponent of equal size from the other camp to come and challenge him. Each man would then take up a crouching stance, fencing with one hand to force an opening and then suddenly seizing the other's neck with his free hand. Legs were used to trip an opponent, and the style was decidedly catch-as-catch-can. Here and there contestants would pause in their struggles to rub their hands in the sand for a better grip; and occasionally, among the younger ones, there would be a sudden flare-up of temper by the loser after he had been thrown, which would bring groups of supporters aggressively rushing forward, swinging their blue and red plastic belts (a very new ornament in the traditional dress) until the *Balagwe* descended with their ropes and put a stop to the fracas. Bouts—at least half a dozen were going on all the time—were decided by throwing an opponent so that both his hands touched the ground, or by a man turning his back on the other, whereupon the winner was enthusiastically congratulated by his kinsmen; but with the emotionless face of a Wimbledon competitor he would quietly accept the acclamations of his brother villagers. These would then again parade round the ring with that brazen stride of pride, after which the winner would return to the arena to await another challenger.

The brilliance of the scene was enhanced by the Mbula youths, resplendent in their customary Farei dress and quite striking with their huge stature and variety of *gizo* matted hair-styles. Naked down to their hips, their strong bodies augured poorly for their would-be opponents. Around their loins they wore the magnificently coloured triangular cloths, mostly dark blue or green, garlanded with woollen fringes and festooned with bright, canary-yellow streamers. Many had long white stockings or leggings of plaited grass to complete the variegated spectacle.

About four-thirty the wrestling came to an end and the dancing began. For this it has always been the custom for the youths to adorn themselves superbly, with enormous 'Red Indian' head-dresses of stork feathers, rush corselets, and a thick mass of white goatbeards on their wrists and forearms. But this year word had gone round that a certain authority frowned upon the traditional coiffure and plaited hair (*kitso*), with the result that the festival was deprived of one of its finest features. So the men compromised with exotic hair fashions, without the magnificent feather ornaments, and in their hands they all carried short swords or knives or sticks.

The women were not to be outdone in the art of toilet. In their braided hair they had leaves and ribs of pieces of beaten copper, like the keel of a cuirassier's helmet. Over their left arms they carried a piece of cloth (a 'piece' in the canteen sense of a 6- or 10-yard roll), or perhaps a singlet or even a tennis shoe, and in the right hand each bore a spear, the point impaled on a small wedge of wood to prevent accidents. On the right ankle was fastened an iron rattle which beat out the rhythm of the dance.

Each village had been dancing separately, but now they all came together in the arena, forming an enormous circle that slowly shuffled and stamped its way round and round. The band, dressed like the village elders in baggy white trousers of calico, numbered a dozen drummers, using double-membrane drums and small single-membrane pottery drums with the lower end open, and four tireless xylophonists. This xylophone is made of four cow-horns, tipped with beeswax and mounted on a wooden framework, which act as resonators and over which is hung a row of wooden blocks. These the players struck with two forked sticks, giving out an intriguing and genuinely xylophonic sound.

Round and round the dancers stamped, their bodies bent to a crouch, thumping out the regular one-step with their anklet instruments, the men shaking their swords to the tune and the women their spears. Many of the women danced with closed eyes, nodding their heads as if in a trance. As the dancers jerked by, the twentieth-century incongruities forced themselves on the unwilling eye: the very second-hand trilby challenging the peerless, period-piece loincloth, the pair of spectacles lurking under the artistic coxcomb of hair, the cheap plastic belt of red (a colour till recently taboo to Nzeanzo) wound in splendid isolation round an intricately cicatriced abdomen, and the primeval rhythm beaten out by the canteen gym shoes.

After about an hour of the dancing, the Kisami and the elders of Farei entered the arena and sat down in the centre. The dance stopped. Nzo Bellato, the orator of the priestly lineage, rose and, clasping in his right hand a short knife surmounted by a rattle and decked with hibiscus fibre which he shook up and down to emphasize his words, addressed the people in a staccato, sing-song intonation. The object of his speech was to remind them that the prowess and glories of Nzeanzo were ever to be marvelled at; to warn them that the sexual licence granted at Farei (assignations are often made for that day) was not a permanent state; that jealousy and anger must be effaced from the hearts of all this day; and to invoke Nzeanzo for his protection over the sowing and the coming harvest.

The speech, except for the shrill ululations from the elders that underlined the more important points, was heard in perfect silence by the crowd. When it was finished, all the *Balagwe* gave a fusillade of cracks from their ropes. Then the people of Farei alone, led by the Kisami with his sceptre of hippopotamus hide covered with crocodile skin on his shoulder, performed their own dance in honour of Nzeanzo. Each of the elders carried two of the god's staves, one lying across his left shoulder and the other jerking and gyrating in the air to the rhythm of the dance. While this was in progress Mbamto herself appeared for the first time on this public day, accompanied by four other women. By tradition her hair should be worn long, as short hair would be a sign that Nzeanzo had repudiated her, but today her hair was short. This solecism was explained as being due to the lack of manatee oil (only one of these sirenian mammals had been caught at Numan this year), of which there was only enough to dress her short hair. She wore a skirt of dark blue cloth, sandals, and anklets of leaves smeared with red ochre, and in her hand she carried a forked stick. Mbamto made only a brief appearance, and with her return to her compound the ceremonies of the second day were brought to a close.

By the third day most people had gone back to their villages. But the faithful children of Nzeanzo, the Mbula, remained to ride forth and hunt a few *barewa* (gazelles) for the Kisami, who as a reward offered them gifts of beer. Dancing and wrestling continued informally throughout the day in the village, and in the evening another mass dance was held. By then, however, few people remained beyond the villagers of Farei; and they had to turn their immediate thoughts to their planting, for it is a tradition that rain will fall on one of the days of the festival.

APPENDIX D

AN INITIATION CEREMONY[1]

INITIATION rites are a common feature of the pagan tribes of Northern Nigeria. They mark the entry of a boy to manhood, and correspond to the 'age of adolescence' rather than to the 'years of discretion'. 'Puberty is the great transition between childhood and physical maturity', writes the Senior Lecturer in Religious Studies at the University College of Ibadan, 'and is therefore an occasion for considerable ritual . . . without passing through such initiation ceremonies young people could not take part in the adult life of the tribe.' This important physiological advent of puberty often coincides with an equally important change in social status within the tribal unit. These rites are based on the motif of entry into manhood: the boy puts away childish things, he leaves the compound and cares of the womenfolk in the family, and he takes his proper place in the tribe as a complete man.

Among the Marghi tribe, who inhabit Northern Adamawa and Southern Bornu, the *mba* initiation ceremony is of peculiar interest in that it is twofold, its twin complementary stages relating the acceptance into manhood (initiation) with the pre-consummation of manhood (betrothal). The eastern Marghi, like most of the pagan peoples in that area of the Northern Cameroons, claim descent through the Sukur dynasty from the holy village of Gudur in what is now French Cameroons. They migrated to the Yedseram valley some time in the eighteenth century, that is to say, before the *jihad* of Usman dan Fodio, and, despite subsequent invasions by the Bata and the Fulani, retained their tribal entity so that they now number about 100,000, 45,000 of whom live in Adamawa Province. Consequent upon the gradual detribalization and increasing Muslim and mission influences, many Marghi customs are lapsing while others have undergone varying degrees of modification, so that within the same village-area and even within the same hamlet we come across uncertainty and divergent opinions on traditional practices. But the *mba* ceremony of initiation and betrothal continues to be observed in its essentials, and these notes attempt to present its principal features as it is practised among the Marghi of north-east Adamawa.

Among those Marghi peoples who claim Sukur origin the actual initiation is a separate rite known as *dukwa*, which takes place when a boy is between the ages of 14 and 17. It is a group function, in contrast to the second half of the *mba* ceremony which is performed individually, and is held in August or September, towards the end of the rains and

[1] Reproduced by permission of the Editor of *Nigerian Field*.

just before the early corn (Marghi: *jiga*; Fulani: *njigari*) is harvested. The father of each boy who is due to undergo the initiation kills a cow, a sheep, and a goat, and on the day before the rites begin a family feast is prepared for the initiate, who is required to shave his head. On the first day of the ceremony, which lasts a whole month, the youths race up to one of the hills behind their village—the majority of the Adamawa Marghi live along the western spurs of the Mandara range—to the *Ntsika Dukwa* (rock of initiation), where the first boy to reach the summit (provided that he belongs to the royal *zuriya* or lineage) is elected as their leader. Here they strip naked, smearing their bodies with a mixture of red ochre and mahogany oil, and spend the day in singing and dancing on the hilltop. This ochre is much used by the Marghi women for their normal adornment, and in the initiation ceremony it provides a welcome protection against the rain, for he who shivers in the chilly mists of the mountains will be mocked by his fellow-initiates because his father could obviously not afford a good feast of meat. In one hand the initiates carry a grass-cutting sickle (Marghi: *thlahu*; Fulani: *wafdu*) and under the other armpit a small piece of broken calabash with which to cover their private parts in case any stranger penetrates to the hilltop. Nominally the area is taboo and the boys will shoot grass arrows at the young girls should they stray to peep; and when they descend in the evening they have licence to 'shoot' at all the maidens. They continue thus for seven days, by day indulging in youthful sport in the mountains and at night returning to the parental compound. Here food is brought to the youths by the young girls of the village, two of them attending each boy.

At the end of seven days spent in the mountains, the boys leave the hilltops and put on the regalia that at once informs the stranger to a village that the *mba* ceremony is in progress. Each youth girds his loins with a smooth, black goatskin, and round his waist he ties a thin leather girdle adorned with groups of white cowrie shells, from which is suspended a small bell that tinkles as he walks and will ward off leopards and evil spirits. He wears an open-mouthed, iron bangle on his elbows, and round his forehead, neck, and ankles are twisted skeins of blue beads, lent to the initiates by the girls who have been ministering to them. More black necklaces (Marghi: *shuwa tagu*; Fulani: *babaji*) are massed round the neck, while the ankle beads are attached by a string to an ornamental ring on the middle toe. Also suspended from the neck are such charms as an *anini*, a brass amulet the size and shape of a small banana, and a scent bottle. A sickle is hooked over the shoulder on a sling of plaited, black, grass-string, and in his hand the boy carries a Marghi throwing-knife. This is the *danisko* or handbill of the tribe, an exact replica of which appears in a sketch by Barth among the notes of his 1851 journey to the kingdom of Fumbina (Adamawa) and which he again observed among the Marghi of Isge, on the Adamawa-Bornu boundary. The boys spend the remaining three weeks, thus dressed, in their fathers' compounds. The actual initiation ceremony ends with another feast and shaving of the head, after which the boy is considered to have 'received *mba*' and may now, as a man, exercise his right to marry.

The betrothal ceremony, which is properly *mba* (tying to, hence 'betrothed') takes place between six months to a year later, when the nomadic Fulani are passing through with their herds to find richer pasture-land for the dry season and the price of a cow is therefore lower. A girl will be chosen by the boy's father, possibly from among the two who attended on the youth during the initiation period. She is referred to as the *mba-mbamba*, the wife tied by an essentially religious rite. In the boy's father's compound a shelter of cornstalks is erected, known as the *mba ulla*. After a cow has been eaten at the large family feast, the boy and his *mba* partner smear themselves with the traditional Marghi red ochre and mahogany oil, and take up residence in this grass shelter. The boy has a friend with him and the girl brings another girl with her, who are thus witnesses to the *mba* betrothal as well as acting as chaperons. This party spends a week in their shelter: no sexual intercourse is permitted, and though the girl will grind corn for her 'husband' she will not cook for him. After a week of gluttony, during which time they parade together for people to witness the betrothal and welcome all friends with copious meals, both parties will shave their heads again and the girl will then return to her parents. In some villages, on the night before the final feast, the boy and girl will go to a crossing of the paths, where they will place the stool on which they both sat when being anointed with ochre, and invoke the blessing of their *tsafi* (fetish) for a prolific union. At one village, Palam, the boy used to visit the compound of the Til or local chief to obtain a charm for fertility. He would approach a hole in the rear of the Til's compound backwards, clasping his hands behind his back and inserting them into the opening. The Til would place a clod of clay in his hands and the boy would then depart, without setting eyes on his chief.

The status of the *mba* wife deserves further consideration. Although a Marghi is bound to undergo the *mba* ceremony before he is allowed to marry, he is under no compulsion to marry the girl who acts as his partner in the betrothal rite. There may not be any serious intention on the part of the boy's family for the girl eventually to become his wife; indeed, one of the leading authorities on the Marghi tribe declares that he has come upon cases where the *mba-mbamba* was too intimately related to the boy ever to have married him. Often, of course, it is she whom he marries as soon as she is nubile; but whether or not she becomes the real wife, the *mba* wife is always looked on and referred to as his 'wife'. Other wives are known as *mala nuhu* or women that are taken, but she alone is 'the woman of the promise' whereby she acquires the right to refer to her partner in *mba* as her 'husband'. Upon the latter's death she must return to his house to mourn him, participate in his funeral rites, and perform certain ceremonies that are governed by the customs of his clan. In the spirit world a man's wife is always the girl with whom he celebrated *mba*, even though in this life he never lived with her or if, when she reached maturity, another man 'married' her in the usually accepted social sense.

Even Marghi who have been educated by missions do not reject all their traditional customs and still insist on the observance of the *mba* ceremony before they marry, though they have naturally shorn the rites of the more pagan trimmings which are incompatible with their up-bringing, such as the two pieces of broken gourd that should always be kept by one's bed and on which a chicken must be sacrificed on each anniversary of the end of the *mba* rites.

Such are the outlines of the *mba* ceremony as practised by those Marghi who claim Sukur origin, such as Gulak and Duhu. Indeed, with one exception, all the other sub-tribes of the Adamawa Marghi and many of those in Bornu practise the *mba* betrothal ceremony along the customary lines here described, though they no longer indulge in the preparatory initiation rites, which are peculiar to the Mandara lineages. Among these Sukur-dynasty lineages alone is the separate *dukwa* obligatory; for the other Marghi clans, the *mba* ceremony by itself assumes the double significance of initiation and betrothal. The important exception to this is the *mba* ritual observed by the Gadzama clan. These Marghi, who are centred round Lassa, have not coalesced to the same degree as the earlier immigrants and show a marked Muslim influence (for instance, they practise circumcision, wear gowns instead of the characteristic leather loin-cloth of the original Marghi settlers, and bury their dead at once rather than follow the prolonged Marghi mourning rites), and this is reflected in their *mba* customs. After the boy has worked for a year for his bride-to-be, he brews six jars of beer for his future father-in-law, who will accept them if he considers his daughter has reached marriageable age. They then spend one week (at Wamdeo the period may extend from one to three months) in the *mba ulla*, beginning on a Friday, at the end of which he will be given the traditional Marghi *gumbara* of black and white striped cloth to wind round her body, while the youth himself will put on long trousers, shoes, and a gown. The absence of ochre-smearing, the observance of Friday, and the preference for alien clothes are further examples of a strong Muslim influence. The marriage is sealed by a small girl touching the lips of both parties with a sliver of cornstalk dipped into a calabash of millet-gruel flavoured with groundnuts.

APPENDIX E

SOME JUDICIAL OATHS IN ADAMAWA[1]

THIS appendix deals briefly with some of the principal oaths recently or still current in pagan *siyasa* (tribal courts) in the Adamawa Province of Northern Nigeria, with particular reference to those used among the peoples of the Trusteeship Territory contained in the north-east of that Province. The gradual spread of Muslim and mission influences, coupled with the fragmentary detribalization consequent upon contact with the world outside the tribal area, has inevitably led to modification and even abolition of several customary tribal oaths; but apart from those that have been prohibited as being repugnant to natural justice and equity, many interesting and valuable oaths exist today, whose influence in keeping the peace and settling litigation is remarkable.

The Marghi have three oaths to which their *siyasa* normally have recourse. These are, in ascending order of solemnity: Shafa, Kamale, and Guti. Most important men possess a *shafa*, and each court carefully guards its own (at Madagali it is kept in the prison). The basic component is a small bundle of the leaves of the *Combretum verticillatum* tree (Hausa: *tarauniya*), a tree with white spikes of flowers and four-winged fruit. Its leaves are silver-coloured on the underside. Wrapped up in these leaves is an assortment of sacred objects, the whole *shafa* being tied together with grass rope and bound to a stick. The *shafa* I examined at Gulak revealed the horn of a waterbuck, the horn of an hartebeest, a left-foot shoe that had belonged to a leper, and an arrow that had been fired but had missed its target. Other ingredients also recognized as constituting *shafa* are: a wart-hog's bristle, a hair from a lion's tail, a porcupine quill, blades of a red grass, a thorn of the *gawo* acacia, a piece of the stick traditionally used in grave-digging, and bugs and lice which are usually sprinkled on top of the leaves and their contents. The Marghi assessor of the Madagali Alkali's court assured me that the power of his *shafa* was considerably enhanced by the inclusion of a monkey's skull among the articles wrapped up in the dried *tarauniya* leaves. To swear on *shafa*, a piece of naked steel (either a spear or a knife) is generally laid on top of the bundle, and the accused says to his accuser, in front of the court elders: 'If I have wronged you, may *shafa* seize me; but if I have done you no wrong, may *shafa* seize you.' He will then step over the *shafa*, which has been placed at his feet while he swears. Meek, in his *Tribal Studies*, tells us that if misfortune strikes the swearer this is a clear sign of his guilt and *shafa* must again be produced. This time it is

[1] Reproduced with permission from 'On Swearing', *Africa*, vol. xxv, 1955.

the plaintiff who speaks: '*Shafa*, you have shown this man to be in the wrong. Release him now from your power that he may pay me.' The guilty party must then step over *shafa* and pay compensation. If, however, the plaintiff should fall ill or otherwise suffer an evil visitation after the first oath has been taken, then it is he who must confess to the accused that he bore false witness and must pay suitable compensation. There is some doubt whether an oath on *shafa* can be rescinded, but I have met a few elders who declare that this may be permitted if the original swearer has the exceptional temerity to step backwards over *shafa* and touch it lightly with his foot. *Shafa* may also be used to guard crops, and the bunch of leaves, possibly mixed with earth from an ant-hill, can be seen tied to a cornstalk in the corner of a guinea-corn farm as a warning to would-be pilferers; or it may be placed on a head-load that the bearer has had to leave temporarily on a bush track. Anyone interfering would expose himself to the wrath of the tutelary deity.

Kamale is the name of an awe-inspiring finger-peak that attracts the eye for many miles along the Yedseram valley, one of the group of crystalline granite pinnacles that dominate the frontier escarpment between the Cubunawa District of Adamawa and the Kapsiki area of the French Cameroons about latitude 11°. It rises almost 700 feet from its base, the last 400 feet being an unscalable mass of sheer rock-face. The hill is known locally as Chirgi, with its near-by wife-peak of Hum-tumale (*Hum* = hill, *Male* = woman; hence *Hum-tu-male* = wife of mountain) and its several grotesque hill-children. At the foot of this magnificent pinnacle—like Jebba rock, a natural *juju* place—is Khumtla, the ancient, thin-necked fetish pot. It is to this grove that the disputants are sent by the court. Each party must buy a cock (a profitable monopoly for the *mai-gunki* or priest?) with which he repairs to the shrine. The priest will address the sacred pot, invoking its spirit to strike down the guilty one and protect the innocent. Both cockerels are then released to fight. The owner of the one which first climbs on to the sacred pot is held to be innocent. 'The decision', comments Meek, 'can be manipulated by the priest, who contrives to give drink secretly to the pullet of the man whom he adjudges to be guilty. The other chicken, impelled by thirst, mounts the pot which has been previously filled with water.' This oath is used by many of the neighbouring French tribes as well as by the Marghi and Higi from the British Cameroons. Some adherents have maintained to me that the victorious cock will leap down and kill the other cockerel; others claim that the victor has its throat cut and is eaten by the priest, its blood being poured over the sacred pot; while one man declared that the innocent party's chicken would swell to the size of an ostrich in order to slay its rival.

The third Marghi judicial oath is the Guti ordeal. About a mile due east of Husara, a small village at the north end of the Uba hills, there is a *fadama* (marsh) through which winds a stream. In the reaches of this stream is a deep pool, about 30 feet across. This pool is inhabited by the spirit Guti, who will prevent a guilty person from swimming across. Both parties to a dispute will kill a cockerel among the reeds on the western bank and will call on Guti to seize the guilty one; then they strip and dive in. The innocent person will reach the opposite bank without mishap, but the guilty one will become mysteriously paralysed in mid-stream. Some believe that a huge snake seizes him, and that the water, normally tranquil, begins to bubble angrily. He remains thus floundering until his adversary beseeches Guti to release him. It may be a guilty conscience that causes a person to panic, as was often the case in the Saxon 'corsnæd' or trial slice of bread and cheese administered at the altar with the curse that if the accused were guilty God would send the archangel to prevent him swallowing. Certain it is that Guti is much feared and respected. I have known very few cases tried here, and have seen a woman at Mbeco court deny her guilt when *shafa* and Kamale were proposed but immediately plead guilty as soon as the court decided that the case merited the severity of the Guti ordeal. Again, I have heard of an appeal against a decision of the Guti spirit, referring to an ordeal some twenty years earlier, yet at the very suggestion of a retrial by Guti the appellant shuddered and confessed that he had indeed committed perjury. It is quite in order for the litigants to appoint substitutes to swim if they themselves are non-swimmers, in which case they sit behind their chosen swimmers and place their hands on their backs to help Guti, in her near-omniscience, to recognize the vicariously guilty party. This, however, has encouraged the ordeal to degenerate into a professional swimming-race, and responsible Marghi opinion, though reluctant to abolish such a puissant and traditional ordeal, admits that the 9s. now (1954) demanded by the substitute swimmers has tended to invalidate the efficacy of the test. Guti was for a time prohibited because of the supposed presence of crocodiles. It is resorted to in the dry season only, as in the rains the whole area becomes marshland.

The Higi, another of the leading tribes in Northern Adamawa, also use the *shafa* and Kamale oaths—*shafa*, indeed, is common to the Bura, Chibbak, Babur, Njai (Barth's 'Zani'), Gude, Kilba, and several other Mandara hill tribes. The Higi *shafa* used by the Kankafa court includes in its bunch of *tarauniya* leaves an arrow-shaft and a strip of cloth torn from the black *riga* of a burial shroud. This emphasis on the dead suggests an awe of the spirit world, characteristic of oaths in many other countries. The litigant is sworn on it in the same way as with the Marghi *shafa*. Another oath used by the Higi is that of Pulilaffo, a shrine on the northern face of the Mokolo massif which gives on to the Bazza-Vi route. Accompanied by the *arnado* or village headman of Pul, both parties will address the tutelary godling that inhabits the sacred grove, and then swear their innocence on a wide rock on which they stand. Whichever party later suffers a misfortune, such as an illness in his household, or a fire among his crops, is adjudged to be the guilty one. The Higi also used to practise a form of sasswood ordeal known as *uwar makera*, but this oath has been prohibited everywhere by the Administration and is no longer countenanced by the native courts.

Among the Njai of Maiha District *shafa* can be used by the courts, but there are a number of shrines, each of which is said to contain a guardian snake, on which oaths are more usually sworn. Examples are the invisible Gogei idol at the Lugdira shrine and the Darba cult at Pakka. Consequent upon the move of the District Headquarters and strengthened by the recent approval of the Njai tribal court, the most important oath is now that of Madafangan, near Mayo Nguli, which has become the leading public cult. It is supposed to have been handed into the care of the *arnado* Nguli by the first Njai chief, a Madagali hunter, who brought it from mystic Sukur. On the way to the shrine the litigant may undergo a preliminary *tsafi*: if an edible wild animal crosses his path, such as a deer or crested duiker, then he may proceed to Madafangan, as his case is favoured; but should he encounter some unclean beast, such as a hyena or jackal, then there is no point in his trying to bluff the Madafangan deity. Another tradition is that if the litigant meets a waterbuck, red baboon, or a Gambian oribi, it is a good omen; but a red-fronted gazelle that wags its tail, a cat, or a flock of rising guinea-fowl are bad augurs and he dare not go on to the shrine lest he fall dead at the threshold. On reaching Madafangan the priest will instruct him to remove his goatskin and don a pure white cloth before he approaches the shrine, which consists of a baobab tree, a rock, and (supposedly) a snake. It is a well-known fact among the Njai that, however calm a day it is, a wind will always blow lustily at the shrine just before the litigant makes his oath: 'If I did this wrong, may the fetish bring ruin on me and my family and my household.' A similar oath, *Buba'en* (place of baobab trees), can be taken at a shrine called Mudurusa, between Humbitode and Kumbo'on on the River Kae.

The Kilba are another tribe who use *shafa* as their simplest form of oath. With them the oath can be taken by touching the sacred object, which at Hong consists of an arrow, an ant, a left-footed native sandal, blades of a tall, coarse, reddish grass (*Cymbopogon giganteum*; Hausa: *tsaure*; Fulani: *wajalo*), and a curved thorn of the *kaidaja* or riverain mimosa, all wrapped in the silver leaves of the common *shafa* tree. Another *shafa* I met with here consisted of seven snake-heads, a misfired arrow, a broken sickle, and a knife. *Shafa* can be sworn on anywhere, and many important householders keep their own. In the old days a Kilba would have to triplicate his oath as added security. Having taken his oath on *shafa* in public, he would be escorted to the shrine of Garga, which reposed in the house of the Til or chief at Hong Lamurde, the royal capital (*Lamurde* = royal town). The Garga shrine is made up of a number of iron implements contained in a pot with a very narrow mouth embedded in earth up to its neck and closed with a small earthenware cover. For full effect, a libation of sacrificial blood (preferably that of a black cow) would be sprinkled over it before the oath was taken. On his final swearing, the litigant must turn his face towards Lim, the virtually unscalable granite *bloc* on the summit of the Hong massif, about 2 miles south of the village. Here is the actual shrine, a narrow cave cleft in the rock-face, lofty and remote, in which resides another sacred pot, embellished with four slivers of local iron similar in design to the traditional Kilba female pubic ornaments. Recourse is also had to Lim in times of drought after the first sowing, when the blood of a ram is spilled at the cave-mouth and the meat is devoured by the Hedima, who is in charge of the cult.

The second Kilba oath is that described as the Cock's Test, which takes place at the Njai village of Humbitode in the contiguous Maiha District. By the Humbitode hill the spirit dwells, in a baobab tree near a spring. Both litigants set forth with a cock, and the one whose cock crows first is declared to have won his suit. The cocks may crow anywhere along the bush path, whereupon it is said that the liar's cock's crest will at once turn white and droop in shame. Should neither cock crow before they reach Humbitode, both parties are credited with telling the truth and the oath is declared void. Barth, in his journey to Adamawa in 1851, gives an account of 'a curious ordeal on the holy granite rock of Kobshi', though he relates this oath to the Marghi tribe, whereas Kobochi is a centre of the Njai in the French Cameroons and Strümpell's Kobochi vocabulary corresponds with modern Njai.

When two are litigating [he writes], each of them takes a cock which he thinks the best for fighting: and they go to Kobshi. Having arrived at the holy rock, they set their birds a-fighting, and he whose cock prevails in the combat is also the winner in the point of litigation. But more than that, the master of the defeated cock is punished by the divinity, whose anger he has thus provoked; and on returning to his village he finds his hut in flames.

The Rhum oath of the Kilba was sworn by the River Rhum near Kopri, in the presence of the priest and the accuser: if the man told the truth, fish and crocodiles would emerge from the river and lie on the bank. Korta is another oath, the responsibilty of a lineage at Jedinyi, but here the oath is not taken on the iron symbols but on a shard (*kwasko*) of the sacred pot. A further medium, similar to *shafa* in that it is a household tutelary deity but different in that it is not used by the court, is *katu*. A small strip of locally smelted iron is placed in a brand new calabash filled with a paste of flour and water. The swearer calls on the fetish to kill him if he is not telling the truth and drinks the concoction. *Katu* may also be used as an amulet, in which case the iron is set between two potsherds and smeared with a red ochre cross. A similar ochre mark on a corn-bin, or a broken calabash filled with chickens' feathers, can also be used to warn off thieves from stealing crops.

The Gude of Mubi District (called Cheke by Meek, from their Fulani nickname meaning 'zana-mats') use *shafa*, on which they spill the blood of a hen before stepping over it to take the oath. *Shinta* (Gude: broom) is another tribal oath. The accused will put out his left foot, the priest joins the tips of two native brushes and draws them three times round the calf (or neck, according to some sources) of the accused. If he is guilty, the tips of the brooms will refuse to separate—and what priest does not know how to mix a glutinous paste so that the bristles will adhere to each other? Another customary oath was that of Nzangwana (Hausa: *yin tarko*; Fulani: *zamawal*). The hunters would make an enormous net, then the rest of the villagers would go out into the bush with spears, arrows, and sticks to drive all game towards the net where the tribal elders would be sitting in judgement. If a gazelle or leopard, a rabbit, hedgehog, or duiker was caught, the accused was held to be innocent; but if a bush-cat, monkey, snake, or hyena was ensnared, then the man's guilt was established. If it was a ground-squirrel, however, there was considered to be an error in the accusation and the case had to be retried.

The Tur and Wagga, who frequent the mountains at the north-eastern tip of Adamawa Province where it marches with Bornu Province and the Anglo-French international boundary, swear on Hololo. This is a cairn of boulders, before which the swearer stands naked and asks the monolith for the truth to be shown. He will then, per some elders, place his hands on the stone and turn a cartwheel to seal the oath. Should he or his household later suffer any illness or misfortune, his guilt is established. The *shafa* cult of the other tribes in these hills is unknown to them, but a grass called *lidzo* is held to be sacred, which a dead man's children will tie round their wrists to ward off their father's ghost.

The Bachama of Numan Division have two principal oaths. The first is at Boleng, where the litigant will drink out of a hollowed stone a concoction made from ground leaves of one of the amaryllids and the fur of a bush-cat (a favourite totem of the Mbamo group). 'If I did this thing, let the fetish seize me,' declares the swearer. Should he be guilty, the bush-cats will come prowling and howling round his hut at night, and he will fall ill. The bush-cat also helps any Mbamo to discover who has stolen from him by crying outside the thief's house. The other

Bachama oath is at Nafarang, the hillock opposite Imburu on the River Benue, whose spirit, should a person swear a false oath, will cause him to swell as though with child till he dies.

The Hona and Bura in the Guyaku-Garkida area swear upon Pasha. This is the name of an iron bar kept in the *juju* grass hut at Dingai. The swearer will make the priest a present of beer and then take in his hand the proffered Pasha, a rod of rough iron some 30 inches long, with rings of iron threaded at one end and a handle rounded like a ball-shaped knob. It is presented to the man to swear on, wrapped in a grass covering, as only the priest may look on it uncovered. The Bura merge with the Pabir tribe in the part of Bornu Province adjacent to Northern Adamawa, so that their interesting oaths of Melim and their ordeals connected with cacti do not properly fall within this study.

The Verre pagans used to employ the common poison ordeal, either of sasswood or a concoction of loofah seeds. Another of their oaths is an appeal to Ula, their god of sun and hunting. A man will seize his bow, hold it up to the sun, and cry out, 'If I lie, may I die this day,' and immediately go off to the bush to hunt some dangerous wild beast, such as a lion or leopard.

The Mambila, who inhabit the vast, fertile plateau of southern Adamawa that joins the Northern Trust Territory to the Cameroons proper, have three main oaths. These are described here in a corroborated but second-hand note, whereas the analysis of all the previous tribal oaths has been based on personal research. I have also come across two accounts of a fourth oath which, however, is quoted with the caution that neither of the recent students of the Mambila has met with its practice. The most common oath is that sworn on the *jiru* grass. This is a short, tough grass, not unlike the English rat's-tail fescue (*Festuca myurus*) or its allied broom grasses, which is so sacred that it is rarely hoed out of a path (e.g. that leading up to a rest-house) but rather a deviation is made around it. It is at its most effective when it is displayed with its root and (best of all) complete with seed-heads, but a bunch of its blades is carried by many Mambila elders. To quote a District Officer who has a considerable knowledge of this tribe: '*Jiru* is commonly wielded at boundary disputes by excited participants. Its function is somewhat analogous to that of the crucifix to the Catholic.' Meek adds that before invoking the *jiru* to punish him if he is lying, the swearer will strike his breast three times with the grass. It may be carried by itself or protected in leaves or chicken feathers.

Another oath, used by the Southern Mambila *siyasa* at Mbamnga, is referred to as Yung, which is the name of the *tsafi* bell. The President of the Court takes this fetish bell, which is his prerogative and is rung in front of him wherever he goes, and fills the two cones with water. He then scrapes up a pinch of earth, pours it into each cup, and spits in it.

Drinking a little, he says: 'May what you now say be the truth or the *juju* will kill you,' and sips again. The man taking the oath then repeats the statement that he is required to swear to, drinks, repeats the formula quoted above, *mutatis mutandis*, and drinks some more.

As a substitute for the severe sasswood ordeal, the Mambila have recourse to a vicarious ordeal, where chickens are substituted for human beings. The two parties will present themselves before the priest or a man who knows how to brew a sasswood concoction and the poison will be administered to their fowls. These will then be killed in the cruel Mambila fashion of slitting the bird across the beak and allowing it to bleed to death. The first to die denotes the guilty owner.

One of the most sacred oaths is said to be that sworn on Ngub Shoa (*shoa* = fetish), which in its first instance is a charm against witchcraft, so prevalent in Mambila affairs. The symbol consists of a cock's head affixed to the pointed tip of a four-foot-long stick of Ngub bark, which is set in the ground. The shaft is decorated with bunches of dried *jiru* grass and the coarse fruit of the common *Gardenia ternifolia* (Hausa: *gauden kura*). The head of the cock should always face east, the direction from which all witchcraft is believed to emanate. To settle a dispute, a man may demand to prove his innocence on his adversary's Ngub Shoa. The owner of the sacred symbol will grasp some blades of *jiru* grass in his left hand and with his right decapitate the chicken. According to which way the headless chicken falls, the man's innocence or guilt is established.

INDEX

Adamawa Division, 2, 3, 81, 104, 106, 125–51,152, 166
Emir of, *see* Lamido
Emirate, 3, 67, 99, 100, 105, 125 ff., 150, 180, 188, 203
Province, 1–14 *et passim*, 82, 99–100, 150, 180 ff., 198
Administration, British, 3, 55–69, 99–124, 150, 164–5, 172
French, 38, 45, 81
German, 66, 67, 79–80, 93
Native, 100, 106, 108–9, 120, 146, 166, 167, 189, 190
Pre-British, 147–9, 161–3, 174–7
Agriculture, 8, 34, 109, 110, 163, 183, 184, 186, 187, 189
Ahmadu (Lamido), 145–6
Air services, 116, 184, 187
Alantika hills, 4, 11, 17, 19, 82, 133, 184
Alexander, Boyd, 91–3, 144, 200
Alkali, 46, 104, 107, 163, 189.
Amadu (Governor of Chamba), 135–6
Atlantic Charter, 85

Bachama (tribe), 2, 17, 18, 45, 49, 64, 65, 67, 121, 122, 157, 166, 167–9, 170, 174, 175, 177, 178, 179, 182, 208, 209, 210, 211, 223
Baikie, W. B., 29–31, 53, 155, 169
Bamenda Province, 3, 19, 81, 82, 97, 125
Bamum (tribe), 130, 133
Banyo, 19, 20, 32, 33, 34, 39, 54, 75, 80, 108, 127, 128, 131, 133, 143
Barclay, G. N., 61, 62, 63, 64, 164, 199
Barth, H., 27–9, 53, 130, 138 139, 149, 193, 215, 222
Bata (tribe), 2, 17, 65, 129, 131, 132–3, 138, 148, 166, 167–9, 170, 174, 178, 179, 188, 190, 208, 209, 214
Bauchi Emirate, 15, 16, 21, 91, 127, 154
Province, 4, 55, 153
Bauer, F., 88–9, 192
Benue Province, 3, 9, 55, 99, 125, 152
river, 3, 4, 8–9, 28, 29, 34, 38, 39, 43, 54, 55, 77, 89, 99, 115–16, 117–19, 152, 153, 166, 177, 178, 224
Betrothal, 214 ff.
Bismarck, 79, 80

Bobo Ahmadu, 58, 59, 136, 144–5
Bornu Kingdom, 15, 22, 28, 39, 48, 138
Province, 1, 4, 55, 67, 99, 125, 214
Boundary Commission (1904), 67, 79, 90; (1907), 12; (1912–13), 90–1
Bröunum, Dr., 121
Buba Yero (Emir of Gombe), 16, 131, 153, 172

Cameroons Baptist Mission, 124
Cameroons, British, 86, 99, 219
campaign, 70–9, 99, 150, 180
French, 8, 15, 18, 81, 188, 201, 214
German occupation of, 60, 79–81, 184
Mining Corporation, 187, 188
Northern, 60, 76, 80, 103, 214
Southern, 81, 82, 125, 150
see also, Trust Territories, Boundary Commission, League of Nations
Cannibalism, 68, 92, 164, 174
Caravans, 34, 40, 54, 66, 104
Cattle, 8, 40, 109, 111–12, 126, 149, 174, 187, 216
Cattle-tax, 102, 103, 104
Census, 1, 15, 124, 152, 166
Chamba (tribe), 2, 4, 16–17, 81, 82, 130, 133, 135, 161, 182, 188, 191
Patrol, 82–3
Chiefs, 18, 21, 22, 132, 148, 149, 161, 162, 168, 171, 173, 174, 175, 179, 198, 209, 216
federation of, 100, 167
Christianity, 15, 124, 166–7
see also Missions (Christian)
Church of the Brethren Mission, 120, 123–4
Circumcision, 217
Coffee, 109, 110, 189
Congress of Berlin, 41
Cotton, 39, 109, 110–11
Councils, advisory, 165
chiefs', 149, 162, 183, 190
District, 151, 165, 179, 190
Native Authority, 151, 160, 165, 190
Outer, 151, 165
Town, 100, 151
Village, 100, 151

226